BODY

Intelligence

BODY
Intelligence

Lose Weight, Keep It Off,
and Feel Great About Your
Body Without Dieting!

EDWARD ABRAMSON, Ph.D.

McGraw·Hill

New York   Chicago   San Francisco   Lisbon   London   Madrid   Mexico City
Milan   New Delhi   San Juan   Seoul   Singapore   Sydney   Toronto

The *McGraw·Hill* Companies

Library of Congress Cataloging-in-Publication Data

Abramson, Edward E.
  Body intelligence : lose weight, keep it off, and feel great about your body without dieting! / by Edward Abramson.—1st ed.
    p.   cm.
  Includes bibliographical references and index.
  ISBN 0-07-144206-5
  1. Weight loss—Psychological aspects.   2. Food habits.   I. Title.

RM222.2.A235   2006
613.2′5—dc22   2005000996

    2 3 4 5 6 7 8 9 0   FGR/FGR   0 9 8 7 6 5

ISBN 0-07-144206-5

McGraw-Hill books are available at special quantity discounts to use as premiums and sales promotions, or for use in corporate training programs. For more information, please write to the Director of Special Sales, Professional Publishing, McGraw-Hill, Two Penn Plaza, New York, NY 10121-2298. Or contact your local bookstore.

This book is printed on acid-free paper.

This book is dedicated to Morris, Helen, and Bob Abramson.
May their memories be for blessing.

CONTENTS

PREFACE

This book and the idea of body intelligence were born out of my frustration when trying to discuss effective methods of weight control. Whether I was presenting a workshop for health professionals, leading a weight-control group, working individually with an eating disordered patient, or just in casual conversation, whenever I suggested that dieting was a flawed strategy that didn't result in permanent weight loss, whoever was listening automatically assumed that I was in favor of abandoning all attempts to lose weight. It seemed that there were only two alternatives: go on a diet and greatly restrict your food choices while feeling hungry and deprived much of the time *or* give up all efforts and accept your current weight as being "natural for you." Body intelligence is a third alternative. It is a new way of understanding the nondieting strategies that promote permanent weight control. Body intelligence is based on a large body of scientific research studying weight regulation along with my experiences with people who have successfully lost weight and maintained their losses.

Many people have contributed to this book. Hundreds of patients in hospital and outpatient settings shared their eating and weight struggles with me. Some of their stories, with identifying details altered, are briefly described in this book. Going back to my graduate school days, I am indebted to Richard Wunderlich, Ph.D., for introducing me to the joys and frustrations of doing research on eating, dieting, and obesity. At California State University–Chico, Marv Megibow, Ph.D., and Paul Spear, Ph.D., encouraged my work with weight issues. More recently,

Kris Picklesimer, Ph.D., was helpful when I was establishing my Lafayette, California, practice. My agent, Shelley Roth, helped to refine and focus my proposal and was supportive throughout the entire process of writing this book. Judith McCarthy and Michele Pezzuti, my editors at McGraw-Hill, offered feedback and many useful suggestions. Their genuine enthusiasm helped me maintain motivation when it seemed that "the light at the end of the tunnel" wasn't getting any closer.

Several colleagues, friends, and family members helped with suggestions, thought-provoking discussions, or general support during the process of writing *Body Intelligence*. I'm particularly indebted to Alan and Nancy Bernstein; Scott Cheesman; Ron Rifkin; Barbara Deutsch; Lewis Dobson of Te Anau, New Zealand; and Jennifer Johnson. I'm also grateful to Anne Abramson, M.S.W., my daughter, who was especially helpful with the sections on children; Jeremy, my son, for his computer advice; and Crystal, my wife, who always serves the salad first.

BODY
Intelligence

CHAPTER 1

DIETING VERSUS BODY INTELLIGENCE

The next time you're in a shopping mall, or walking down a crowded street, take a good look around. How many overweight people do you see? According to the Centers for Disease Control and Prevention (CDC), more than 64 percent of adults are overweight and about fifty-nine million (one in three) are obese. A Rand Corporation study shows that between 1986 and 2000 the number of morbidly obese people (more than 100 pounds overweight) has quadrupled, bringing the total to a whopping four million. This startling increase in weight has occurred despite the fact that 64 percent of American men and 78 percent of American women are on a diet or watching their weight. Since this wasn't always the case, how did the majority of us get fat? And if you are among the overweight majority and dieting isn't working for you, how do you join the slender minority?

Despite the gloomy statistics, many people, including a large number of formerly overweight individuals, are able to maintain a desirable weight without dieting. A *Consumer Reports* survey of thirty-two thousand readers found that four thousand were able to maintain an average loss of thirty-seven pounds for five or more years with "self-directed lifestyle changes." These changes include a new set of behaviors and attitudes that are necessary for permanent weight control. Since these changes are less restrictive than the typical diet, they are more likely to be maintained indefinitely. This more effective approach can be described as *body intelligence*.

Consider Cindy, a thirty-three-year-old, divorced social worker. Currently she weighs 110 pounds and is 5 feet, 2 inches tall. But Cindy wasn't always so slender. When she got married at age twenty, she weighed 165 pounds. She joined a softball team at work, but at 165 pounds she didn't hustle very much. Three years later she suffered a miscarriage, became depressed, and her weight ballooned to 185 pounds. Cindy saw a psychologist, worked through her grief, and started to understand why she was eating so much. Although she kept a diary to record her eating, she never went on a diet. Ten years later I asked Cindy how she lost all the weight. Her response was:

I don't worry about eating anymore. Gaining some control over my eating was difficult in the beginning. It was hard for me to figure out why I kept gaining weight, but after I saw the psychologist and kept an eating diary, I realized how I was using food and it gradually became easier to give up some of the eating. When I was in therapy I never dieted or had a list of forbidden foods. Instead when I was eating, I would ask myself, "What am I doing?" Then I'd figure out why I wanted to eat. Once I did that, I'd be satisfied with a smaller amount of food, or sometimes I would decide that I really didn't need to eat anything. Now, this way of thinking has become automatic. I don't struggle with food. I just eat when I'm hungry.

Cindy never joined a weight-loss program and wasn't on a diet. She wasn't anorexic or bulimic. She enjoyed eating, especially Mexican food. At her lower weight, she played softball more often and was more active during the game, but she wasn't an exercise fanatic.

Was Cindy just lucky enough to have inherited a tendency to be thin? There is no way to precisely determine anyone's genetic predisposition to obesity (there are more than 250 genes that can contribute to weight), but Cindy's father wasn't thin and both her mother and her maternal grandmother were overweight, so it's unlikely that she has a gene that made her slender. The best explanation for her ability to keep her weight in the normal range is a set of behaviors, habits, and attitudes that can be called *body intelligence*.

Marty, a married, fifty-six-year-old high school teacher also exhibits body intelligence, although his background is quite different from

Cindy's. He is 6 feet tall and weighs 177 pounds. He is not skinny, but he's not fat either—although he jokes about his rounded abdomen. "I guess the only six-pack I'm ever going to have is a six-pack of Budweiser."

Marty is no culinary ascetic. He loves ice cream, and his favorite meal is spaghetti with lots of garlic bread to mop up the extra sauce. He wasn't a jock in school, isn't particularly athletic now, and is definitely not a compulsive runner. He's not on a diet and he doesn't have any forbidden foods. Does he have "good genes" or is there some secret to his ability to manage his weight?

Marty's parents and his brother were all overweight, which suggests that he also has at least some of the genes that make gaining weight easier. If you asked Marty the secret to his success, he would tell you that there is no secret, he's not doing anything out of the ordinary, he's just "watching his weight." But questioning him more closely would show that "watching his weight" actually refers to several specific practices, habits, and attitudes: *body intelligence*.

What Is Body Intelligence and How Do You Get It?

In his bestseller *Emotional Intelligence*, Daniel Goleman suggested that the traditional view of intelligence as a purely cognitive function was far too narrow. He used the term *emotional intelligence* to bring together several threads of research showing that emotions and social relations were important parts of intellectual performance. Body intelligence is a similar reconceptualization for weight. Rather than an exclusive focus on the nutritional qualities of the food you eat, body intelligence integrates research on the psychology of eating and appetite, body image, and exercise to provide a more complete view of weight regulation. There are three components of body intelligence.

- *Eating intelligently: you know why you want to eat and only use food to satisfy that particular purpose.* You'll be surprised to find that only a small part of your eating is actually determined by physical hunger. With awareness and new habits much of your eating can be reduced or avoided.

- *Looking at your body intelligently: you develop a nonpunitive, positive—but realistic—image of your body.* Thinking irrationally about your body may be one of the reasons why your previous attempts to lose weight have failed. It's hard to persist when you don't see all the expected changes. Developing a healthy body image will help you to set realistic goals so you won't get discouraged and you will be able to maintain your motivation.
- *Using your body intelligently: you become comfortable with activity and reasonable physical exertion.* Most likely, your previous attempts to exercise were unpleasant. When you understand the source of your discomfort you will be able to find an easier way of including physical activity in your daily routine.

Similar to Cindy and Marty, people with body intelligence are not on a diet, but they are not carefree, or unconcerned, about what they eat either. They may fantasize about having a movie star's body, but they allow themselves to feel good about the body that they do have,

---

A FEW WORDS ABOUT WORDS

When describing your weight, do you use words such as *large*, *heavy*, or *full-figured*? Typically the use of these or similar words is intended to reduce the negativity and self-consciousness associated with such words as *fat* and *obese*. To increase body intelligence you need to become comfortable discussing your weight and body image without embarrassment. Since we'll be focusing on them for the next two hundred or so pages, it would be helpful to have language that we can agree on.

First, *fat* is a perfectly acceptable three-letter word. It refers to adipose tissue that supplies the body with energy when needed. It also keeps you warm in the winter; and if you're female, it's essential for the curves defining your gender. If you cringe every time you hear the word *fat*, you need to desensitize yourself to it. Fat's just adipose tissue—it has nothing to do with your personality, your moral character, your industriousness, or any other attribute other than adiposity. If you are still uncomfortable with this harmless word, try to neutralize its effect on you by saying "fat" over and over until it sounds funny and loses its meaning.

The words *overweight* and *obese* are best defined using Body-Mass Index (BMI) cutoff scores. The Body-Mass Index is the ratio of height to weight that replaces the old height-weight charts that were difficult to use and were based on questionable life insurance company data. Body-Mass Index is a method of estimating body fat that is usually accurate, although very muscular men may appear to be fatter than they really are. For both men and women, a BMI above 25 is considered overweight, while 30 or above is obese. Use Figure 1.1 to find your BMI, or if you are near a computer, go to nhlbisupport.com/bmi for a calculator that will figure it out for you.

To use the table in Figure 1.1, find the appropriate height in the left-hand column then move across to your weight. The number at the top of the column is the BMI at that height and weight. Pounds have been rounded off.

Using the BMI calculator, Cindy's current BMI is 20.1, which is in the normal range, while at her heaviest her score was 33.8, clearly in the obese category. Marty's BMI is 24, within the normal range, but just below the cutoff score for being overweight.

even with its imperfections. Likewise, they may not be exercise fanatics or even enjoy exercise, yet they have developed routines in their lives that enable them to be physically active. With body intelligence comes the recognition that there is no single miracle cure for fat. Instead you develop habits and attitudes that become second nature and help you comfortably and permanently regulate your weight.

Your Dieting History

If you are one of the many people who have gained weight despite years of habitual dieting, it's time to stand back, look at your dieting history

FIGURE 1.1 Body-Mass Index (BMI) Chart

Body Weight (pounds)

BMI Height (inches)	19	20	21	22	23	24	25	26	27	28	29	30	31	32	33	34	35	36	37	38	39	40	41	42	43	44	45	46	47	48	49	50	51	52	53	54
58	91	96	100	105	110	115	119	124	129	134	138	143	148	153	158	162	167	172	177	181	186	191	196	201	205	210	215	220	224	229	234	239	244	248	253	258
59	94	99	104	109	114	119	124	128	133	138	143	148	153	158	163	168	173	178	183	188	193	198	203	208	212	217	222	227	232	237	242	247	252	257	262	267
60	97	102	107	112	118	123	128	133	138	143	148	153	158	163	168	174	179	184	189	194	199	204	209	215	220	225	230	235	240	245	250	255	261	266	271	276
61	100	106	111	116	122	127	132	137	143	148	153	158	164	169	174	180	185	190	195	201	206	211	217	222	227	232	238	243	248	254	259	264	269	275	280	285
62	104	109	115	120	126	131	136	142	147	153	158	164	169	175	180	186	191	196	202	207	213	218	224	229	235	240	246	251	256	262	267	273	278	284	289	295
63	107	113	118	124	130	135	141	146	152	158	163	169	175	180	186	191	197	203	208	214	220	225	231	237	242	248	254	259	265	270	278	282	287	293	299	304
64	110	116	122	128	134	140	145	151	157	163	169	174	180	186	192	197	204	209	215	221	227	232	238	244	250	256	262	267	273	279	285	291	296	302	308	314
65	114	120	126	132	138	144	150	156	162	168	174	180	186	192	198	204	210	216	222	228	234	240	246	252	258	264	270	276	282	288	294	300	306	312	318	324
66	118	124	130	136	142	148	155	161	167	173	179	186	192	198	204	210	216	223	229	235	241	247	253	260	266	272	278	284	291	297	303	309	315	322	328	334
67	121	127	134	140	146	153	159	166	172	178	185	191	198	204	211	217	223	230	236	242	249	255	261	268	274	280	287	293	299	306	312	319	325	331	338	344
68	125	131	138	144	151	158	164	171	177	184	190	197	203	210	216	223	230	236	243	249	256	262	269	276	282	289	295	302	308	315	322	328	335	341	348	354
69	128	135	142	149	155	162	169	176	182	189	196	203	209	216	223	230	236	243	250	257	263	270	277	284	291	297	304	311	318	324	331	338	345	351	358	365
70	132	139	146	153	160	167	174	181	188	195	202	209	216	222	229	236	243	250	257	264	271	278	285	292	299	306	313	320	327	334	341	348	355	362	369	376
71	136	143	150	157	165	172	179	186	193	200	208	215	222	229	236	243	250	257	265	272	279	286	293	301	308	315	322	329	338	343	351	358	365	372	379	386
72	140	147	154	162	169	177	184	191	199	206	213	221	228	235	242	250	258	265	272	279	287	294	302	309	316	324	331	338	346	353	361	368	375	383	390	397
73	144	151	159	166	174	182	189	197	204	212	219	227	235	242	250	257	265	272	280	288	295	302	310	318	325	333	340	348	355	363	371	378	386	393	401	408
74	148	155	163	171	179	186	194	202	210	218	225	233	241	249	256	264	272	280	287	295	303	311	319	326	334	342	350	358	365	373	381	389	396	404	412	420
75	152	160	168	176	184	192	200	208	216	224	232	240	248	256	264	272	279	287	295	303	311	319	327	335	343	351	359	367	375	383	391	399	407	415	423	431
76	156	164	172	180	189	197	205	213	221	230	238	246	254	263	271	279	287	295	304	312	320	328	336	344	353	361	369	377	385	394	402	410	418	426	435	443

Source: Adapted from Clinical Guidelines on the Identification, Evaluation, and Treatment of Overweight and Obesity in Adults: The Evidence Report.

to see what has gone wrong, and then find a better alternative. To start, for each of the following ten questions circle the best answer:

1. How often are you dieting?

    Never   Rarely   Sometimes   Usually   Always

2. What is the maximum amount of weight (in pounds) you have ever lost within one month?

    0–4   5–9   10–14   15–19   20+

3. What is your maximum weight gain within a week?

    0–1   1.1–2   2.1–3   3.1–5   5.1+

4. In a typical week, how much does your weight fluctuate?

    0–1   1.1–2   2.1–3   3.1–5   5.1+

5. Would a weight fluctuation of five pounds affect the way you live your life?

    Not at all   Slightly   Moderately   Extremely

6. Do you eat sensibly in front of others and splurge alone?

    Never   Rarely   Often   Always

7. Do you give too much time and thought to food?

    Never   Rarely   Often   Always

8. Do you have feelings of guilt after overeating?

    Never   Rarely   Often   Always

9. How conscious are you of what you're eating?

    Not at all   Slightly   Moderately   Extremely

10. How many pounds over your desired weight were you at your maximum weight?

    0–1   1–5   6–10   11–20   21+

You have just completed the Revised Restraint Scale, a measure of the tendency to diet that has been used in many research studies. To calculate your restraint score, give each of your responses a 0, 1, 2, 3, or 4. For each question, assign it a 0 if you circled the response in the first column on the left (typically "Not at all," "Never," or "0–4"). If you circled the second response it would be 1; the third response is 2; the fourth is 3; and the fifth is 4. Then add the numbers for the ten items to arrive at your restraint score.

For women a restraint score of 16 or above generally indicates a restrained eater or chronic dieter, while men scoring 12 or higher are considered restrained eaters. Several dozen studies have demonstrated that chronic dieting doesn't result in weight loss. Although restrained eaters report that they eat less than nondieters, and they have greater fluctuations in their weight, over time they don't actually lose weight.

In addition to the failure of dieting to produce weight loss, there are several unexpected negative consequences. Instead of relying on the internal, physical cues of hunger to determine when and what to eat, the chronic dieter is dependent on an externally imposed list of approved foods and quantities. As a result, the normal regulation of eating is disrupted. As long as he or she adheres to the diet, weight loss is possible, but once the diet is finished, the ex-dieter no longer has the internal guidelines and may overeat or even binge. For example, studies have shown that when a nondieter eats a high-calorie meal, he or she is likely to compensate by eating less at the next meal. In contrast, when a dieter overeats, he or she will continue to overeat. This "oh what the hell, I've blown my diet, I might as well keep eating" phenomenon results in periods of unrealistic eating restraint with accompanying irritability, bad moods, and difficulty concentrating, followed by periods of excessive eating with feelings of guilt, self-reproach, and lowered self-esteem. It's the classic pattern of up-and-down, yo-yo, dieting. A University of Toronto study found that people who had high scores on the Restraint Scale gave themselves permission to eat *more* before they were going to start a new diet. The research shows that dieters don't lose weight, but they do make themselves miserable trying.

Compare Cindy's and Marty's body intelligence to Allison's dieting. Allison S., a thirty-two-year-old, divorced secretary, scored 27 on the Restraint Scale. She described a lengthy history of dieting attempts going back to her early adolescence. Her mother, who was also a habitual dieter, became concerned about Allison's inability to lose her "baby fat" when she was ten years old and put her on a diet. In addition to restricting the foods that Allison could eat, Mrs. S. often lectured her about the importance of being slender. When Allison gave in to the inevitable temptations, Mrs. S. expressed disappointment and reminded her that slenderness was a prerequisite to being pretty, popular, and successful. Throughout her adolescence, Allison dutifully attempted to follow whatever diet her mother suggested, but inevitably any weight that was lost was regained, often with a few additional pounds.

After graduating, Allison married Derek, her high school sweetheart, and went to work as a secretary. Her husband took over where her mother left off, pointing out new diets to try, reminding her not to eat forbidden foods, and making "humorous"—but pointed—comments about her body, particularly her thighs. Trying to please Derek, Allison joined Weight Watchers and lost twenty pounds, but after several months she became discouraged when her weight plateaued and Derek was still unhappy with her thighs. She tried bestselling diet books and diets she found in women's magazines but any weight lost was eventually regained. Despite the continuing setbacks, Allison never gave up hope. A friend at work had lost some weight with an "all natural" dietary supplement, so Allison went to a health food store. The enthusiastic clerk sold her several herbal products and gave her detailed instructions on their use. Again, Allison was disappointed.

In addition to failing to lose weight, Allison exhibited many of the unfortunate side effects of dieting. When on a diet Allison felt deprived and was frequently hungry. Inevitably when she went off the diet, she would eat all the foods that she had been craving and then felt guilty and hopeless. Also, Derek complained that Allison was "bitchy" when dieting. Although there were many other sources of conflict with Derek, Allison acknowledged that she had more of a temper when on a diet.

To change eating behaviors and for many of the exercises in this book it will be helpful for you to use a separate notebook—we'll call it your *Body Intelligence* notebook—to record your thoughts, scores, and answers. Review your dieting history by writing the answers to the following questions in your notebook.

- Are your experiences more like Allison's, Marty's, or Cindy's?
- How often are you on a diet?

- What was your most successful diet?
- What did you feel like physically/emotionally during that diet?
- Did you try to ignore your hunger?
- When did you go off the diet?
- Looking back, what made you give it up?
- After you went off the diet, did you splurge or treat yourself to the goodies that you missed while dieting?
- How did you physically/emotionally feel after the diet?
- How long was it before you regained the weight you lost on the diet?
- If you have been a restrained eater and had some or all of the negative experiences with diets are you ready to do something different?

Instead of waiting for the next miracle diet, maybe it's time to disengage from the whole dieting process and, instead, work on increasing your body intelligence.

Perhaps you're not convinced. Maybe you are pinning your hopes on a scientific breakthrough that will make dieting, exercise, or any effort unnecessary. Surely someone will discover a "cure" for obesity.

Looking in All the Wrong Places

When you see an article in the newspaper about obesity does it grab your attention? It seems that the search for a "cure" for obesity is in the news every week. You've probably read several of the hundreds of articles reporting new medical findings about obesity and weight control. You may be a little skeptical of some of the claims but still hold out hope that, this time, someone has discovered a painless method for losing weight.

In a December 1994 front page article titled, "Researchers Link Obesity in Humans to Flaw in a Gene," Natalie Angier from the *New York Times* reported that "Eventually, the finding might lead to novel and more effective therapies for weight problems" although the ". . . researchers caution that it will take at least 5 to 10 years to translate the preliminary results into a medication." Unfortunately, those ten years have passed without a useful medication. The early enthusiasm led Amgen, a biotech company, to pay $20 million for a license to develop medications based on these findings. So far, there is no drug. Obese mice injected with leptin, a protein hormone related to the "obesity gene," had significant weight loss, but when humans received leptin injections the weight losses were minimal.

More recently, you may have read about ghrelin and Peptide YY3-36, hormones that are involved in hunger. It has been suggested that drugs decreasing ghrelin levels might help people lose weight. Likewise, Peptide YY 3-36 may reduce hunger pangs. When administered in a nasal spray, Peptide YY 3-36 could reduce appetite, although it will be years before any drugs based on these hormones are approved and marketed. Even if any of these discoveries results in a treatment, it is likely to affect only one of the many variables that contribute to eating. According to Dr. Jules Hirsh, a Rockefeller University obesity researcher quoted in Denise Grady's *New York Times* article, "Hormone Linked to Appetite, Weight Control" (May 23, 2002), "There are so many redundant loops that something else may take over to restore the fat that people want to lose." While it would help to have fewer hunger pangs, the amount you eat when you're not hungry but are bored or stressed wouldn't change. Even with new discoveries, it's unlikely that there will be a complete "cure" for obesity in the foreseeable future. Instead of waiting, you can start now to increase your body intelligence.

It's been suggested that obesity is similar to a fever. In the same way that you could have an elevated temperature for dozens of different reasons, you can put on weight for dozens, or maybe hundreds, of different reasons. Since obesity in humans has many genetic, psychological, and social causes it is unlikely that any single treatment, by itself, will make an obese person slender. To lose weight it's not necessary to know each of the many reasons for weight gain, but it is helpful to understand the mechanisms that make it easy to put on the pounds.

Evolution Versus the Happy Meal

Hundreds of thousands of years ago when the human race was getting started, our ancestors depended on hunting and gathering for their

MEDICAL WEIGHT LOSS

As of the end of 2004, there are two prescription medications (sibutramine and orlistat) approved for long-term use, two approved for short-term use (phentermine and diethylpropion), several waiting for FDA approval, and countless over-the-counter drugs and nutritional supplements that claim weight loss or "fat-burning" results.

The two long-term medications are intended for obese adults (BMI above 30) who are also dieting and exercising. Sibutramine, sold as Meridia, is similar to many of the widely used antidepressants that raise the level of neurotransmitters in the brain producing feelings of fullness. Orlistat, marketed as Xenical, acts on the gastrointestinal tract to block the absorption of fat. Both drugs result in more weight loss than placebos but only work as long as the patient continues taking them. There may be side effects, but they can be managed with medical supervision.

Phentermine combined with fenfluramine (fen-phen) was very popular in the 1990s until fenfluramine was withdrawn from the market because the combination caused heart valve disease. By itself, phentermine doesn't cause this problem. Both phentermine (sold as Ionamin, Fastin, or Adipex) and diethylpropion (Tenuate), another drug that increases the neurotransmitter norepinephrine, produced more weight loss than placebo treatments but have the potential for abuse. As a result they are only approved for short-term use, typically less than twelve weeks in any year.

Over-the-counter drugs usually contain ephedrine (ephedra, mahuang) or caffeine (guarana, kola nut), which are stimulants that may temporarily suppress appetite or increase metabolism. Ephedra was the main ingredient in several well-known herbal remedies taken by 2.5 million Americans. It is especially risky, having been implicated in the deaths of several professional and college athletes, and it may have caused 100,000 people adverse reactions. As a result the FDA banned it in 2004.

Other than testimonials showing an ecstatic customer proudly displaying the huge pants he or she used to wear, there is no evidence that over-the-counter drugs or nutritional supplements, such as chromium picolinate and chitosan, are effective weight-loss aids. It is undoubtedly true that someone permanently lost weight using these products. It is also true that someone else lost weight using a rabbit's foot, sugar pill, or another type of placebo.

The most radical medical weight-loss method is bariatric surgery. According to one estimate 144,000 of these operations were performed in 2004. The most common procedure, the Roux-en-Y, reduces the size of the stomach so that it can hold only two tablespoons of food and bypasses a large section of the small intestine so that less digested food can be absorbed. Surgery is not recommended for people with a BMI less than 40 or for those who are severely depressed or have an eating disorder. Between 10 and 20 percent of patients experience complications that require additional surgery and about 1 percent die from the procedure, but nearly 90 percent report losing more than half of their excess weight. The surgery isn't magic. Dr. Alan Wittgrove, medical director of the bariatric surgery program at a leading San Diego hospital, noted in the August 14, 2003, *USA Today* that, "People eat for many reasons other than hunger . . . hunger is also psychologically regulated, and we don't operate on your brain." In other words, patients must be willing to make drastic changes after surgery. With a tiny stomach patients can only eat tablespoon portions of food and they are expected to exercise to maintain their losses.

It is clear that there are no panaceas for weight loss. In order to be effective the medications and surgery require many of the same lifestyle changes that are needed for increased body intelligence. The medications, especially sibutramine and orlistat, can be helpful in the short term if you are obese (not just overweight), you can tolerate possible side effects, and you plan to take the drugs while you increase your body intelligence.

food. Given the vagaries of animal migrations, weather, and other forces of nature, early humans were confronted with occasional feasts followed by famines in which there were no animals to kill or plants to gather. To survive, our ancestors had to fill up whenever the opportunity presented itself and hope that the accumulated fat stores would enable them to survive the inevitable lean times that followed. Back then eating as much as you could, whenever you could was adaptive. Those early humans who were successful in storing fat survived and produced offspring with fat-storing skills; those who were less successful perished.

Over the course of hundreds of thousands of years, humans have developed several overlapping mechanisms for efficiently conserving energy in the form of fat so that they could survive and produce offspring. While you might not appreciate this genetic legacy that makes gaining weight easy and losing weight hard, we have to accept that without it, none of us would be here to complain.

The inherited predisposition to accumulate fat served our ancestors well, but they didn't have to live in an environment in which food is cheap, plentiful, and easy to get. Our genetic makeup leaves us poorly equipped to deal with a world with twenty-four-hour drive-up fast-food outlets serving cheap, tasty, supersized, high-fat, high-calorie foods. We weren't designed to deal with ubiquitous vending machines, microwaveable instant meals, TV remotes, and garage door openers. According to Dr. David Katz, a professor at the Yale School of Medicine, we are as out of place in our current food environment as a polar bear would be in the Sahara in the middle of summer. We could shave the bear's fur, provide cold liquids to drink and a fan to sit in front of, but the bear still won't be able to comfortably adjust to this environment. Scientific efforts to find a pill to lower his body temperature or otherwise alter a bear's biological constitution would be doomed to failure because the different mechanisms intended to keep warm are an intrinsic part of being a polar bear. The mechanisms that enable us to store energy as fat are just as much a part of our human nature.

Although it sounds pessimistic, recognizing that we were designed to cope with an unpredictable food supply is also liberating. The difficulty you've had losing weight is not a result of some personality defect or deficiency of your character, it is your biological self trying to cope with an environment that it was not designed to live in. You might be able to use medications to make small changes in your biology, but you will still be living in an environment that is hostile to weight loss. On the other hand, with body intelligence you can make significant changes in your environment so that there will be less conflict between your genes and your environment. You will be better able to regulate your weight.

What's in Your Genes

If evolution resulted in humans who are very efficient at storing fat, what hope is there that you can lose weight? Dr. George Bray, an obesity researcher, offered the simplest answer when he said, "Genes load the gun; the environment pulls the trigger." The 250 or more genes may determine how hungry you get, how much food it takes before you feel satisfied, how efficiently the food will be converted into energy, how much activity will be comfortable for you, and how much energy you'll expend doing the activity, but it is the environment that will provide you with food and the opportunity to be active or sedentary. Regardless of your genetic makeup, you're more likely to eat in an environment that offers a wide variety of easily accessible, tempting foods and less likely to be active in an environment that doesn't make physical demands.

If you have been a chronic dieter (check your score on the Restraint Scale again) and you haven't lost weight, could the problem be your genes? While we know that, in general, genes can make it easier or more difficult to gain weight, we don't know how to measure the genetic component of weight for any one person.

Nature

You can easily see the resemblance between overweight parents and their children, but it is hard to know if the similarity is due to similar genetics. The resemblance might not be due to genes but rather to similar environments resulting in families eating the same food and having comparable physical activities. To try and resolve this nature versus nurture argument, geneticists have compared the similarity in body weight of pairs of identical twins, who have exactly the same genetic makeup, with pairs of fraternal twins, who have similar but not identical genes. These studies have found the strongest evidence for the inheritability of weight. Identical twins were much closer in weight than fraternal twins. These findings suggested that about 70 percent of weight is determined by genetics. Other studies have compared the weight of adopted children with the weight of both their biological parents and their adoptive parents. The adoptees were more similar to their biological parents, again pointing to the role of heredity in determining weight, but this time the researchers estimated that weight is only 30 percent determined by genetics.

Whether weight is 70 percent or 30 percent determined by genetics (or some other number in between), you shouldn't get discouraged about losing weight. Since evolution takes place over tens of thousands of years, genetics doesn't explain why there are so many more overweight people than there were twenty years ago. Most likely, the recent changes in our way of life are responsible for the sudden obesity epidemic. In 1995, a committee of the Institute of Medicine of the National Academy of Sciences issued a report that concluded:

> *Although it is clear that genetics has a modest influence on obesity on a population basis, by far the largest amount of the variance in body weight is due to environmental influences.*

While there is nothing you can do about the part of your weight determined by genetics, there is plenty you can do about that part of your weight attributable to your environment.

Nurture

Numerous studies demonstrate that, as people from all parts of the planet adopt an American lifestyle, they gain weight. For example, the Pima Indians of Arizona have some of the highest rates of obesity in the United States. A genetically related Pima tribe living in Sonora, Mexico, that follows a more traditional, non-American lifestyle, has a much lower prevalence of obesity. Even pets aren't immune from the effects of living in an environment with plentiful food and few demands for physical activity. One-quarter of American cats and dogs are over-weight, again suggesting the influence of environment over that of genetics.

Are you asking yourself whether it's your heredity or your environment that's responsible for your weight? The best answer is that it is a mixture of both, but there is no precise way of telling which is more important for any one person. Future research won't answer your question either, since any findings will be an average for the whole population rather than an estimate for any one person. The best we can do is to make a crude estimate based on your response to the following questions.

- *When did you first become overweight?* If you were heavy as a child or adolescent, it is more likely that genetics plays a significant role in determining your weight.
- *Are your parents obese?* If both your parents are significantly over-weight, it is likely that you may have inherited a predisposition to gain weight. If one parent is overweight, it is less likely that you've inherited this tendency. If neither parent is overweight, the chances are greater that your weight gain is mostly due to lifestyle.
- *When you have lost weight on previous diets, how long were you able to maintain the losses?* If your weight slowly increased, it was probably caused by gradually reverting to your previous eating habits. On the other hand, if you regained the lost weight within a short period, it is more likely that your body was rebelling against the unnatural caloric restrictions you temporarily imposed on it.

Keep in mind that, even if it appears that you are genetically predisposed to gain weight, your genes don't set a specific weight—they set a range of possible weights you can comfortably maintain. Your body intelligence will determine where in that range your weight will fall.

Nature Again

Your genetic makeup will partially contribute to your weight, and it does determine which part of your body will accumulate any excess fat you may have. Fat distribution—which part of your body will get bigger if you gain weight—is inherited. If both parents have big stomachs and you gain weight, it is likely that you'll tend to gain weight in your middle rather than on your hips and buttocks. If you accumulate fat in your abdomen, doing sit-ups endlessly won't change this pattern. You will just have very strong muscles underneath your abdominal fat. Body wraps, steam baths, and "miracle spot reducers" can't change your genetic makeup either. To get a completely flat stomach you'll have to lose so much weight that other parts of your body may look gaunt or too thin.

Cindy, the 110-pound social worker, didn't think of herself as overweight or fat but has reconciled herself to having less-than-perfect thighs. Likewise, Marty knows that the only way he can have a perfectly flat stomach would be to drastically reduce his eating. From past experience he knows that this is not realistic. In college he was fifteen pounds lighter but still didn't have a flat stomach. He is content to maintain his weight in the normal range even though he would prefer to have a smaller gut.

Why Body Intelligence Is Important

Your ancestors didn't need body intelligence. They were more concerned with food scarcity than excess fat. Your grandparents might have had less need for body intelligence because they weren't confronted with countless twenty-four-hour fast-food franchises, and even if they didn't work on a farm or in a factory, the daily routine required more physical activity. Although there have always been "stout" men and "plump" women, their numbers were small and frequently excess weight was viewed favorably. Depending on the historical period and the culture, the overweight male could be displaying his prosperity, while the overweight female was seen as voluptuous. Unlike her skinny sisters, she would be highly valued for her ability to do chores around the farm and she would be seen as attractive because her rounded form suggested reproductive competence. As long as she continued to work around the farm, there was little likelihood that she would become seriously overweight. As a result many of the health risks associated with obesity were unknown a hundred years ago.

APPLES VERSUS PEARS

In addition to the amount of fat you have on your body, the part of the body where the fat accumulates can have significant health consequences. Some people are shaped like an apple because they store most of their fat in the upper body, typically in the arms, chest, and abdomen. Others are pear shaped, accumulating fat in the lower parts of the body, especially the hips, buttocks, and thighs. Men are more likely to be apples while the pear shape is more common in women. Unfortunately for men, the apple shape is associated with significantly greater risk of cardiovascular disease and diabetes. The pear shape is associated with less serious problems such as varicose veins.

There are two methods for measuring fat distribution. The first method is simply to measure your waistline while standing upright. Health risks are greater if you are a male with a thirty-eight-inch or larger waist or a female with a thirty-five-inch or larger waist.

The second method measurement, waist/hip ratio, is calculated first thing in the morning by measuring the circumference of the waist at its smallest point between the rib cage and navel, and then dividing that number by hip circumference, at the widest point around the buttocks. A ratio greater than 1.0 for men and 0.85 for women is associated with increased health risks.

All of that changed in the second half of the twentieth century, and by the 1980s the United States and much of the Western world started to experience the current obesity epidemic. Increased body intelligence will be necessary to navigate through this "toxic environment" that threatens to make us all obese.

How to Increase Body Intelligence

You have no control over the genes that set the upper and lower limits of your weight. To paraphrase Dr. Bray, the gun was loaded before you were born, but the decision to pull the trigger or not is up to you. Most people need additional information if they are going to avoid pulling the trigger. The basic principle, eat less and exercise more, is well known. What is less well known are the reasons why it is so difficult to do. Once you understand the different reasons for eating, and become aware of how you use food, you will find that some of these needs can be met without eating. As you develop alternative ways of meeting these needs, you will lose weight. When you have a realistic, but nonpunitive view of your body, you will avoid much of the discouragement that has undermined your previous weight-loss efforts. A healthy body image will enable you to convert the new eating behaviors into permanent habits. Similarly, understanding the bad feelings associated with exercise will help you get past these feelings so you can develop a routine that is not painful and which actually may be enjoyable.

In Chapter 2, we'll explore the three components of body intelligence and how each one develops, so that you can see where your attitudes and habits came from. In Chapter 3, we'll describe three reasons for eating and explore the physiological and psychological processes that occur when you are "hungry." In Chapter 4, we'll explore the relationship between eating and emotions such as anxiety, depression, anger, boredom, and loneliness. Understanding your unique emotional patterns will enable you to develop methods to handle emotions that don't involve eating. In Chapter 5, we'll examine dieting and your weight-loss goals. You will learn how the psychology of dieting has affected your past efforts to lose weight and how to free yourself from this type of thinking. We also include a discussion of dieting controversies, such as the value of low-carbohydrate versus low-fat diets. In Chapter 6, you'll develop an eating plan that avoids the pitfalls of your past diets, regardless of their nutritional adequacy. By the time you are halfway through this book, you will be able to recognize the reasons why you want to eat. You will be able to alter the environment to reduce many of the external stimuli that trigger your eating while ensuring that when you do eat, you are satisfying the intended purpose.

In Chapters 7 and 8, we'll examine and refine your beliefs about your body. Having a realistic view of your body is an essential part of body intelligence; it will help keep you motivated so that you can maintain your new eating and activity habits. In Chapter 9, we'll address difficulties with exercise and how to overcome the barriers that keep you from being active. In Chapter 10, you'll find out where you are in the process of becoming active as well as what practical methods can help you move on to the next stage. Chapter 11 is for parents who want to prevent obesity and insure that their children develop body intelligence. In Chapter 12, you'll discover ways to help promote body intelligence in schools, at work, and in the community. In Chapter 13, you'll explore how to avoid the predictable causes of relapses so that your weight loss becomes permanent. In References, you'll find a chapter by chapter listing of sources used in writing this book.

CHAPTER 2

WHERE DOES BODY INTELLIGENCE COME FROM?

Y ou had no say in picking the genes that partially determine your weight. You can't blame your parents either since they are just passing down to you what they inherited from their parents, but accepting your genetic boundaries does not mean being fatalistic about your weight. When you were born, you had all the body intelligence you needed to regulate your weight within your genetic boundaries. As an infant your eating was determined by your physical need for nourishment, you liked your body, and you were comfortable with physical exertion. As you grew and got to know your parents and then the larger society, something happened. In addition to your need for nourishment, your environment now influenced eating. You started eating even though you weren't hungry. You became increasingly unhappy with your body and uncomfortable with activity. In this chapter there are several opportunities to reflect on your childhood experiences that will help you make the changes necessary to reclaim your body intelligence.

Recall from Chapter 1 that there are three components that make up body intelligence: eating intelligently, looking at your body intelligently, and using your body intelligently. In this chapter, you'll examine your unique patterns of development for each of the three components. Understanding how each developed and the roles that your parents, your peers, and the larger society played will help you untangle some of the childhood experiences that diminished the body intelligence that you had at birth. Although some of the habits and beliefs that undermine body intelligence were learned years ago, with persistence they can be changed. The first step is to identify these patterns and understand how they developed.

Eating Intelligently

Let's start with individual developmental factors contributing to intelligent eating, the first component of body intelligence. One word of caution: if you are a parent, it's natural that you will think about your children as we review the development of body intelligence. Try to restrain this tendency. Chapter 11 is filled with practical suggestions for raising a child with body intelligence, so for now, focus your attention on your own upbringing.

Learning to Eat

Think about your childhood experiences. Do you remember hearing any of these statements?

- Don't waste food. Think of all the starving children in China (or Africa or wherever).
- Finish your vegetables (or meat or milk) if you want to grow up to be strong (or pretty or healthy).
- Don't eat that, you'll spoil your appetite.
- You can't have dessert (or watch TV) unless you finish everything on your plate.
- Good boy (girl), you've finished everything. Now you're a member of the clean plate club.
- You don't have to eat it all. Just try a little bit.
- I spent all afternoon making this just for you. The least you can do is try a little.
- You need to eat a good breakfast before you go to school.

There are many reasons why your parents tried to regulate your eating. They could have been concerned about your nutrition or had fears that you would get sick if you didn't eat the right foods or get enough vitamins. They might have worried that you would eat too much and get fat. Some parents have strong moral beliefs about food. For example, in one of my workshops I casually suggested that instead of eating their children's leftovers, parents should throw them away. An older nurse who had been hungry as a child living in Europe after World War II expressed sincere outrage at the thought of wasting food this way. Other parents may enjoy a particular food and want their child to share the enjoyment, or they might encourage their child to eat a food associated with a cultural or religious celebration. Some parents may feel that the efforts they put into preparing the food obligate the child to eat it.

If you give it some thought, you probably can recall many well-intentioned attempts that your parents made to influence your eating. Some of your eating habits and beliefs about eating are a result of direct parental instructions, but parental influence actually starts long before the first time you were told to eat your vegetables.

Losing Your Body Intelligence

Like all good mammals, we were born to drink milk, but our taste preferences may start before birth. There is evidence that based on the mother's diet, the fetus can distinguish some flavors in the amniotic fluid as early as twelve to fourteen weeks' gestation. Although the findings aren't definitive, the exposure to a variety of dietary flavors before birth may increase the acceptance of foods in infancy. If you weren't exposed to different flavors before you were born, you might have been more resistant to new foods so your mother might have had a greater need to encourage you to eat.

Your mother's decision to breast-feed or bottle-feed could have influenced your taste preferences in childhood. Mother's breast milk carries a variety of flavors depending on her diet. If you were breast-fed you were exposed to different flavors, while if you were bottle-fed there was less variety. Accepting new foods may be easier for breast-fed babies while bottle-fed babies might have become fussier eaters. Also important for the development of body intelligence is the role that early feeding plays in learning how to regulate your food intake. If Mom gave you the bottle, she could see how much formula you drank so she could decide when you've had enough. If she gave you the breast, she had no way of knowing how much you drank. She just waited for you to get tired and nod off, or just let the nipple slide from your lips. With breast-feeding you decided when you were full. With bottle-feeding your mom or dad knew how much you had consumed and helped you make the decision to stop. Research suggests that infants are good at determining how much they need to eat, but if you were bottle-fed as an infant there may be less of a connection between feeling full and stopping eating.

Eating Under the Influence

Once you started transitioning to solid foods, your tastes and habits started to develop and there was more opportunity for parents and others to influence your choices. Initially you preferred sweet or salty foods, rejecting sour or bitter foods and most any new foods that you hadn't tried before. Although fear of new foods frustrates parents, that fear was probably adaptive for our prehistoric ancestors since the fear helped them avoid eating poisonous or nonedible substances. Most children learn to like new foods after having been persuaded to try them. Although children may require some encouragement to try new foods, there is evidence showing that when left to their own devices, young children do a good job of knowing how much to eat. For example, in one study children were fed either high- or low-calorie meals. The Penn State researchers found that the kids who had the high-calorie meal ate less at a second meal, suggesting that they could regulate their intake without help.

In addition to encouraging their children to try new foods, parents frequently discourage eating snacks or junk foods. Answer these questions in your notebook:

- Do you remember any foods that your parents tried to prevent you from eating?
- Did their efforts succeed?
- Now that you're an adult, how do you feel about these foods?

Usually when parents try to prevent a child from eating his or her favorite food, the preference for that food increases. When the parents aren't around and the forbidden foods are available, the child will indulge, and sometimes lose control and binge on the food. Think about your own experiences with parental prohibitions and restrictions. Although I'm not advocating unlimited access to snack foods, if you could have had candy bars (ice cream, cookies, or your favorite treat) whenever you wanted, they might not be as appealing to you as they are now.

The pattern of chronic dieting described in Chapter 1 frequently can be traced back to well-intentioned parental attempts to control a child's eating. At least one study demonstrated that girls (but not boys) were fatter when their parents tried to exert more control over their eating. In 2002, psychiatrists Robert Berkowitz and Albert Stunkard reviewed the research on parental control of food intake and concluded, "Prompting and rewarding eating behavior may override a child's self-regulation of food intake and foster overfeeding. Reduction of food prompts and rewards at mealtime may help to lower the risk of childhood obesity. This issue requires further study."

Kelly S. is a good example of an obese young adult who spent much of her childhood struggling with her parents over her eating. When I first saw her, she was a twenty-two-year-old college dropout who weighed 230 pounds. For as long as she could remember, her parents were concerned about her weight. Her mother, who was frequently dieting, would share her diet foods with Kelly and prohibited Kelly from eating desserts and snack foods. With some embarrassment, Kelly described how she would wait until her parents were gone to sneak the goodies her mother had banned. Several times her mother returned unexpectedly to find Kelly devouring a bag of cookies and gave her a stern lecture and threatened to punish her. Other times, when the infraction was not as pronounced, Mrs. S. would just express disappointment in Kelly's lack of "willpower." When Kelly was in third grade, Mrs. S. was frustrated by Kelly's inability to lose weight so she put her on a diet and set weight goals for her. Kelly responded by sneaking more prohibited foods, which in turn led Mrs. S. to periodically search Kelly's drawers and closets for the contraband goodies. Kelly always "won" these contests. Whatever Mrs. S. did to restrain Kelly's eating was ineffective; Kelly always managed to eat what she wanted with a little extra to spite her mother.

Kelly's example and ample research demonstrate one very important principle: *Eating is one of the few things in life that is entirely under your control.* Short of tying you down and force-feeding you (a less brutal, but equally coercive method is sometimes used in the hospital treatment of anorexics) or locking you up and denying you food, ultimately no one else can determine what or how much you will eat. Body intelligence requires the recognition that, while other people may have opinions about what you should or shouldn't eat, regardless of how well intentioned these people may be, *you* will make the decisions.

Much of your adult eating is determined by something other than physical hunger (see Chapter 3). This nonnutritive eating gets started early. As a baby you knew how to eat intelligently. Your well-meaning parents intervened to get you to try new foods, but in the process they may have taught you that you shouldn't trust your own judgment. As you came to increasingly rely on external cues to determine your eating, you lost some of your body intelligence.

Does Kelly's example or any of the parental directives trigger any thoughts about your upbringing? To help clarify your thinking, in your notebook take a minute to write down several lessons about eating that you learned from your parents.

But let's not blame Mom and Dad for all your difficulties with eating. They were only the nearby agents of a culture intent on getting you fat.

The Culture of Fat

McDonald's and large food conglomerates such as Kraft Foods spent $15 billion (that's *billion*, with a "B") in 2002 marketing their products to children. Not very many of these dollars went to promoting broccoli and bananas. American children spend more time watching television than they do in school, playing, or doing anything else except sleeping. The average child sees ten thousand food advertisements each year (more than twenty-seven every day), mostly for fast food, sugar-laden cereals, soft drinks, or candy. In addition to advertisements on children's TV programs, there are ubiquitous product tie-ins such as SpongeBob SquarePants popsicles and Scooby Doo cookies. Even if your parents didn't attempt to control your eating, advertisers would try and probably succeed. Research published in the journal *Pediatrics* showed that almost one-third of the six thousand children studied eat fast food each day. This is likely to be responsible for six extra pounds per child per year.

In addition to your parents telling you to finish everything that's on your plate when you were a child, you had cartoon characters, advertisements, and product tie-ins encouraging you to eat high-calorie, sugar- and fat-laden foods. At least when your parents were trying to control your eating, they frequently encouraged you to eat vegetables, fish, or meat. Ronald McDonald wants you to eat cheeseburgers and fries washed down with a soda or shake.

Ronald and his corporate colleagues not only want you to eat their offerings, they also want you to eat them in ever-larger quantities. The portions, calories, and fat grams of fast-food meals have been steadily increasing since McDonald's introduced the Happy Meal. The original order of french fries was about two ounces and 200 calories. A "large" order with about 320 calories was introduced in 1972. In 1982 a supersized order became available containing 540 calories and twenty-five grams of fat. Usually the larger-sized servings are priced in such a way that buying the regular size seems wasteful, because for just a little more money, you get considerably more food.

Throughout childhood and adolescence the constant inducements to eat large quantities of high-fat, high-calorie foods further undermine the body intelligence you were born with. External cues rather than your innate body intelligence increasingly determined when, what, and how much you would eat. Try to recall messages about eating that you got from television, advertising, or other media.

Using Food to Feel Good

When you are an infant, having a full tummy feels good. A few minutes earlier you were hungry. It was a very unpleasant experience, you cried loudly, your mother or father fed you, and you felt better. But what happens if you are crying for some other reason? Maybe your diaper needed to be changed or you were cold or frightened, so you cried. Dr. Hilde Bruch, a pioneer in the study of eating problems, suggested that a competent mother would be able to tell when her infant is crying from hunger rather than crying because of some other type of discomfort. The mother, making this distinction would comfort the child when necessary but would only offer nourishment when the infant was hungry. The child would associate eating with physical hunger, but not with any other discomfort. On the other hand, a less competent or a distracted mother might not make this distinction. As a result, the infant is fed whenever he or she cries regardless of hunger. The infant then learns that food provides the all-purpose solution to any uncomfortable situation.

When the child grows up, he or she won't be able to distinguish between physical hunger and other types of discomfort. As an adult when he or she is feeling unpleasant emotions, such as being sad, lonely, stressed, angry, or bored, it's likely that food will be used to make the bad feeling go away. Eating to soothe emotions further diminishes body intelligence.

Learning the Rules of Eating

Young children rarely eat alone. Early in childhood your parents, day-care providers, and friends teach you the "rules" of eating. You learn the structure of eating (breakfast, lunch, and dinner versus continuous snacks), the context of eating (eat in the dining room, not the bathroom), and the appropriateness of foods and food combinations (cereal instead of ice cream for breakfast; marshmallows don't go in soup). As you get older, you want to have more say over what you eat, but now your decisions will be influenced by the larger culture. If parents have difficulty finding the right balance between providing structure versus allowing you to make the choices, eating may become an arena for power struggles. Especially if you are female and your mother is concerned about her own weight and diet, she may feel the need to control what you eat even if she isn't as heavy-handed as Kelly's mother was. As parents increase control over their child's eating, the child's ability to regulate his or her eating decreases. Often the foods that the parents are trying to discourage become more attractive, while the foods the parents are promoting become disliked.

You started life eating intelligently. You ate when you were hungry and stopped when you were full. Mom and Dad tried to help guide you by exposing you to new foods, being concerned about your nutrition and weight, and discouraging wastefulness. In the process, they may have taught you to rely on external rather than internal signals to regulate your eating. Slick marketing helped you develop a taste for high-calorie, high-fat foods in ever-increasing portions, while simultaneously you came to associate eating with relief from uncomfortable emotional states. Food, eating, and the sensations of fullness now are associated with more than just replenishing your body's supply of nutrients. It's portrayed as something to bond over. External cues and internal emotions have become increasingly important in determining when and how much you will eat.

Looking at Your Body Intelligently

Most infants and toddlers like their bodies regardless of any imperfections they may have. Somewhere around age five or six, many children—especially girls—start to express body dissatisfaction and a drive to be thinner. In one study of middle-class girls, 30 percent of nine-year-olds, 55 percent of ten-year-olds, and 65 percent of eleven-year-olds were concerned that they were too fat. African-American girls tend to be more satisfied with their bodies even though, on average, they are heavier. For most girls the weight gain brought on by puberty further increases dissatisfaction with the body, but it is especially difficult for girls who mature early. Early maturing boys tend to be proud of their more masculine bodies, but girls who mature early are often uncomfortable with their rounded shape. They are likely to have a worse body image and try to diet to lose the "fat" to look more like their prepubescent friends.

Think back to your own childhood. When did you first become dissatisfied with your body? How old were you when you started thinking that you were too fat? Since a realistic, but nonpunitive body image is essential for body intelligence and long-term weight regulation, it is important to understand how your attitudes about your body developed.

Mom and Dad Again

Your parents lay the foundation for your body image. When you become a teenager your peers are more important, but until then your parents provide the most frequent feedback about your appearance. At the very least they pick your clothes, take you to get a haircut, and tell you to smile when they want to take your picture. If they are dissatisfied with your appearance, they will suggest what you need to do to improve. Frequently, the suggestion is that you lose weight. Even though it is usually prompted by a sincere concern about your appearance and health, this type of discussion can have long-lasting, negative consequences.

Bill was a thirty-eight-year-old, high-powered Silicon Valley entrepreneur who owned two rapidly growing small firms. He is a dynamic, take-charge kind of guy, except when it comes to his weight. Bill is 5 feet, 8 inches tall and weighed 265 pounds (BMI of 40.3) and was considering bariatric surgery. When I asked Bill about his childhood weight history he said that, although he was a "chubby" kid, it was "no big deal" until he was eight. His stepmother, concerned that he would become fat like his biological mother, had him take his shirt off and took his picture. When the pictures were developed a week later, she showed it to him so that he would recognize how heavy he had become. She put him on a diet.

Thirty years later Bill told me that he was "devastated" after this conversation with his stepmother. He has been concerned about his weight ever since. Despite repeated attempts to diet, a bout of bulimia during his adolescence, and his religious adherence to a rigorous exercise routine, Bill can't seem to stop "eating too much" and feeling bad about the way he looked.

The effects of parental comments aren't always as profound as they were with Bill, but research shows that comments can have a direct effect on the body image of children in elementary school. In addition, dieting mothers may affect their daughters' body images by setting an example of dissatisfaction. When a mother disparages her own body, or is preoccupied with diets, it is likely that her daughter's body image will also suffer.

Friends, Barbie, and Television

Once you were sent off to kindergarten, more people were offering their opinions about the shape of your body. Teasing and jokes from peers may have made you self-conscious and started your preoccupation with dieting with the hope that a slimmer body would increase your popularity. A 2000 study reported in the journal *Sex Roles* found that 75 percent of third-grade through fifth-grade children had been teased about their appearance or called ugly. The teasing didn't have a great effect on boys, but girls were more likely to have lower body esteem as a result.

Kerry, a forty-three-year-old bank employee, was raised in what she described as a "Leave It to Beaver" family. Her parents were happily married, they lived in a pleasant suburban neighborhood, and none of the three children had any more than the usual problems growing up. When she was eleven, she was swimming in the backyard pool with her brother Mike and his friend. Getting out of the pool, Mike told her she had a "bubble butt." The friend laughed and Kerry was embarrassed. The name stuck. Mike and many of the kids in the neighborhood called Kerry "bubble butt," or just "bubbles," whenever they wanted to get a reaction from her. More than thirty years later, she is still self-conscious about her buttocks and continues to search for the right combination of diet and exercise that will solve the problem.

Even if you were lucky enough to have avoided the barbed comments of your siblings and schoolmates, you will have been exposed to more subtle messages telling you that your body is flawed. Think about the magazines and books you read, the movies and TV shows you watched, the movie and music stars you idolized, and even the toys you played with. Since 25 percent of the models in some magazines meet the weight requirements for anorexia and the average Miss America had a BMI of 18.5, you probably didn't look like them, but can you remember trying to or wishing that you could? If you read teen magazines, compared yourself to movie stars, or played with Barbie (or GI Joe), it was quite likely that you felt too fat and became self-conscious about your body.

Although there is no evidence directly linking Barbie with the development of a poor body image, about 90 percent of American girls aged three to eleven own at least one Barbie and fewer than one in one hundred thousand women have body proportions similar to this toy. If Barbie represents some ideal of female beauty, virtually all the girls that play with her will feel that their bodies are unsatisfactory. The effect is less pronounced for boys, but they don't entirely escape the influence of popular culture. Action figures portray an unrealistically muscular physique that will be unattainable for most of the boys playing with them.

It doesn't matter if it was parental comments, peer teasing, or comparing yourself to Barbie that caused you to be unhappy with your body. Regardless of the cause, as your body dissatisfaction grows the likelihood that you will diet increases. For most teenagers dieting will only produce additional weight gain and more body dissatisfaction. For example, one study of 692 ninth-grade girls who were followed for three years found that the girls who dieted or used more radical weight-loss methods such as appetite suppressants or laxatives were *more* likely to gain weight than equally heavy girls who didn't use these methods.

While the role of the media in contributing to body dissatisfaction is undeniable, research suggests that some children are more susceptible to these messages than others. Early positive experiences such as success in athletics or parental acceptance of weight and body shape can increase body intelligence by "inoculating" a child so that the media images have less impact. On the other hand, parental criticism or peer teasing may leave the child vulnerable to the unrealistic images of slender beauty portrayed in the media.

Give some thought to your childhood experiences or exposure to the media. How have these experiences influenced the way you feel about your body now?

Using Your Body Intelligently

If you cringe when you hear the word *exercise*, try to recall how old you were when you started to feel uncomfortable with the idea of physical exertion. If you go far enough back in your childhood, you should be able to recall play activities that involved vigorous movement and activity, but that did not include the sense of dread that you now associate with exercising.

- When you were a kid did you jump rope in school during recess, or before classes began?
- Did you play ball with the kids on the block, run through the neighborhood playing hide-and-seek, ride your bicycle, roller-skate, swim, or hop on one foot playing jacks?

You probably haven't tried to play jacks for a while, but do you still enjoy riding a bike or swimming? If you don't, what happened to transform the fun you had using your body as a kid into the discomfort and avoidance of activity you now feel?

To understand your feelings about using your body, we again have to look at both your individual development and the larger cultural context surrounding your childhood experience, but first let's start with possible genetic contributions.

Loading the Gun

Similar to eating, the amount of physical activity a person engages in may be partially determined by heredity. One study showed that three-month-old infants who later became overweight were 20 percent less active than infants who didn't become overweight. Although there might have been some learning in the first three months, it is likely that some people are born with a predisposition to be more active. Other research has demonstrated that there are inherited differences in the frequency of small, fidgeting types of body movements. While fidgeting is unlikely to produce significant weight loss, this genetic trait could account for between one hundred to seven hundred calories per day, making it easier for some lucky people to regulate their weight. As with eating, genetics may contribute to your comfort with exercise, but it is likely that environmental influences play a more important role in determining how many calories you'll burn up with physical activity.

Pulling the Trigger

Even with a genetic predisposition to be active, it is necessary to be in an environment that allows or encourages activity in order for the predisposition to be expressed. Unfortunately this type of environment is increasingly rare. Elementary school children in California average fifteen minutes per week of organized exercise even though the state mandates one hundred minutes per week. Even if you had more frequent gym classes when you went to school, did you participate or did you try to avoid some of the activities? It is likely that many of your attitudes about exercise were developed before you got to school. As with eating, when you were young your parents played a critical role in establishing your activity habits.

Parents exert influence directly by encouraging, nagging, rewarding, and punishing their child's activities, but they may indirectly have a greater impact by modeling, supporting, and participating in physical activity. Look back at your childhood and try to remember your interactions with your parents about activity. Were they supportive? If you were involved in athletics, did they encourage your participation, take you to practice, and come to your games? Children who are active are more likely to feel supported by their parents than inactive children. Were your parents active themselves? One study found that children between the ages of four and seven years old who had active parents were six times as likely to be active when compared with peers who had inactive parents. Unfortunately, most kids don't have active parents. Fewer than 30 percent of parents of elementary school children exercise three or more days per week. Parental exhortations to exercise will be ineffective if the parents' behavior communicates that activity is unpleasant or not very important.

Mark is a good example of an inactive child who grew up to become an inactive adult. As a child, his father encouraged him to "go out and play," but Mark's dad was rarely active and did not participate in any activity with him. Mark recalled one occasion when he asked his father to play ball with him when he was six. His father reluctantly agreed, but shortly after starting to toss the softball, the father invited a neighborhood child to play, and then excused himself. When Mark was eleven years old, his father persuaded him to sign up for Little League baseball, but once Mark agreed his father showed little interest. In high school, Mark volunteered for clerical work so that he could avoid gym class, and he remained inactive throughout his teen years. Now, as a young adult, Mark has joined a gym several times because he recognizes the need to exercise to lose weight. Each attempt has been unsuccessful because "it's boring, I hate to sweat, and I feel awful when I'm out of breath or when my muscles can't make the weights budge."

The Tyranny of Screens

When you were a child, how much television did you watch? On average, American children spend twenty-four hours each week watching television. Three of the five years between the ages of twelve and seventeen are spent watching television, videos, or DVDs, or staring at computers and video games. In one study of third and fourth graders, less time spent in front of screens was associated with significant decreases in BMI, waist circumference, waist-to-hip ratio, and eating while watching. In addition to subjecting children to unrealistic body images and countless advertisements for food that are likely to increase eating, watching takes up the free time that could be spent doing something active. As an added "bonus," watching television may decrease the resting metabolic rate causing fewer calories to be used. Instead of watching the tube, you would have been better off reading, doing your homework, or almost any other passive activity. If kids aren't getting much exercise in school and they are spending most of their free time watching a screen, is it surprising that they are uncomfortable exercising when they become overweight adults and are trying to lose weight?

Examine your childhood experiences with physical activity. Can you recall experiences that influenced your current attitudes about exercise?

Where Does Your Body Intelligence Come From?

For the sake of convenience I have discussed the development of body intelligence in terms of each of the three components separately, but in the real world there is an interaction of the components as you develop. Teasing and media images can increase body dissatisfaction leading to dieting that results in weight gain that makes physical activity more difficult so body dissatisfaction increases . . . it can be a never-ending cycle. The result is a continuing erosion of body intelligence. On the other hand, supportive parents who encourage healthy eating without being too controlling and who help their children understand the unreality of some of the images portrayed in the media—while modeling, encouraging, and supporting their participation in sports and physical activity—can increase their child's body intelligence.

Review your answers to the questions posed in this chapter and consider your childhood experiences in light of the information presented. Think about:

- Your parents' attitudes about food and eating
- Whether you were breast-fed or bottle-fed
- Your parents' attempts to control your eating
- The effects of the media on your food choices
- The use of food as a source of comfort
- Your parents' dissatisfaction with your appearance or weight
- Negative comments from peers about your appearance or weight
- Dissatisfaction when comparing your appearance or weight to media images
- Lack of parental modeling and support for physical activity
- The impact of excessive TV watching

If you have identified some of the sources of your current eating, body image, and exercise behaviors, you're on your way to restoring your body intelligence. Remember, the goal is not to assign blame. Even if it were possible to fairly apportion responsibility, nothing would be accomplished. Instead, what we want to do is see how your long-standing patterns developed. With this understanding, the mystery and potency of the patterns decreases and your ability to alter them and rebuild body intelligence increases. Let's start with eating. In Chapter 3, you'll examine your reasons for eating.

CHAPTER 3

WHY ARE YOU EATING THAT?

If I asked you why you were eating something, the likely answer would be, "Because I'm hungry." But what exactly is *hunger*? Is it an uncomfortable rumbling in your stomach that demands your attention? In that case, any palatable food will do as long as it makes the hunger pangs go away. Maybe it's not a rumbling in your stomach, but you have a hunger in your mouth, a craving for a specific sensation that requires a particular food such as ice cream, potato chips, or even Brussels sprouts. Or maybe your stomach is quiet and you don't have any cravings. In fact, you weren't even thinking about food until you walked by the cookie stand in the mall and smelled those freshly baked chocolate chip cookies. Suddenly you've developed a hunger that can only be satisfied by Mrs. Fields.

To develop body intelligence you need to look more carefully at what is happening when you say you are hungry. The typical use of the word *hunger* could encompass many different explanations for the desire to eat. Since body intelligence includes understanding your motivations for eating, in this chapter we explore the specifics of the various reasons for eating and learn the signs that will help you identify which type of hunger you are experiencing. When you know exactly why you want to eat, you will be able to fulfill that need—often with less food. Sometimes you'll be able to take care of that need without eating anything. For example, there's no point in having that candy bar when the reason that you are eating has nothing to do with the taste of chocolate. Even if you are a confirmed chocolate-lover, if your stomach is reminding you that it has been four hours since you ate, you might be just as satisfied with more nutritious food.

Consider the following three examples.

- Sara is a junior in college. It is 11:30 A.M. and she is in her English class listening to her professor's analysis of a Shakespeare sonnet. She feels her stomach rumble, hears the noise it makes, and hopes that the guy sitting next to her didn't hear it. She starts to plan what she will eat for lunch and checks the clock to see how long it will be before the class is over. As soon as the professor dismisses the class, she heads to the cafeteria in the student union and orders a chicken tostada.
- Cal finished dinner an hour ago. His wife is getting their two small children ready for bed. He is sitting on the sofa watching "Monday Night Football." During the halftime break, a commercial for Doritos comes on. He gets up and looks in the kitchen for something to eat. He finds a bag of potato chips, grabs a beer, and is back in his seat before the second half starts.
- Margo is bummed. Although she has been in sales for some time, she recently passed the real estate exam and started working for a local broker. She had been showing houses to a fussy couple who couldn't seem to agree on what they were looking for. She called them this morning to schedule a showing of a house that she knew they would love. The wife told her that the couple had made an offer on another house, using a different broker, and the offer had been accepted. Margo hung up the phone, started wondering if she had made a mistake switching careers, and helped herself to a handful of candy that was sitting in a bowl on a coworker's desk.

Sara, Cal, and Margo illustrate the three most common reasons for eating: eating to satisfy physical hunger, eating prompted by external cues, and eating to soothe unpleasant emotions. In this chapter we'll take a closer look at eating prompted by hunger and eating in response to external cues. Then in Chapter 4 we'll explore emotions and eating.

Physical Hunger

If you've ever missed a meal or two you know that hunger is an unpleasant experience that increasingly dominates your life. While there is little debate about the unpleasantness of a growling stomach and light-headedness there is disagreement among scientists about the cause. The traditional view is that hunger pangs are caused by a decline in the body's energy supply. Your hypothalamus (located in the middle of your brain) signals that your blood sugar is too low while the contractions from muscles around your stomach let you know that it's running on empty. (Sometimes, the stomach noises that go along with the contractions let everyone nearby know, too.) According to this view, when you eat, you increase blood glucose (sugar) and the hunger goes away.

An alternative view holds that being hungry has nothing to do with food deprivation. According to this view, even if you're slender you have enough energy stored in your body fat to last for at least a month. If you're obese you could go for a year without eating, living off of your fat. What causes hunger isn't a lack of nourishment, it is a result of changes that occur in the body when there is food available and you are anticipating that you will eat. As the expected mealtime approaches, insulin is released from your pancreas. The insulin removes glucose from the blood and you feel hungry, but if you don't eat anything the glucose returns to normal levels by itself. According to this view, when Sara is sitting in her class watching the clock, her expectation that lunch is imminent triggers the insulin release. If she had been disoriented and didn't know what time it was or how long it had been since she last ate, the insulin wouldn't have been released and she wouldn't feel hunger.

If hunger were just a result of food deprivation, you would expect hunger to get more intense as you missed more meals, but this rarely happens. If you can ignore your hunger pangs, eventually they'll go away. When you miss lunch you'll feel stomach contractions but an hour or so later, it's likely that your stomach will calm down. You won't feel those contractions again until dinnertime approaches and your pancreas again secretes insulin. If you persist in not eating (and I'm not recommending that you do), the hunger pangs will go away after about five days of starvation. Anorexics who have been on a prolonged hunger strike are not lying when they report that they're not hungry even though they haven't had anything to eat for days or weeks. I've had the experience of working with an anorexic woman who insisted that she wasn't hungry even though she hadn't had anything to eat for four days. During our session my stomach started growling because I was a half an hour late for lunch.

Dr. Paul Rozin, a University of Pennsylvania researcher, clearly demonstrated that psychological variables could easily override physical hunger cues in determining food consumption. He studied two men who had severe amnesia resulting from brain injuries. Their memory loss was so profound that neither man could remember events that happened a few minutes earlier. Dr. Rozin fed the men lunch, waited less than a half hour, and then offered them a second meal. Although they had just had lunch and were full, neither remembered the earlier meal so they ate the second meal. Physical hunger wasn't responsible for this eating. The sight and smell of food, combined with the inability to remember the recent meals, was enough to trigger eating.

Although the precise mechanisms responsible for hunger haven't been established, what is clear is that hunger is at least partially controlled by psychological processes such as expectations and memory. Although hunger can be an intense experience, it isn't inevitable that you will eat when you have been deprived of food, nor is hunger the only influence that can make you want to eat.

Overriding Your Hunger

Even if you are not an anorexic and don't have amnesia, habitual dieting may leave you out of touch with your physical hunger. Being on a diet usually requires that you ignore or override hunger so that you can limit your eating. If you get good at it, the connection between hunger and eating is lost and your eating is determined by the meal plans suggested by the diet's author. Once you've gone off the diet, the ability to use physical hunger to regulate eating doesn't automatically return. Increasing body intelligence requires that you can take an accurate reading of your body's hunger signals. Although there are reasons to eat other than being physically hungry, it is important to know when you are eating because you are hungry and when you are eating for some other reason. Understanding your different motivations will enable you to make deliberate choices about your eating.

Knowing When to Stop

Accurately assessing physical hunger can be difficult if you have been a habitual dieter, but even if you're out of practice, there is no mistaking a sharp hunger pang. So, if a hunger pang is a signal to start eating, what are the signals telling you to stop? Unfortunately, your body's signaling system to tell you that you've had enough is more subtle, and unless you pay careful attention, you may not notice it.

Knowing when you are no longer hungry is important because your need for food fluctuates. Some days you should stop eating sooner; other days you can keep going. For example, if you're a woman, it's likely that you will need between 200 and 500 additional calories each day during the second half of your menstrual cycle. But when the next cycle starts will you continue eating the same amount? Or, if you're a weekend jock, but a weekday desk jockey, will you vary your eating according to your level of activity?

The physical process of satiation (the scientific name for the end of hunger after eating) is complicated. Until recently, most attention was focused on the stomach's swelling after eating, and on the effects of sugar and free fatty acids circulating in the bloodstream. Researchers have found that hormones such as ghrelin and PYY—in conjunction with the hypothalamus—regulate feeding. In the not too distant future researchers will probably figure out the precise formula that predicts satiation. Whatever the complex interaction that determines satiation turns out to be, it is clear that after you've started to eat there is no flashing light and loud bell to tell you that you've had enough. Feeling satiated is especially difficult for bulimics and binge eaters who may consume enormous quantities of food, stopping only when they are interrupted or they feel nauseated. Even if researchers find a drug that will make you feel full with less food, you will still need to identify the feeling of satiation and use this information to decide when to stop eating.

RECOGNIZING WHEN YOU'VE HAD ENOUGH

Can you distinguish between being hungry and being comfortably full? Being comfortably full usually is accompanied by feelings of contentment and well-being. Surprisingly, it doesn't take a lot of food to feel satisfied. For example, if you're hungry in the middle of the afternoon, a 100-calorie snack such as an apple will usually do the trick. If you're not sure when you're no longer hungry, try this exercise suggested by author Dr. Barbara Rolls in *Volumetrics*. Use a scale of 1 (starving) to 10 (so full you can't eat another bite) to rate your hunger before a meal. During the meal stop several times and rate your hunger again. When your rating reaches 5, ask yourself if it's time to stop eating. You'll probably find that your hunger stopped long before the food on your plate is finished. If you decide to continue eating, recognize that you are eating for a reason other than hunger.

External Eating

When Cal grabbed a bag of potato chips to eat while watching football, his stomach wasn't growling, his blood sugar wasn't low, and his hypothalamus was doing fine; his eating had nothing to do with physical hunger. Similar to Cal, most of your eating will take place when you aren't physically hungry but will be determined by either external cues or emotional arousal (see Chapter 4).

To get an idea of your external eating tendencies look at the following statements. Put a check mark next to each statement that is true (or mostly true) for you.

❑ 1. When I am around other people who are eating, I'll eat something even if I'm not hungry.
❑ 2. When I'm shopping I'll buy something I hadn't planned to just because it looks good.
❑ 3. When food smells good I have to try a little.
❑ 4. It's hard to ignore the smell of fresh baked goods.

❑ 5. If a food tastes especially good, I will eat more of it than I had planned to.

❑ 6. If I am hungry I won't eat unless the food tastes good.

❑ 7. If it is time for dinner but I've already eaten, I'll eat dinner anyway.

❑ 8. When I lose track of the time I may forget to eat.

❑ 9. When I go to the movies, I buy popcorn or another snack even if I'm not hungry.

❑ 10. I like to have something to eat or drink while I'm watching television.

❑ 11. I watch TV or read when I eat by myself.

❑ 12. If I were alone, I'd rather snack than eat a regular meal.

❑ 13. It wouldn't be Thanksgiving if I didn't eat too much.

❑ 14. Whenever there's a special occasion I celebrate with food.

According to Dr. Stanley Schachter, the psychologist who first identified external eating, normal weight people eat when they are physically hungry. In contrast, overweight individuals eat in response to external cues such as the time of day or the smell of food. Since we live in a world filled with food cues (food advertisements, restaurant signs, other people eating), external eaters will gain weight. Although the idea that external eating caused obesity created a lot of excitement, after decades of research it appears that the process of gaining weight is more complicated. Dr. Judith Rodin (a former student of Dr. Schachter's) reviewed the research on external eating and concluded:

> Most people are responsive to some external food cues. Indeed, there are people in all weight categories who are highly responsive to these external cues. . . . While a high degree of responsiveness does lead to overeating and weight gain, the final level of obesity attained over the long term is influenced by a great number of factors. . . .

External eating *is not* the single cause of obesity (many normal weight people are external eaters), but it is one source of unnecessary eating. Since external eating is unnecessary eating, increasing body intelligence requires that you control eating by determining which type of cues trigger your eating and learning to avoid eating in response to these cues.

To get an idea of your patterns, go back to the statements you just checked. These statements are examples of the most common types of external eating:

- Visual food cues (items 1 and 2)
- Food smell (3 and 4)
- Food taste (5 and 6)
- Time of day (7 and 8)
- Eating rituals (9 and 10)
- Solo eating (11 and 12)
- Celebrations (13 and 14)

Which type of external cues are most likely to trigger your eating? Keep in mind that these examples represent a small sample of possible external cues. In the rest of this chapter, we'll review a wider range of external eating situations. To increase body intelligence you'll have to minimize all external eating. Let's look at the specific types of external eating in more detail.

Seeing and Smelling

Rebecca, a forty-three-year-old teacher who attended a group I conducted, described the discovery she made one afternoon. On her way home from school, usually between 3:30 and 4:00 P.M., she drove through the take-out window at Taco Bell and ordered one of their smaller burritos to "hold me over until dinner." That afternoon, because of delays due to road construction, she took a different route home. It was after 5:00 P.M. before she realized that she didn't have her customary afternoon snack, and she wasn't hungry. For Rebecca, it was literally a case of out of sight, out of mind. Rebecca figured that, if she could permanently alter her route, she could save the calories from her usual snack.

One Friday afternoon Sam, a fifty-two-year-old real estate appraiser, returned to the office after spending most of the day out in the field. Although he was still full from his substantial lunch, and he was planning on going out to eat with friends in the evening, Sam couldn't resist the brownies a coworker had brought in to celebrate her birthday. If he had just felt the need to eat something to be social he could have had some of the fruit that was available, but the apples and pears didn't smell as good or look as attractive as the brownies.

Think about all the visual food cues you encounter in a typical day. In addition to the fast-food signs and holiday goodies you encounter, there are:

- Food advertisements on television, radio, newspapers, and magazines
- The sight of other people eating
- Candy, nuts, and snacks on tables in your living room, your dresser drawer, your car's glove compartment, and your coworkers' desks
- The smells of cooking or baking food
- Appetizing pictures on packaged food wrappers
- Vending machines in hallways and public places
- Parties and social events with food prominently displayed
- Cruises and all-inclusive resorts where meals and snacks are a main theme and always available

You are being bombarded. It is impossible to tally the number of visual food cues you see each day, but the number is surely in the thousands. Although some environments have fewer visual food cues—a library for example—you can't completely escape from them. Even in a library you still might see vending machines, pictures of food in magazines, students snacking, and candy on the librarian's desk.

If you checked the first two statements it is likely that you are responsive to visual food cues. Do you find yourself getting "hungry" when you see an ad for a cake mix or when you drive past a favorite restaurant? It doesn't take much to trigger eating; even small changes in visual cues can do the trick. For example, one study showed that highly external participants ate more cashews when the nuts were brightly illuminated and fewer cashews when the lights were dim.

Think how you can reduce the number of visual food cues in your environment. For example, if you use aluminum foil rather than clear plastic wrap for leftovers, the food will be less visible when you go to the refrigerator. As a result, you'll be less likely to have an unscheduled snack. Several other suggestions for minimizing visual food cues are presented in the "Minimizing Visual Cues" sidebar.

The sense of smell works the same way. When a food has a tempting aroma, people who are responsive to external cues are more likely to indulge, regardless of their physical hunger. The proprietors of bakeries and cookie stands in shopping malls are aware of this phenomenon. They vent their ovens to make sure that external eaters passing by are tempted to sample their high-calorie wares. Body intelligence doesn't require that you hold your breath to avoid pleasant smells. But knowing that you are susceptible to this type of external cue will make it less likely that you will find yourself eating.

Tasting

If you missed a meal and felt the uncomfortable hunger pangs in your stomach, but the only food available was spinach or broccoli, how much would you eat? Would you stop after a few mouthfuls? If you weren't as hungry, but instead of spinach you were offered your favorite ice cream, would you eat more? Especially for external eaters, the taste of food is more important than actual hunger in determining how much food is eaten.

Similar to the rest of the human race, you were born liking sweet tastes and rejecting bitter, salty, or sour-tasting food. In addition to these four sensations, our adult sense of taste includes the smell of food, its texture, and how it feels in your mouth. While there may be exceptions, humans generally prefer foods that are "energy dense"—high in both sugar and fat—to foods that are less rich. We like the sweetness of sugar and the texture and feel that fat provides. Not surprisingly, dense foods are more likely to contribute to weight gain. For example, chocolate and peanut butter provide five or six calories per gram while the same gram of vegetables or fruit will contain less than one-half calorie. Despite their higher caloric content, dense foods do not do a better job of satisfying hunger. To feel full you'll have to eat the same amount of food regardless of whether it is chocolate or spinach. The problem with choosing chocolate instead of a fruit to satisfy your hunger is that you will have consumed about ten times as many calories.

MINIMIZING VISUAL CUES

To control external eating you will need to minimize the amount of food that you see. Although you could try eating in the dark, it is more practical to arrange your environment to reduce the number of visual food cues. Here are a few suggestions:

➤ Store tempting foods on the top shelves of cabinets or bottom shelves of the refrigerator so they will be less noticeable.

➤ Remove foods from every room in the house except the kitchen (no candy dishes in the living room, no chocolates in the top dresser drawer, and no snacks in the car's glove compartment or on the desk at work).

➤ At parties and social events, after you have eaten, stay away from the room with the food.

➤ Don't make phone calls, read, or watch television in the kitchen (or any other place with food cues).

➤ When shopping, avoid the aisles with candies and desserts.

➤ Whenever possible, get up from the dinner table as soon as you have finished eating.

➤ At home, serve reasonable portions of food in the kitchen and bring the plates to the dining table. Don't put serving bowls or platters on the table. If you really want seconds, go back into the kitchen to get them.

➤ If you must have treats in the house, don't buy them in bulk packages. Instead of buying a half gallon of ice cream (or low-fat yogurt), buy single servings such as pops, cones, or cups. It is more likely that you'll have a large serving of ice cream without thinking about it than it is that you'll go back to the freezer and get a second treat without thinking about it.

➤ When eating out, ask the waitperson to take the bread away as soon as possible.

➤ Resign from the clean plate club. Even if it feels a little uncomfortable, leave a small amount of food on your plate to help unlearn the association between the sight of food and eating.

If your eating is determined primarily by taste, an external cue, rather than by hunger, you will gain weight. While everybody has his or her favorite foods, and there is nothing wrong with enjoying eating (see Chapter 6), developing body intelligence requires that you learn how to eat to satisfy hunger while enjoying the taste of less dense foods.

Time

Perhaps the most common external reason for eating without hunger is simply the time of day. The clock on the wall says it's noon, so you eat lunch, or if it's 7:00 P.M., it's time for dinner. If there were no way to tell the time, you might not know when to eat.

It's hard to overestimate the role time plays in eating. Several classic studies have illustrated how time of day, independent of any physical hunger, could determine eating. For example, in one study subjects sat in a windowless room facing a clock that was programmed to either speed up or slow down the passage of time. The subjects ate more or less depending on the doctored clock rather than hunger resulting from the actual passage of time. These findings suggest that, if you tend to be an external eater, the clock may have a greater influence on your eating than your stomach.

If you examine your eating patterns, it is more likely that you will find instances in which you ate because it was mealtime even though you were not physically hungry. For example, Stephanie, a thirty-one-year-old participant in a weight group I conducted, kept track of her eating. Her records for one day showed that after a decent lunch and stopping for snacks at an after-work reception, she went home and had a full dinner. She wasn't particularly hungry, but it was 6:30 P.M. and the rest of the family was eating, so she joined them.

There are many different patterns of external eating. Stephanie's eating was clearly influenced by time, but she was less susceptible to visual and olfactory (smell) cues. Since she was able to see food without having an urge to eat, we decided that it would be safe for her to join her family at the table and sip on a diet soda while they ate. If she had been more responsive to visual cues, it would have been better for her to go to another room until her family had finished eating. Understanding your external eating cues will allow you to develop strategies to minimize their effects.

Eating Rituals

Eating because it is mealtime is not the only example of habits determining food consumption. Eating rituals may develop in certain situations regardless of the time of day. When you go to the movies, do you buy popcorn before taking your seat? Would it feel a little strange to watch the movie without nibbling on something? If this is one of your eating rituals, it doesn't make any difference if you're going to a matinee or an evening show, or if you had a meal right before the movie started. Whatever the circumstances, you will have the popcorn. Popcorn at movies, hot dogs and beer at baseball games, coffee and doughnuts at the morning work break, and milk and cookies after school are a few of the common eating rituals. In addition, most people develop their own, unique eating rituals.

Charles, a forty-five-year-old pharmaceutical salesman, was required to make a 200-mile trip every other week to call on doctors in a town at the far edge of his territory. He dreaded the long drive, especially the hour and a half he had to spend on a lengthy stretch of desolate interstate. After several months, a new Wendy's opened at about the halfway point in the journey. Charles stopped for a chocolate Frosty one day, and he was hooked. It didn't make any difference if he was traveling at 10:00 A.M., 4:30 P.M., or 8:00 P.M. If he had a meal before leaving, the Frosty was his dessert. If he was going to eat when he arrived, it was an appetizer. Regardless of the time of day, or the amount of time that had elapsed since his last meal, every trip included a stop for the Frosty.

Katherine, a thirty-seven-year-old social worker, would come home from work and have dinner with her family. As soon as the dishes were done, she would make herself a huge bowl of popcorn, grab a bunch of grapes (when in season), and get into bed and watch the soap operas she had prerecorded. If popcorn and grapes weren't available, she would search the pantry to find another food she could eat while watching her soaps. The taste of the food wasn't as important as the eating-while-watching ritual.

Think about your own routines:

- Can you find examples of eating that occur in a specific situation regardless of your physical hunger or the time of day?
- Do you need a snack when watching television?
- Is there a task that you routinely perform that is followed by a treat?
- Do you reward yourself with a treat when you get home from work?

The sidebar, "Changing the Ritual," offers some suggestions.

Katherine, the popcorn-eating, soap-opera watcher, rarely paid attention to the sensations of eating popcorn since she was usually involved in her soap opera. It was just a mindless activity that kept her hands busy. To give up this eating ritual, Katherine took up crocheting while watching her soaps. She left the yarn and needles on top of the television so she could grab them before getting into bed. Charles, the Frosty-loving pharmaceutical salesman, prepared a snack before his trip and then stopped at a rest area two exits before the Wendy's. When the weather cooperated, he broke up his drive by taking a little walk and having his snack.

Eating Alone

How often do you eat by yourself? While humans vary in their need for social contact, most of us enjoy eating meals with others and feel odd eating alone. I remember hearing about a monk who was a member of a strict Roman Catholic order. The monk had asked for, and was given, permission to live by himself in a little cottage, as a hermit. Despite his self-imposed isolation, he frequently chose to eat with the rest of the religious community. Apparently being isolated was difficult only at mealtimes.

For many meals, the act of eating is less important than the social contact that is going on. Some social interactions would be awkward,

CHANGING THE RITUAL

Identify one of your frequent eating rituals. This is a type of eating that is not motivated by hunger or mealtimes, but by a specific set of circumstances such as going to the movies or coming home from work. Visual cues may be present, but they are not necessary for some rituals. In your notebook, briefly describe your ritual.

Where does this ritual usually take place? For example, you snack while watching television in the living room, or wherever you usually watch. Write these locations in your notebook.

Plan an alternative to eating when you are in the ritual situation. In your notebook, write down some specific activities you could do instead of eating, such as knitting while watching TV, holding hands in the movies, or drinking a glass of sparkling water when you get home from work.

even impossible, without eating. For example, imagine a young man who has met a woman he'd like to get to know better. It is unlikely that he would suggest that they meet for the sole purpose of checking each other out. On the other hand, suggesting that they get something to eat or drink seems more natural, even though neither may be paying attention to the food they are eating.

If eating with others is one of life's little pleasures, eating alone may be one of life's little pains. When you do eat by yourself, you may find it awkward or mildly uncomfortable and, therefore, may change your eating behaviors to minimize your discomfort. For example,

- If you are eating at home, do you turn on the TV for company, call someone on the phone, or read something to distract yourself?
- If you had to eat by yourself with no distractions, would you gobble the food as fast as possible to get the meal over with quickly?
- Would you avoid a lonely sit-down meal by snacking while standing up?

Any of these behaviors are likely to result in unnecessary eating or poor food choices.

Why are you comfortable doing other things by yourself but uncomfortable eating alone? It is likely that you have accepted the dieting mentality that implies that you have no right to eat, and when you do eat, you should feel guilty about it. When you are eating alone, there is nothing to take your attention away from what you are doing. If this makes you feel guilty then it's likely that you will employ several strategies to distract yourself. Geneen Roth, author of several popular books on eating disorders, suggests that eating

> . . . *doesn't count if you're not sitting down. . . . When you eat and the majority of your attention is focused on something other than the act of eating, tasting, chewing, satisfying, you are as much as pretending that you are not eating.*

Eating out alone can be even more difficult. *Los Angeles Times* travel columnist Susan Spano suggests, "Solo dining in restaurants makes some people so uneasy that they grab meals in food stalls and order room service in hotels to avoid the ordeal." Not only are you painfully aware of what you are eating, but also everyone else in the room can watch you doing it. In addition to the embarrassment of eating in public, you may also feel self-conscious eating alone if everyone else is eating with others. You may feel that you stand out as the only one without a partner. If you're not staying in a hotel and you can't order room service, you might avoid this discomfort by using the drive-thru window at a fast-food restaurant and eating in your car.

Why should you be concerned about being uncomfortable eating alone? Unfortunately, many of the strategies we develop to minimize the discomfort of solo meals can contribute to unnecessary eating. For example, if you snack while standing rather than sitting down to eat a meal, you are more likely to eat high-calorie snack foods. Also, since you are not having a well-defined lunch or dinner, there are fewer guidelines to help you regulate your eating. With your food on your plate you know how much you're eating, but if you're snacking, it's hard to remember if this is your third trip to the refrigerator, or your fourth.

In a study on the effects awareness has on food consumption, University of Toronto psychologists invited overweight and normal weight women to eat a meal as part of a study "measuring performance before and after eating." The subjects were left alone in a small room to eat the meal. Half of the subjects were facing a large mirror on the wall as they ate. For the other half, the mirror was covered. Both overweight and normal weight women ate considerably less when they could see themselves in the mirror. These results suggest that anything that increases your awareness of your eating will be helpful in trying to lose weight. You don't need a big mirror in your dining room, just turn off the television or put the book away while eating. Take your snacks to the table and sit down rather than eating while standing in the kitchen. The exercise in the "Pay Attention to Your Eating Behavior" sidebar will help you become comfortable eating by yourself and paying attention to what you're eating.

Celebrating

Try to imagine Thanksgiving without a turkey dinner. How about a child's birthday party without a cake? A wedding reception without hors d'oeuvres, Easter without candy, Passover without matzos, Valentine's Day without chocolate, or the Fourth of July without a barbeque? Without special foods, these occasions would feel unnatural to many people; something would be missing. Physical hunger is rarely the cause of eating Halloween candy or the second helping of turkey at Thanksgiving. The celebration is an external cue that requires that you consume specific foods and, often, that you eat them in large quantities. When you turn down second (or third) helpings of turkey, the hostess might feel slighted or you might be seen as a party pooper.

Celebrating with food can be a major source of weight gain. In one study of dieters, the researchers compared weight gain during the Thanksgiving through New Year's holiday season with weight gain during the rest of the year. The dieters gained five times as much during the holidays. If you have a busy social life and frequently go to parties, receptions, and holiday get-togethers, you can probably gain weight

---

PAY ATTENTION TO YOUR EATING BEHAVIOR

Try this exercise. The next time you are home by yourself and it's time to eat, prepare a normal meal, sit down at the dining room or kitchen table (not in the living room), and eat your meal without television, radio, books, newspapers, magazines, or any other distractions. Just eat. Pay attention to how you feel and the thoughts that go through your mind. Does it feel weird? Are you bored? Do you think you should be doing something useful, instead of wasting your time "just eating"? Are you eating faster to get it over with?

If you experience any unpleasantness, stop and remind yourself that eating, whether you are alone or with other people, is a perfectly reasonable activity. Eating alone, even if you are in a restaurant filled with couples enjoying each other's company, does not imply that you are friendless or unlovable. If you are feeling guilty about "wasting time," remember that even if you eat slowly, eating is a legitimate activity worthy of a little time. If you are bored, focus your attention on the food. Mentally compare it with the last time you had the same dish. Notice the taste (sweet? salty?), the seasonings (spicy? bitter?), the texture (smooth? rough?), and the sensations (crunchy? cool?) as you eat it. Learn to enjoy the quiet time that a solo meal offers. With practice you will become comfortable eating by yourself.

---

effortlessly! As you develop body intelligence, you will recognize the role that food plays in these events and adjust your eating to participate comfortably without adding unnecessary calories.

Jean, a forty-eight-year-old nurse who attended one of my workshops, described the methods she used to regulate her holiday eating. She was particularly pleased with the strategy she used at parties where the food was served buffet-style.

When we've got a big party to go to, I tell Tom [her husband] that I'm going to need his help. I tell him that I'm going to be careful about what

I eat. Actually, I don't rely on him for anything, but just telling him what I'm going to do makes me stick to my plan. Usually most of the food is spread out on the dining room table. I'll do most of my socializing in the living room, the family room, or any place but the dining room. I'll get the food I want from the dining room and take it into the living room so I won't be tempted to nibble. When I'm finished eating, I'll get a glass of mineral water and sip on it while I'm talking with my friends. If I've got the glass in my hands, I feel like I'm participating so I'm more comfortable and it will be harder to nibble when I've already got something in my hands.

By planning ahead, and "going on record" (telling her husband what she was going to do), Jean was able to minimize unnecessary eating at holiday celebrations and avoided gaining weight.

Neutralizing External Cues

After reading the information in this chapter, you should have a better idea of which types of situations cause you the most difficulty. Before moving on, take a moment and consider the following types of external eating. For each that is relevant for you, write two specific examples in your notebook of eating that occurs when you're not physically hungry.

- Situations where the sight of food (or food-related stimuli) triggers eating
- The smell of food(s) that I find irresistible
- A food taste that makes me want to eat more than I need
- A time that I routinely eat even when not physically hungry
- A frequent eating ritual
- How I distract myself when eating alone
- Celebrations that usually result in overeating

Habits don't change overnight. It takes time, attention, and persistence to substitute a new behavior for a long-standing habit. Trying to change too many habits at once will leave you feeling overwhelmed and ready to give up. Instead, look at your answers to the previous questions, pick three that will be the easiest to change, and put a check mark next to them. For each, plan a strategy for changing the habit, and write it in your notebook. Start with a few ideas from this chapter and add your own to create comprehensive behaviors. Specify what you will do differently and make a time line for implementing the steps that will produce habit change. Remember, this isn't a diet with forbidden foods; body intelligence is about changing habits. If you find yourself back in the diet-thinking mode, go back and review Chapter 1.

You should plan on being persistent (although not perfect!) in your efforts. With two or three weeks of practice, you will notice that the new behavior comes more naturally; it doesn't require as much attention to avoid eating when confronted with the external cue. Once this happens, you'll be ready to tackle the next three external eating situations on your list.

Now You Know Why

By now you should have an idea of some of the reasons, other than physical hunger, that you eat. Although everyone eats in response to external cues on occasion, your score on the External Eating Scale and your response to the questions posed in this chapter should help you identify which types of external cues are most likely to make you want to eat. Recognizing these eating triggers is a major step toward developing body intelligence. Often just being aware that, "I'm not hungry, I only want that cookie because it looks good," or "I'm not hungry, I'm eating these cashews because everyone else is eating" is enough to help you decide not to eat. With awareness you may find yourself becoming resentful of advertisers' deliberate use of stimuli intended to make you eat, and then you may decide not to respond. There may be more satisfaction in recognizing the cue and not responding to it than there would have been if you gave in and ate the food being promoted. With increasing body intelligence your eating will become a matter of conscious choice—*you* get to decide if you want to eat—rather than an automatic response to environmental cues. You can increase your body intelligence by:

- Recognizing when your eating is prompted by internal, physical hunger versus an external cue
- Identifying the types of external cues that make you want to eat and learning to avoid eating in response to those cues
- Recognizing the role that eating plays in celebrations and rituals and then planning to reduce the amount you eat in these situations
- Becoming comfortable eating alone so that you can make good food choices and minimize unnecessary eating

CHAPTER 4

BEN AND JERRY TO THE RESCUE

Chris, a forty-seven-year-old nurse, was visiting her friend, Barbara. After a nice dinner at a fancy restaurant, they sat down to watch television. Barbara was eating Ben and Jerry's ice cream when the phone rang. It was Chris's daughter calling to inform her that she was taking her kids and leaving her husband. Seeing Chris's disappointment, Barbara reached over and handed her friend the ice cream and spoon, saying, "Here, you'll feel better."

Betsy was a sixty-two-year-old housewife married to Paul, a farmer who strongly believed in the traditional, subservient role of women. Every morning, before he left the house, he would "remind" Betsy of the tasks she needed to accomplish that day. Since Betsy weighed close to 200 pounds, he also assumed responsibility for directing her food choices. At most meals, he would let her know what she should eat or not eat in order to lose weight. Despite his attempt to control her eating, Betsy's weight remained constant. What Paul didn't know was that as soon as he left in the morning, Betsy started snacking, and continued eating throughout the day.

Josh was a twenty-year-old college sophomore who hoped to go to medical school. The weekend before final exams started he had made a pledge to himself, his parents, and his roommate to spend the whole weekend seated at the kitchen table in his apartment studying for his chemistry final. Unfortunately, Josh didn't really like chemistry and had difficulty with some of the problems he had to solve, but the course was required to get into med school. He had resolved to do well on the final, so he sat at the table trying to study even though his mind would wander. Several times he got up, wandered over to the refrigerator and had a piece of cheese, a spoonful of leftover enchilada, or whatever else he could eat while standing.

Tiffany was a twenty-two-year-old college senior majoring in communications. In addition to her classes, she spent the past year interning at a TV station with the hope that the experience would qualify her for an entry-level position in broadcasting. One day, she received a letter from a TV station offering her a job in their newsroom when she graduated. Tiffany was elated. Although she had been on a diet, she celebrated by eating a pint of her favorite gourmet ice cream in a single sitting.

What do Chris, Betsy, Josh, and Tiffany have in common? They weren't physically hungry when they ate. They weren't eating because it was mealtime or because the food tasted particularly good or because of any of the other external cues that can trigger eating. They were using food to make themselves feel better after having an unpleasant emotional experience, or in Tiffany's case, she was using food to increase an already pleasant emotional state. Usually emotional eating occurs when someone is feeling bad and uses the food to make him- or herself feel better.

Unfortunately, many manufacturers of tempting, high-fat, high-calorie foods know all about emotional eating and use their advertising to encourage it. A recent ad featured fifteen people of differing ages and ethnicities telling why Hershey's chocolate makes them happy ("A girlfriend will leave you, chocolate never will"), ending with a close-up of the word *happiness* imprinted on the candy bar. This linkage isn't limited to American television. I recall seeing a poster at a bus stop in Dublin, Ireland. In large print was "The Power of Emotions" and below it was a picture of a huge ice-cream cone.

Are You an Emotional Eater?

To get an idea of your emotional eating tendencies look at the following statements. In the space next to each statement indicate how often it occurs. Write a 1 for Never, 2 for Seldom, 3 for Sometimes, 4 for Often, and 5 for Very Often.

__ 1. When I am feeling "down" or "blue" a little snack will lift my mood.

__ 2. When I'm depressed I have more desire to eat.

__ 3. If someone disappoints me I want to eat something. _____

__ 4. When I am pressured or working under a deadline I have the urge to snack.

__ 5. I eat more when I am stressed than when I am calm.

__ 6. If I am worried or afraid of something I tend to eat. _____

__ 7. Sometimes when people irritate me I want to get something to eat.

__ 8. I have had something to eat "just to teach him/her a lesson."

__ 9. When I get angry, eating will make me feel better. _____

__ 10. I look forward to eating something when I'm bored.

__ 11. I eat more than usual when there is nothing to do.

__ 12. If time is passing slowly, I look forward to having a snack. _____

__ 13. Being alone increases my appetite.

__ 14. I eat less when other people are around than I do when I'm by myself.

__ 15. Eating makes me feel better when I am lonely. _____

__ 16. I celebrate with food when I'm in a good mood.

__ 17. If I'm feeling really good, I don't worry about my diet.

__ 18. When I'm happy, having a favorite snack makes me feel even better. _____

These statements measure the most common types of emotional eating. Add your scores on items 1–3 and write the total in the space after item 3. This is your depressed eating score. Add your scores on items 4–6 and write the total in the space after item 6 to get your anxiety/stress eating score. Add your scores on items 7–9 and write the total in the space after item 9 to get your angry eating score. Add your scores on items 10–12 and write the total in the space after item 12 to get your bored eating score. Add your scores on items 13–15 and write the total in the space after item 15 to get your lonely eating score. And finally, add your scores on items 16–18 and write the total in the space after item 18 to get your happy eating score. Any score greater than six is a sign that this emotion may be responsible for unnecessary eating.

Next, compare your scores for each of the six types of emotional eating to see which emotion is most likely to trigger eating for you. Later in this chapter, there are guidelines that will help you get a more precise assessment of when and where you are at risk for emotional eating. Once you know the specifics, you will be able to develop a plan to deal with your emotions without using food.

What Type of Emotional Eater Are You?

Becoming aware that you are eating to soothe emotional upsets is the first step in changing a habit. To gain insight into your eating, look at some of the following types of emotional eating.

Emotional eating can take many forms. In its most extreme form, an emotional upset can trigger a full-blown eating binge. When this happens, the eating feels out of control. The type of food doesn't matter, all that's important is to keep eating until the bad feeling goes away. Often the bad feeling doesn't go away; it's just replaced with guilt about eating so much. A Stanford University study showed that negative moods were at least as important as physical hunger in precipitating an eating binge. Many bingers report that they will keep eating until it's just physically impossible to eat more, or that they stop only after something or someone interrupts the food orgy. Bingers can consume massive amounts of food, sometimes as much as ten thousand calories worth, in a single sitting. Although this type of emotional eating is relatively rare (2–3 percent of the adult population; 8 percent of obese adults), the depression that usually accompanies binge eating is psychologically damaging and makes weight loss even more difficult.

Most emotional eaters are not out-of-control bingers. Since the more common types of emotional eating don't involve depression and a loss of control, they are not as psychologically destructive as binge eating, but they still result in unnecessary weight gain. Josh, for example, isn't likely to consume ten thousand calories, but his "grazing"—wandering over to the refrigerator—adds up even if he doesn't eat that much on each trip. Chris, Betsy, and Tiffany are trying to lose weight. Since their emotional eating wasn't included in the diets they were trying to follow, they felt guilty about the unplanned eating. Chris was especially angry with herself. Feeling a sense of futility, she gave up her attempt to diet. So why would Chris, Betsy, Josh, Tiffany, or any other reasonable person use food in this way? Why eat unnecessarily, especially if they are overweight and on a diet?

The Whys of Emotional Eating

You are a reasonable, logical person capable of sensible decision making. You know that emotional eating is counterproductive and you feel bad after you do it, so why is it so hard to control? Chapter 2 explored how body intelligence develops, including childhood experiences linking eating with being comforted. While you can't go back and redo your childhood, one thing you can do to make emotional eating less likely is to give up dieting. Chapter 5 explores the hazards of dieting more completely and will offer an alternative, more intelligent approach to weight control. But now, we need to discuss one of the less well-known problems with dieting: diets will make you more irritable and emotionally volatile. Psychologist/author Carol Tavris suggests that ". . . the irritability quotient in this country would drop if people went off whatever currently idiotic, abnormally restricted diet they were on. . . ." Maybe if so many drivers weren't on a diet there would be less road rage! Constant preoccupation with what you are eating or not eating, feeling deprived because you are missing your favorite foods, and feeling guilty about eating something that wasn't on your diet are stressful. Dieting drains emotional resources that you need in order to cope with the other pressures in your life. Just because you're on a diet you are not absolved of job pressures, financial worries, kid problems, and all the other hassles of modern life. With the constant drain of dieting, you're more easily irritated and feel down more often. So what can you do to make yourself feel better? In a moment of weakness, you eat, knowing that you'll feel guilty later, but for now, you might feel better. This emotional eating might have been avoided if you weren't on a diet, so you can increase your body intelligence by decreasing your dieting. Chapter 6 will show you how to regulate your eating without dieting.

Besides dieting, what else could cause emotional eating? Is it a type of pathology or an addiction? First recognize that, with the possible exception of bingeing, which may be related to clinical depression, emotional eating is not a sign of mental illness or psychopathology. Psychologist Richard Ganley reviewed the research and concluded that emotional eating is reported by 75 percent or more of overweight people in weight-loss programs and may be present in many normal weight people. So, if it isn't pathology, could it be a type of addiction? After all, emotional eating usually involves foods that are high in carbohydrates or fat or both (such as chocolate), and emotional eaters report cravings when deprived of their favorite foods. Is there a chemical dependence or addiction that is the cause of your emotional eating?

While there are some similarities between the cravings an alcoholic has for a drink and your craving for chocolate, there isn't much scientific support for the idea that emotional eating is an addiction. Addictions to substances such as alcohol and heroin are characterized by a physical dependence, severe withdrawal reactions, and increased tolerance for the substance. While there is some evidence that eating high-fat, high-carbohydrate "comfort foods" decreases hypothalamo-pituitary-adrenal activity resulting in improved mood, there is no convincing evidence that these effects are strong enough to be addicting. Even chocolate, the food most often described as addicting, does not cause a true physiological addiction. Although it does contain some psychoactive substances, the amount is very small so it is likely that the chocolate craving you feel is primarily psychological. Chocolate tastes good, and it feels good in your mouth.

Research suggests that the types of food cravings you have are a result of your learning experiences and cultural background. In our culture, chocolate is a special food and is usually associated with love (heart-shaped boxes of Valentine's candy), a reward, or a treat, but in other cultures chocolate might not have these meanings. For example, one cross-cultural study found that women in the United States and Spain craved chocolate while Egyptian women craved savory treats such as meat-stuffed eggplant. If you'd grown up in Egypt, you might have been indifferent to chocolate!

Now, why is this important to you? Very simply, if you attribute your emotional eating to a mental illness, a personality defect, or an addiction, then you are telling yourself that there is an underlying physiological problem *that you can't do anything about*. When you accept these explanations, you become passive. There's nothing to do but wait until the miracle cure is developed. On the other hand, when you recognize your emotions that trigger eating, you increase your body intelligence and you can do something about it. You can find other ways of working through the emotions without food.

How do you know when you are eating something that the reason is an emotional upset? It isn't always possible to establish a clear cause-and-effect relationship between an emotional state and biting into a candy bar. Sometimes eating may have more than one trigger. Here are some questions you can ask yourself to help identify emotional eating:

- *Am I having a meal?* Eating a regular meal at a regular mealtime is probably not emotional eating; having an unscheduled "snack" might be.
- *Am I physically hungry?* If you're not hungry and you are not eating in response to an external cue (see Chapter 3), then it could be emotional eating.
- *Has anything happened recently that was upsetting?* Was there a phone call, a conversation, or even a song on the radio that changed your mood? Did anyone cut you off in traffic or treat you rudely in a store? Were you just sitting there, bored, waiting for time to pass? Even if nothing has happened, have you been thinking about something that might have been distressing?
- *What are the circumstances surrounding this eating?* Emotional eating is less likely in the morning, more likely in the afternoon and evening, less likely when other people are around, and more likely when you are alone.

Identifying Emotions

Once you suspect that your eating has been triggered by an emotion, you will want to know which emotion is at work so that you will be able to substitute something other than eating when you feel that emotion. Now the detective work begins. For the next week keep track of your emotional eating. The simplest way of doing this is with an Emotional Eating Record. Take a three-by-five card, fold it in half, and keep it in

your purse or pocket. Since you're not dieting, don't worry about counting calories, carbohydrates, or fat grams; we're only interested in finding out about your unique emotional eating patterns. To do this, make
four headings on the card, like this:

Time	Location/ People	Food/ Amount	Emotion (or Thought)

You are not going to write down everything you eat. For this exercise, we are not interested in what you are eating for breakfast, lunch,
dinner, or any other planned eating. Only record your unplanned
"snacks," the unauthorized trips to the refrigerator, vending machine,
or wherever the goodies are kept.

It is important that you feel comfortable recording *all* of your emotional eating, so it is probably best to not discuss this assignment with
others. Since most emotional eating occurs in private, it shouldn't be
too difficult to write it down without being observed. The goal is to get
an accurate picture of your patterns. There is no point in "forgetting"
to record any snack. Remember that you will be the only one reading
the cards so you can be completely honest, even if you would be embarrassed if other people knew what you ate. If you think you are going to
be uncomfortable, or ashamed when you have to face the recording of
a week's worth of snacking, now is the time to get over it. Embarrassment and shame are counterproductive when you are trying to change
a behavior—they get in the way of making a realistic assessment of the
work that needs to be done. You will need to give up the guilt and adopt
a neutral, "just the facts, ma'am" attitude toward your emotional eating.

The purpose of the first column, "Time," is to determine when you
are at greatest risk for emotional eating. You will probably find that the
risk is minimal in the morning but increases as the day progresses.
Many people find that there is a specific time—such as the hour after
coming home from work or later in the evening after dinner—when
they are at greatest risk. By keeping track of the time for the next week,
you will be able to see if your emotional eating follows a pattern.

The second column will help you see if there are any specific places
or people associated with emotional eating. Is your emotional eating
more likely to occur in the kitchen, standing in front of the open refrigerator? On the sofa in the living room? After recording her emotional

eating for one week, Cindy, a thirty-four-year-old college re-entry student, found that most of her emotional eating occurred in the car, in the evening, after telling her husband that she was going to the library to study. Any patterns that you can find will be helpful in planning to reduce emotional eating.

The "Food/Amount" column will reveal the types of food you use to soothe emotional upsets. Don't become overly preoccupied with the amount you're eating; we just need an approximate measure of quantity.

Finally, the last column requires that you record how you are feeling. This may be the most difficult to identify. Even though we have hundreds of terms to describe our emotions, often it is hard to describe in words just how we are feeling. Are you stressed, anxious, uptight, afraid, fearful, worried, tense, or paranoid? If none of those descriptions fit, how about sad, depressed, blue, down in the dumps, low, or bummed? Maybe you are angry, mad, annoyed, or irritated. You get the idea; emotions are confusing and the language of emotions isn't much help. To get a handle on the emotional morass, let's look at the emotions that have been most closely related to eating and, for each, describe some of the outward signs along with the physical responses that goes along with them. Table 4.1 describes some of the most common emotions that have been associated with eating.

Although Table 4.1 describes the emotions most commonly linked to eating, your experiences may not fit neatly into one of these categories. Your eating could be triggered by an emotion that's not on the list, such as guilt or shame, or a combination of emotions. For example, Betsy was clearly angry with Paul for being so controlling. She thought that he was being unfair when he told her what to do and had thoughts about getting back at him by eating forbidden foods and gaining weight "just to teach him a lesson." In addition to her anger, she also was anxious. Having been raised in a traditional family, Betsy learned that "nice" girls don't get mad and went to great lengths to avoid expressing anger. So, in addition to feeling angry with Paul, she also felt anxious because she was afraid that something bad would happen if she allowed herself to be angry. Her eating served both to decrease her anger and to soothe her anxieties. Likewise, you may find that an instance of emotional eating has more than one cause. Or, you might find that none of the terms described in Table 4.1 fit for you. You know that before you started eating you were feeling something; you're just not sure what it was.

Difficulty defining emotional states is very common, especially for men, who usually have had less experience talking about their emotions. If you had difficulty identifying the emotion that triggered eating and recorded your thoughts instead, go back and review your thoughts. If you thought, *Where did I leave the peanut butter?*, try to recall what you were thinking about *before* you had the urge to snack. Compare the thoughts with the Mental Clues in the fourth column on Table 4.1. Although they won't be identical, it's likely that you will find that the theme of your thought matches one or more of the Mental Clues. For example, if you were having a negative thought about yourself, you were probably feeling depressed. If you were worried about something difficult or unpleasant coming up, you were probably anxious.

Now, review your week's Emotional Eating Records and see which type of emotion is most likely to trigger eating. Once you know your emotional triggers, you will be able to use cognitive therapy methods to gain control. Refer to your three-by-five cards and use your notebook to answer the following questions. This will be your Emotional Eating Summary.

1. When are the times I'm most likely to be an emotional eater?
2. Where is my emotional eating most likely to occur?
3. Who are the people (if any) who were most likely to be around before or during my emotional eating?
4. What are the food(s) I am most likely to eat in response to an emotion?
5. What are the emotions or thoughts most likely to trigger eating?

You will need to refer back to your Emotional Eating Summary as you complete the activities necessary to control emotional eating. If you have read this far without recording your emotional eating for a week, it's okay to keep reading *as long as you do your recording for the next week*. Don't assume that, because you understand the principle, you can safely ignore this assignment. Patterns of emotional eating aren't always obvious. Rosemary, a participant in one of my groups, resisted this assign-

Table 4.1   Emotions That May Trigger Eating

Emotion	Definition	Physical Clues	Mental Clues
Depression also: sad, down, blue, bummed	Unhappy feelings resulting from a loss of a valued person, relationship, possession, or self-esteem	Tears, slowing movement, tiredness, increased body pain, slumped posture	Thoughts of guilt, worthlessness, shame, hopelessness or pessimism about the future
Anxiety also: stress, afraid, tense, worried	A sense of uneasiness, fear or apprehensiveness about something that will happen in the future	Increased heart rate, sweating, difficulty breathing, "butterflies" in the stomach	Something awful is going to happen, may be specific ("the plane will crash") or just vague uneasiness
Anger also: mad, hostile, annoyed, irritated, pissed off	Intense feelings resulting from a sense that you have been injured, treated unfairly, or threatened	Stiffening of the body, clenched jaw, increased blood pressure	Thoughts of striking out or attacking, desire to get even or revenge, thinking about the incident repeatedly
Boredom also: monotonous, dullness	Distress resulting from a lack of stimulation or repetition of uninteresting activities	Restlessness, fidgeting, yawning	Time seems to pass slowly, frequent daydreaming, easily distracted
Loneliness also: aloneness, isolation	Distress resulting from the perceived lack of satisfying social relationships	Avoidance of social situations, awkwardness around others	Thinking that you have been abandoned or rejected by others
Happiness also: joy, cheerful, elated, upbeat, euphoric	Highly pleasant state of well-being and contentment	Smiling, laughing, extra energy or drive, outgoing	Positive, optimistic thoughts, increased self-esteem

ment because she had been in insight-oriented therapy for several years. She felt that she understood her psychological makeup and knew that she ate when she was stressed. To humor me she reluctantly agreed to do the assignment anyway. At the next meeting she reported that, in addition to stress eating, she found herself eating after conversations with her mother, especially when her mother offered unsolicited advice. As we discussed this type of eating, it became apparent that her mother's well-meaning advice made her angry, and she ate to suppress these feelings. Without the Emotional Eating Records she would have never made this connection.

Fat Thinking

When we have a negative emotion, it's natural to look outside of ourselves to find the cause. You are stressed because of all the work that you have to do by Friday. You are depressed because your partner ended your relationship. You are angry because that idiot telemarketer interrupted you while you were cooking and now the rice has burned. The truth is that the source of the emotion is not outside; it is inside, in between your ears. As the bumper sticker crudely proclaims, "S—t Happens." But when it does, it's not necessary for you to become anxious, depressed, angry, or otherwise stressed (and then eat to feel better).

No one is suggesting that you won't have a reaction to the unpleasant events that happen in your life, but how you think about these events will determine the type and degree of emotional response you will have. After a divorce or the end of a romantic relationship it is perfectly reasonable to feel sad about the loss. However, if you then think that you will never find another person to love you because you are unlovable (or have some other permanent defect of character) you will sink into a more pervasive depression. Negative thinking causes the depression, not the external event that you are thinking about.

Cognitive therapies as developed by Dr. Aaron Beck and Dr. Albert Ellis offer an approach to changing your thought patterns so that you don't feel so miserable when bad things happen. The basic premise is that if you become aware of your automatic thoughts (the things that you tell yourself), you will find that some of these thoughts are irrational. Once you recognize the irrationality of some of the things you are telling yourself, you will be able to substitute more rational thoughts and feel better, and the need to eat will decrease. (For a more thorough discussion of cognitive therapy, read *The Feeling Good Handbook* by David Burns, M.D.)

Alice's Emotional Eating

Alice was a forty-six-year-old, single mother of two and a very successful sales professional. In addition to her six-figure earnings, she had received recognition for her work locally and was written up in a national business publication. Despite her accomplishments, Alice was unhappy with herself primarily because she weighed 244 pounds. But she was also unhappy because she felt that she wasn't an adequate mother, and before she gained the weight, she'd had an affair with a married man. I asked Alice to record her emotional eating for a week. At our next meeting she reported that most of her emotional eating took place at night after putting her kids to bed. Reviewing the definitions in Table 4.1, she decided that the primary emotion leading to her eating was loneliness combined with some sadness.

Alice was using food to nurture herself. She was busy during the day making sales calls (sometimes missing lunch), doing paperwork, preparing dinner, helping the kids with their homework, and getting them ready for bed. Her schedule was hectic. During the day she was usually around people, either taking care of clients or her son and daughter. In the evening, after the kids went to bed, she was alone with no one to take care of her. The eating was an attempt to restore the energy she used up during her stressful day, and it was something nice she could do for herself since no one else was going to do it. I asked her to describe her thoughts before and during her nighttime eating.

When I finally get the kids to bed, I think, Finally, I get to do something I want to do. *I grab a snack and turn on the TV. Pretty soon I start thinking about the hassle I had with Jenny [her daughter], and then I feel guilty because I lost my temper when I found out she was lying to me about finishing her homework. Once I feel bad, I start to think of other mistakes I've made. The thing that comes up most often is the affair I had with Jim [a married man] and how badly that ended. Even though I've finished my snack, I'm thinking about what else I can get to eat, and pretty soon I'm up and in the kitchen.*

I asked Alice about anything else she could do, other than eating, either at night or during the day, to take a break and reward herself. She proceeded to tell me about her hectic schedule, and all the reasons why she couldn't devote any time to herself.

To help her break out of this pattern of bad moods followed by eating, I asked questions to help her recognize the irrational, automatic thoughts that caused the moods and eating. Using Dr. Burns's ten forms of Twisted Thinking (as shown in the sidebar "Twisted Thinking"), Alice recognized her irrational thoughts and, after some discussion, identified the distortions and found more rational alternatives.

Here are Alice's automatic thoughts, the type of twisted thinking implicit in each thought, and more rational alternative thoughts.

Alice's Automatic Thoughts

Automatic Thought	Distortion	Rational Thought
"I don't have the time to nurture myself."	*Should statement* "I should be productive all the time."	"I am productive. I've earned the right to nurture myself for a few minutes."
"I'm a bad mother because i lost my temper with my daughter."	*Labeling* "Bad mother" *All-or-nothing thinking* "Never lose your temper"	"Jenny [the daughter] was being particularly difficult. Usually I can handle her bad moods."
"I'd like to be in a relationship, but I'd choose a married man again."	*Jumping to conclusions* Fortune-telling	"It was a different time in my life. I wouldn't make the same mistake again."
"I might as well finish the leftover spaghetti. I'm always going to be fat anyway."	*All-or-nothing thinking, Jumping to conclusions*	"If I avoid the spaghetti I'll still be fat, but at least I'll be making progress."

Are any of these twisted thoughts familiar? To become aware of your automatic thoughts, look in your notebook at your response to question

5 in your Emotional Eating Summary (the emotion or thought that is most likely to trigger eating). Now, make three columns. In the first column write in the automatic thought most likely to be associated with your emotional eating. Check the Mental Clues column of Table 4.1 for help identifying your automatic thought. Next, referring to the "Twisted Thinking" sidebar, note the type of distortion implicit in the automatic thought and write that in the second column. Finally, substitute a more rational alternative thought and enter that in column three.

After you've identified irrational automatic thoughts and substituted more rational alternatives, you will need to work at catching yourself whenever the irrational automatic thought pops into your head and make an effort to remind yourself of the alternative rational thought. It will take more than a few repetitions before the new thought becomes automatic. It will help to speed the process if you know when automatic thoughts are most likely. Check your answers to questions 1, 2, and 3 in your Emotional Eating Summary so that you can prepare yourself for these times and situations. For example, knowing that after a fight with your spouse you are likely to have an irrational thought and eat to make yourself feel better will enable you to substitute a more rational thought and avoid the urge to eat.

If you are alone when an automatic thought occurs, it is helpful to argue with yourself out loud. Since no one is nearby, you don't need to feel foolish talking to yourself. Just remind yourself why the automatic thought is distorted, and announce the more rational alternative thought. If your automatic thoughts are likely to occur in a particular place (see question 2 in your Emotional Eating Summary), you can make a sign or put up a Post-it note to remind yourself of the rational thought. The basic idea is to repeat the rational thought as often as possible until it becomes automatic. You will find that when the new, more rational thoughts prevail, the negative emotions decrease, and with them, some of the urge to snack.

Alternatives to Emotional Eating

In addition to changing the irrational thinking, a second strategy for decreasing emotional eating is to develop other methods of nurturing

TWISTED THINKING

Dr. Burns identified ten forms of Twisted Thinking.

1. **All-or-nothing thinking.** "I'm either on a diet or off my diet;" one cookie means "I've blown my diet."

2. **Overgeneralization.** "I'll *always* be fat" or "I'll *never* lose weight." Using *always* or *never* to describe your behavior is usually an overgeneralization.

3. **Mental filter.** Focusing on only one aspect or detail of a larger picture. You avoided doughnuts during coffee break and had a sensible lunch and dinner, yet all you think about is the ice cream you ate before bedtime.

4. **Discounting the positive.** You walk for thirty minutes three times each week but think, "It's no big deal, other people walk every day."

5. **Jumping to conclusions.** Fortune-telling or making unwarranted predictions about the future. After eating an unplanned snack you think, "What's the use, I'll never be able to lose weight."

6. **Magnification-Minimization.** You unrealistically increase the importance of negative experiences and minimize the positive ones. You are preoccupied with your "flabby thighs" but don't think about your attractive facial features.

7. **Emotional reasoning.** You assume that your emotions are an accurate reflection of reality. You are ashamed of your tummy, so you assume that you've done something shameful.

8. **Should statements (also must, ought, have to).** While it is perfectly reasonable to have desires, preferences, and goals, the idea that there is a rigid standard that you (or anyone else) should meet is irrational. For example, "I shouldn't eat *any* fried foods."

9. **Labeling.** Just because you do something dumb doesn't mean you are a dummy. For example, it is irrational to label yourself as "lazy" if you miss an exercise session.

10. **Personalization-Blame.** It is irrational to hold yourself (or someone else) responsible for something that isn't under your

(or ther) control. Thinking, *If I stuck to my diet I could get rid of this potbelly* is unrealistic. You have control over how much you eat, but you don't have any control over the locations in your body where fat will accumulate.

yourself when you're feeling bad. First, recognize that everyone, even the most macho cowboy or a Marine drill sergeant, has times when they need to be nurtured. When you were a young child, if your parents were reasonably attentive, your mom or dad would see that you were upset and ask you what was the matter. Depending on the situation, they would get a Band-Aid for your boo-boo, hug and hold you, or just comfort you in some other way (hopefully not with milk and cookies!). Now you're an adult and it's unrealistic to expect Mom to hug you when you're having a bad day at work. Instead of relying on food as a substitute, you can develop a plan to nurture yourself. You can go to the source of your discomfort and confront it directly rather than using food to pacify yourself. Admittedly, it takes a little more planning and effort to nurture yourself instead of raiding the refrigerator or making a detour through the drive-up window at McDonald's, but it's worth it.

The first step is to accept the basic premise that it is perfectly reasonable for you to take the time to do something nice for yourself. When I suggest this in my workshops and individual sessions, the emotional eater will usually have a reason to explain why she can't do whatever it is that will make her feel better. Alice's rationale of "I don't have enough time to . . ." is typical. Given her hectic schedule, it was inevitable that she would resist self-nurturing activities because "I don't have the time." When we discussed her schedule and the time snacking and brooding about the snacking took up, it became clear that time wasn't the main obstacle to self-nurturing. It was her feelings of being unworthy. She always needed to do something else first, something that was more important, before she could get around to taking care of herself.

Taking a few minutes to be nice to yourself is seen as a waste of time or self-indulgent. The underlying thought is usually that you aren't worth the expenditure of time, other demands are more important.

Does any of this sound familiar? Are you "too busy" to take a few minutes to be good to yourself? Would you feel awkward or self-conscious if you spent a little time doing something nice for yourself? If any of this sounds familiar, recognize the twisted thinking in these statements. Similar to Alice, you are making "should" statements. You are assuming that you should be doing something else more worthwhile instead of addressing your very real human needs. If you examine this thinking, you will recognize that it is unreasonable to expect yourself to be productive all the time. Even an automobile, or other mechanical device, has downtimes for maintenance. You are also entitled to a little downtime for maintenance! Besides, if you add up all the time you spend thinking about eating, preparing and eating your snacks, and then being distracted later by feelings of guilt and self-recrimination, you will find that you could have taken a break to nurture yourself instead without losing any time. You might also find that devoting a little time during the day for self-nurturing recharges your batteries so that you have more energy and are more efficient at performing your daily activities.

The second rationale for resisting the idea of self-nurturance is more difficult to combat. It is hard to derive any benefit of doing something nice for yourself if, all the while, you are feeling guilty because you think that you don't deserve it. If you've had these thoughts, ask yourself why you don't deserve to do something nice for yourself.

Usually the assumptions that underlie this guilty feeling revolve around being fat. This is a mental filter because you are only considering your weight and ignoring all the good things that you do or have accomplished. It may also be emotional reasoning if you feel embarrassed about your weight, so you are thinking that you've done something embarrassing that disqualifies you from being nice to yourself. You may be telling yourself that you need to lose weight before you have earned the right to nurture yourself, or that because of your weight you would be embarrassed or exhausted if you did whatever it is that would be nurturing. Recognize how self-defeating this type of circular reasoning is. You need to be nice to yourself to lose weight, but you can't be nice to yourself until after you've lost the weight!

In your notebook, create a table with three columns. Write down your automatic thoughts about self-nurturing in the first column, the distortion in those thoughts in the second column, and more rational alternative thoughts in the third column.

Now, if you have corrected your automatic thoughts about self-nurturing, you can make a plan to integrate self-nurturing rituals into your daily routine. The sidebar "My Plan for Self-Nurturing" will help.

After you have developed your list of self-nurturing activities, go back to your Emotional Eating Summary. Notice the time(s) and place(s) where emotional eating is most likely to occur. Which of your self-nurturing activities can you substitute for eating at that time and place? To formalize your plan, write down in your notebook the time and location when you are most tempted to eat and then list alternative activities you might try.

Focusing on Specific Emotions

Changing your automatic thoughts and developing self-nurturing habits are general strategies to combat emotional eating. Both are highly effective in reducing emotional eating but neither occurs instantaneously; they require repetition before becoming habits. While you are working on your automatic thoughts and learning to nurture yourself, it will be helpful to develop a plan for dealing with the specific emotions that make you want to eat. After recording your emotional eating for a week, you should have some idea of which emotions are your triggers (check your response to question 5 in the Emotional Eating Summary). If you identified more than one emotion that triggers eating, choose one to work on first. The next step in increasing body intelligence is to find effective methods of coping without eating, which are addressed in the "Specific Emotional Coping Methods" sidebar.

Fun Without Ben and Jerry

When you've done the assignments in this chapter you will know how your emotions trigger eating and you will have several strategies for coping without eating. Becoming aware of your emotional eating patterns is a very important first step. Awareness makes habit change pos-

MY PLAN FOR SELF-NURTURING

In order to make self-nurturing a frequent, automatic part of your day, it is necessary for you to find activities that are brief and can be easily integrated into your routine. Start by thinking about things you enjoy doing. Don't get too grandiose. You might enjoy seeing a Broadway musical or flying to Paris for the weekend, but we are not looking for memorable events here, just small activities that provide a pleasant break in your routine. Would you enjoy stopping what you are doing for ten minutes and using this time to:

➤ Phone or e-mail a friend
➤ Read a magazine article
➤ Play with pets
➤ Polish your nails
➤ Putter in the garden
➤ Surf the Net
➤ Pray or meditate
➤ Walk around the block
➤ Practice yoga or dance moves
➤ Play a computer game
➤ Sit in the sun
➤ Write a diary
➤ Doodle or draw
➤ Look at a photo album
➤ Knit, sew, or crochet

There is nothing magical in any of these activities. The list is just intended to get you thinking about activities that you could plan to add to your daily routine when you need to be nurtured and are temped to eat. In your notebook, develop your own list of activities that would be nurturing. If you can only think of one or two, write them in now and, in the next week, notice the kinds of things that you enjoy doing and add them to the list.

SPECIFIC EMOTIONAL COPING METHODS

The following practical activities can help you deal with your emotions without eating.

Depression
The single best activity for coping with depression is physical activity. Chapters 9 and 10 will help you overcome your reluctance to exercise and develop a plan for making exercise a part of your lifestyle, but for now we are only interested in the mood-elevating properties of physical activity. The good news is that the activity doesn't need to be strenuous—you don't have to elevate your heart rate and you don't even need to sweat in order to improve your mood, you just need to get up off the sofa and move. Go for a walk, turn on music and dance, or ride a bike.

Anxiety
There are several methods you can use to reduce anxiety and stress. In addition to the methods you are working on for changing your twisted thinking, you can train your body so that you experience less physiological arousal when you are in a stressful situation. Breathing, muscle relaxation, and stretching exercises all help quiet your internal organs.

➤ *Breathing exercises.* Take a deep breath, filling your lungs till the bursting point, hold the breath for three to five seconds to feel the tightness in your chest, and then exhale slowly, paying attention to the relaxation that comes with releasing the tension. Repeat several times.

➤ *Muscle relaxation.* Start with your right hand. Make a fist. Clench the fist, concentrate on the tension for five to ten seconds, and then relax the muscles, noticing the difference between tension and relaxation for fifteen to twenty seconds.

(continued)

Do it a second time and again notice how different the muscles feel after they're relaxed. Repeat this tense-hold-release-relax sequence for different muscle groups in your body. Although it might take twenty to thirty minutes to cover all the muscle groups on the following list, you can abbreviate your muscle relaxation exercises to fit the time you have. The sequence is: clench right hand, clench left hand, bend right arm at elbow, tighten triceps, bend left arm at elbow, tighten triceps, stretch right arm outward, stretch left arm outward, hunch shoulders forward, push your chin into your chest, close eyelids tightly, raise eyebrows as high as possible, arch your back and push your chest out (skip this if you have back pain), push buttocks against the chair, pull your stomach in as far as possible, with your feet on the floor point your toes toward your face, and then push your toes down against the floor. While this sequence sounds formidable, once you've practiced a few repetitions, it is not difficult.

➤ *Stretching.* Standing, reach upward with both arms as high as possible, and then roll your feet forward so that you are standing on your tiptoes. Resume a normal standing posture, spread your feet apart, and reach up with one arm while sliding the other arm down the leg so that one arm is stretched up while the other is stretched down. Finally, clasp your hands together behind your back and pull your hands down and out; then relax.

Anger

The theme of anger is being treated unfairly by others. It may be a useful emotion if it motivates you to make a constructive change, but it can also be harmful. It is especially important to check for twisted thinking when you are feeling angry. If your thinking is rational, not based on personalization/blame or should statements, then take a time-out to let the physiological arousal subside. (The breathing, relaxation, or stretching exercises can be helpful here, too.) Then, go to the person who has treated you unfairly and in an assertive, but not aggressive, manner let him or her know how you would like to be treated in the future.

Boredom
Sometimes there is no escaping boring tasks. Try though you might, there is no way to make ironing interesting. When you are confronted with this (or any other) boring task, the temptation to get a snack to break up the monotony can be irresistible. To reduce this temptation, try to move your boring tasks to times and places where food is unavailable, or at least difficult to get. For example, take your ironing and a portable TV out to the garage so that snacking is more difficult. If you are a student confronted with a boring assignment, do the assignment in the library rather than at home with the refrigerator nearby.

Loneliness
Eating is a poor substitute for love or companionship, yet when you are lonely food seems better than nothing. With the advent of e-mail, instant messaging, and Internet newsgroups, anyone regardless of their geographical isolation, lack of social skills, or fear of rejection can establish some type of contact with fellow humans. While Internet dating can be fraught with peril, joining a newsgroup or chat room revolving around one of your interests should be safe. Likewise, joining groups that share a common interest or taking a class could provide opportunities to socialize. Since forming new relationships takes time, plan on using your self-nurturing strategies to help get through the times when you are feeling lonely.

Happiness
If you use food to add to your good mood, I don't want you to reduce your happy feelings in order to decrease your caloric intake. Instead, develop alternative rituals to celebrate your good mood that don't involve food.

sible, but by itself, awareness is not sufficient. Time and effort are required to implement the strategy for each emotion. You can't expect that you will do it perfectly each time. It may help you to recognize that controlling emotional eating doesn't mean that you will have to forgo the favorite foods you have used to soothe or nurture yourself. In Chapter 6 you will see how you can continue to eat them for enjoyment rather than to make yourself feel better.

CHAPTER 5

NEVER GO HUNGRY

I n the last two chapters, the three triggers for eating were described: physical hunger, external cues, and emotions. I presented methods for reducing external and emotional eating, but did not discuss the topic that is the focus of most diets: what to eat and what to avoid eating. To increase body intelligence, it is necessary to make food choices without reverting to the usual dieting mentality. No food or category of food is forbidden. Instead you will develop your own guidelines for choosing food to meet your needs and deciding how much of it to eat to satisfy that need. Although it will require some deliberate thought in the beginning, with practice this process will become automatic. Our task in this chapter is to examine the assumptions of dieting so that you can understand your previous difficulties controlling your weight. Without the typical dieting mentality you will be free to develop a more intelligent method for determining what and how much to eat.

What's Wrong with This Picture?

The preoccupation with dieting is a widespread cultural phenomenon. At least 55 percent of women and 29 percent of men report dieting within the past year. The frequency of dieting among girls between the ages of eleven and sixteen is even higher. Dieting is becoming more prevalent among children. About 25 percent of eleven-year-old girls have already made at least one attempt to lose weight. Surprisingly, you don't have to be fat to be on a diet. One study found more normal weight people on a diet than there are obese dieters and about 10 percent of underweight women are dieting. Not only are Americans preoccupied with dieting, we are exporting this concern. Studies show that teenage girls in Iran, Saudi Arabia, and the Pacific Islands are more likely to diet as they have more contact with American society and become more affluent.

Despite all this dieting, Americans are fatter than ever. More than twenty years ago, Dr. William Bennett and Joel Gurin wrote *The Dieter's Dilemma*, a book reviewing the scientific evidence showing that dieting is an ineffective strategy for controlling weight, yet the sales of diet books (more than seven million copies of *The South Beach Diet* alone) and "buzz" about the latest diet craze continues unabated. It's hard to avoid getting distracted by the claims and counterclaims when friends are talking about their experiences with various diets and you read about them whenever you pick up a newspaper or magazine. When you look at the larger picture and understand the psychological processes involved in dieting, you will be able to comfortably ignore media hype about the latest diet and continue to focus on increasing body intelligence.

The Great Debate

In my workshops and clinical work, the first issue that comes up is the comparative merits of low-carbohydrate and low-fat diets. It seems that everyone either has tried the Atkins or South Beach diets or knows someone who claims to have lost weight while on one of these diets. In a government-sponsored forum held in 2000, Dr. Robert Atkins and Dr. Dean Ornish debated the best way to lose weight; the high-protein, low-carbohydrate approach propounded by Atkins (South Beach, Sugar Busters) versus the low-fat, high-carbohydrate diet favored by Ornish (American Heart Association, McDougall). All they could conclude was that:

- Americans are too fat
- Exercise is good
- Sugars and white bread are bad

Although Dr. Atkins died in 2003, the debate continues on an almost weekly basis with newspaper articles reporting the results of studies comparing low-carb versus low-fat diets. Unfortunately, the debate often takes on an almost religious tone with believers accusing nonbelievers of nutritional apostasy. According to Dr. Gary D. Foster, the director of the weight and eating disorders program at the University of Pennsylvania, "These people are believers . . . evangelism creeps in." Even the cause of Dr. Atkins's death has become part of the debate. Nonbelievers claim that he weighed 258 pounds when he died and was unable to follow his own diet.

In trying to make sense out of this dispute, it's helpful to recognize that it has been going on for years and is unlikely to be settled anytime soon. Jean Anthelme Brillat-Savarin, a French attorney, advocated a low-carbohydrate diet in a book he published in 1825. To critics of his low-carb regimen he warned,

Very well then; eat! Get fat! Become ugly and thick, and asthmatic, finally die in your own melted grease.

At about the same time, Sylvester Graham (popularizer of the crackers bearing his name) preached against gluttony, "the greatest of all causes of evil," and advocated vegetarianism, the ultimate low-fat diet, as a cure. Obesity, illness, and mental deficiency were attributed to eating meat and other animal products.

The demonizing of fat or carbohydrates has spread from dieters to the general population. In contrast to the 1980s and 1990s when consumers were avoiding fat because there was a general sense that it was unhealthy (remember how popular low-fat cookies were?), currently 40 percent of consumers are trying to cut back on their consumption of carbohydrates regardless of their weight. More than 700 low-carb products have been introduced (including low-carbohydrate marshmallows) to take advantage of the predicted $25 billion market. This is big business. An 80 percent stake in Atkins's company was sold for $533 million after he died, but the *New York Times* reported that by the end of 2004 half of the low-carb dieters had abandoned their diets and the company had laid off 40 percent of its workforce.

Low-Carb Versus Low-Fat Diets

There have been several studies comparing low-carbohydrate diets and low-fat diets but the findings have been inconclusive. For example, one pilot study conducted in Cambridge, Massachusetts, found that low-carbohydrate dieters lost more than low-fat dieters even though they consumed an extra 300 calories per day. In addition to supporting the Atkins approach, this study cast doubt on the conventional belief that a calorie is a calorie, instead suggesting that low-carbohydrate calories don't count as much. In contrast, another study found that any 1,500-calorie per day diet will produce short-term weight loss, but the Atkins diet produced greater loss of water rather than fat, and the water weight was regained when the diet ended. Several studies found that Atkins dieters lost more weight than low-fat dieters in the short term, but at the end of the year there was no difference in weight loss. Finally, a recent study compared the Atkins, Ornish, Weight Watchers, and Zone diets. This study found that sticking with any of the diets for a year produced an average 5 percent reduction in body weight, although a third of all the dieters gave up on their diets.

One concern about the Atkins diet is that it is high in saturated fat and low in fiber. Both are associated with an increased risk of heart disease. Recently followers of the late Dr. Atkins issued a "clarification," which suggests that dieters should not eat unlimited quantities of saturated fat and that vegetables, fruit, and brown rice are now acceptable. The recommendations were revised to limit saturated fat to 20 percent of total caloric intake.

Confused? Tina, a forty-eight-year-old insurance salesperson, didn't know what to do. She had been watching her fat intake while enjoying frequent meals with pasta or rice. Her mother reported that she had lost ten pounds following the Atkins diet and encouraged Tina to try it. The next day Tina had her fast-food hamburger wrapped in lettuce leaves instead of a bun and served sausage and marinara sauce without pasta for dinner. A week later, Tina lost four pounds but the craving for pasta was overwhelming. Two weeks later, Tina was back to her original weight. Now she wasn't sure what to avoid, carbs or fats.

It will take years before there is a definitive answer to the low-fat versus low-carb controversy. At this point it is safe to say that both approaches contain some truth and some exaggerations. Fats found in fish, nuts, and some vegetables are healthy, and foods with some fat taste better and will keep you feeling satiated longer. On the other hand, saturated fats are thought to contribute to heart disease, fat has nine calories per gram while protein and carbohydrates have four, and fat in your diet will convert to fat on your body more easily than protein or carbohydrates. The low-fat approach is supported by findings that extremely low-fat diets can reverse heart disease, and evidence demonstrating that obesity is rarely found in traditional Asian societies where white rice is a staple of the diet. On the other hand, simple carbohydrates such as sugar, white flour, and white rice are absorbed quickly, causing increased production of insulin that speeds the conversion of calories into body fat and leaves you feeling hungry again. Complex carbohydrates found in fruits and vegetables, brown rice, beans, and whole-wheat bread contain fiber that, in addition to helping maintain regularity, is digested slowly, preventing the spike in blood sugar and insulin response. Until there is definitive proof, it appears that a balanced diet with a careful selection of healthy fats and carbohydrates is the best strategy.

Dieting Follies

Although most of the recent controversy has revolved around the Atkins versus Ornish approach, many other diets have been promoted for weight loss. The editors of *Health Magazine* recently published a book that reviews twenty-two diets, but this just scratches the surface. There are diets proposed by celebrities (Duchess of York, Suzanne Sommers), diets organized by geography (Scarsdale, Beverly Hills, South Beach), diets emphasizing a particular food (peanut butter diet, cabbage soup diet), and diets from organizations (Weight Watchers, Pritikin). There are also meal replacements (SlimFast) and various fasting regimens. Some of the diets are dangerous, while many others are just unrealistic. For example, the Beverly Hills Diet essentially advocates weight loss by eating enough fruit to cause diarrhea. Another weight-loss plan was based on your blood type (A, O) despite the complete lack of evidence linking blood type to weight. More plausible, but still not very practical, are diets that restrict caloric intake to a level that can't be maintained for any length of time. For example, *The 5-Day Miracle Diet* limits your eating to 800 calories a day. Even if you could restrict your consumption to 800 calories, it wouldn't be a good idea since weight losses exceeding two pounds per week are likely to result in breakdown of lean tissue. You'd be losing muscle in addition to fat.

Total fasts are dangerous because they can cause an electrolyte imbalance that affects cardiac functioning. Fasting is counterproductive because lean muscle mass is lost in addition to fat tissue. The heart is a muscle that may be weakened with continued malnourishment. Fasting leaves you feeling dizzy, weak, and lethargic. As a result you are likely to reduce your physical activity leading to further muscle loss.

Less dangerous and possibly more useful are meal replacements, either powdered-diet formulas such as SlimFast or frozen low-calorie meals widely available in supermarkets (Healthy Choice, Lean Cuisine). In one study, men using meal replacements lost an average of seventeen pounds in twelve weeks, while it took women twenty-four weeks to achieve the same result. Meal replacements and frozen meals are convenient, avoid the need to count calories, and often provide fewer calories than dieters would consume even when they are "being good" and following their diets. They also reduce the number of food cues, which can be helpful for external eaters (check your External Eating Score in Chapter 3). Despite these advantages, there are several problems. The liquids may not provide enough fiber to maintain regularity; they may leave you hungry, setting you up for overeating when it is finally time for solid food; and, over time, they are monotonous and don't help you change eating habits. Unless there is also an increase in body intelligence, any weight lost will be regained when you go back to eating regular food.

Roger, a forty-two-year-old accountant, decided to try one of the liquid meal replacements instead of having his usual lunch. He liked the chocolate favor and tried to think of it as a milkshake so that he wouldn't feel deprived, but he was hungry by the middle of the afternoon. The first few days he was able to tolerate the hunger, but by the end of the week he was eating more during his morning coffee break to "fortify" himself. By the end of the second week Roger concluded that he was eating as much or more with the meal replacements and went back to his usual tuna fish sandwich for lunch.

The Dieting Secret

Some of the results of any diet are not due to the foods or combinations of foods that are restricted. The underlying rationale for a diet, be it glycemic index, blood type, or whatever, may be irrelevant. The dieting secret is that all diets restrict your food choices. Some that emphasize a specific food like grapefruit or cabbage soup give you very few food choices. Others allow more foods but curtail one type of nutrient. Whether it's fats or carbohydrates that are prohibited, the effect is the same: your choice of foods is restricted. A review of fifty-eight studies, published in the journal *Psychological Bulletin*, concluded that humans and animals ate more when they were given a variety of foods and less when there were fewer choices. The authors explain,

> Both people and animals will eat more food when a meal or diet contains greater variety of food, which can eventually cause weight gain. So it isn't surprising that a typical American diet that consists of a large variety in foods like sweets and snacks is linked to being overweight.

When there are fewer foods available it is likely that your total consumption will decrease so you could probably lose weight on an all-Twinkie diet, but please don't try.

You don't have to be on a diet to make use of these findings, just try to minimize the variety of food at any one time. When you go out to eat, avoid buffet or smorgasbord restaurants. At regular restaurants order fewer courses. If you must have snack foods in the house, only have one type. Without going on a diet or prohibiting any foods you can lose weight by restricting the number of different foods available.

Your Dieting History

Check your score on the Restraint Scale from Chapter 1. Especially if you have been a restrained eater (a score 16 or above for women; 12 or above for men) it will be necessary to examine some of your assumptions regarding diet and weight loss. Increasing body intelligence usually requires looking at, and then abandoning, some long-held beliefs about dieting.

Review your dieting history. How often have you been on a diet? Recall your most successful diet. What did you feel like while dieting? Did you try to ignore your hunger? How did you feel while on the diet? When did you go off the diet? Looking back, what made you give it up? After you went off the diet, did you splurge or treat yourself to the goodies that you missed while dieting? Did you have one last splurge before you started the diet? How did you feel after the diet? How long was it before you regained the weight you lost on the diet?

The Life Cycle of a Diet

If you are like most dieters, you approached the diet with a mixture of skepticism and hope. While you know that previous diets were unsuccessful, you hoped that maybe this time it would be different. You read about the diet or, perhaps, had a friend who was singing its praises, so you decided to give it a try. With your initial enthusiasm it wasn't too hard to follow the guidelines and after a few days, you lost some weight. The initial skepticism is overcome, you expect continued weight loss, and anticipate the joys of being thinner. Unfortunately, most of this early weight-loss results from water loss, especially if you're on a low-carbohydrate, low-calorie diet. Since there's only so much water you can safely lose, the rate of weight loss slows at about the same time as the effort required to restrict your eating increases. After two weeks, resisting your craving for chocolate chip cookies becomes much more difficult. Since the scale is not rewarding you with rapidly decreasing weight, your enthusiasm wanes and you give up. You eat the cookie and then think, *Since I've blown my diet, I might as well finish the rest of the box.*

My intention in having you recall your dieting history is not to make you discouraged or to suggest that failure at dieting is a rationale for giving up all attempts at weight control. Rather, we can identify the flaws in typical dieting strategies in order to develop a more effective alternative.

Dieting Attitudes

Dieting is more than just changing your eating. When you are on a diet your thinking changes, too. Review the following seven statements. Put a check mark next to each one that represents a thought that you have had about dieting.

❑ Dieting is all or nothing. I'm either on or off a diet.
❑ Dieting is always painful. When I'm on a diet, I'm aware that I'm being deprived of my favorite foods and I'm frequently hungry.
❑ Diets never work for me. Even when I'm enthusiastic, there's a little voice inside that says, "Who are you fooling? You're always going to be fat."
❑ I have to be hard on myself to stick to a diet. Hating the way I look and being angry with myself whenever I slip is necessary to keep myself motivated.
❑ It's not fair. Other people can eat whatever they want and stay slim. Why do I have diet?
❑ I always fail at dieting. Even when I lose weight I never reach my goal.
❑ Since I've failed at dieting I have (choose one or more): no willpower, no self-discipline, a weak character, a personality defect, a neurosis, a lack of moral fiber . . .

If you checked any of these statements it is necessary to look at these attitudes critically to increase body intelligence since any of these beliefs will undermine a weight-loss effort. These widely held beliefs are based on irrational assumptions. To develop a plan for controlling eating, it is necessary to correct the twisted thinking implicit in these beliefs. As we examine each statement, it will be helpful to refer back to the Chapter 4 sidebar "Twisted Thinking."

Dieting Is All or Nothing

This type of all-or-nothing thinking guarantees failure. No one is a perfect dieter. Everyone will deviate sometimes, so if you interpret your slip as a dieting failure, you will become discouraged and it will become a dieting failure. On the other hand, with body intelligence you know that permanent weight control is not achieved by an all-or-nothing diet. You can figure out what was responsible for the slip and then change the circumstances contributing to the unnecessary eating. Despite the slipup you can resume your efforts and continue making progress.

Dieting Is Always Painful

This is an overgeneralization. As with any habit change, weight control requires effort, but as you make gradual changes, many of the new behaviors become automatic. For example, much of the difficulty associated with dieting comes from trying to resist cravings for foods forbidden on a diet. The eating plan presented in Chapter 6 does not prohibit any food. If you really want rocky road ice cream, you can have it. Once you understand what you are hoping to get from a specific treat, you can plan to satisfy that need without damaging your weight-control efforts. Also, many cravings follow a negative mood. As you work on the emotions described in Chapter 4, the frequency and intensity of food cravings should decrease. With body intelligence, working on your weight will require effort but need not be painful.

Diets Never Work for Me

This type of thought is an example of fortune-telling. At first glance, there is some justification for this pessimism. You may have seen the often-quoted statistic that 95 percent of dieters will fail to lose weight, or if they should succeed, they will regain the weight in a few years. This statistic comes from a study published in a medical journal almost a half century ago. We've learned a lot about nutrition and exercise, and developed cognitive and behavioral methods since then. A *Consumer Reports* survey of nineteen thousand people in commercial weight-loss programs such as Weight Watchers found that more than 25 percent of the participants were able to lose weight and maintain the loss for at least two years. Another study found that half of the Weight Watchers participants who reached their goal weight were still lighter after five years. A recent random telephone survey found that 20 percent of the formerly overweight respondents had lost an average of forty-two pounds and maintained the loss for seven years. Clearly, weight loss isn't easy, but many people with a history of unsuccessful previous attempts have succeeded in losing weight. It is irrational to assume that it will be impossible for you.

I Need to Be Hard on Myself to Lose Weight

Usually there is an irrational "should" statement implicit in this type of thinking. If you are angry with yourself every time you slip and have a forbidden food, you are telling yourself that you *should* never slip. This type of perfectionism is unrealistic. Many habitual dieters also feel that they need to hate their "ugly fat" or put themselves down in some other way in order to stay motivated. This is unfortunate since self-hatred isn't healthy or useful for anyone. The "shoulds" and put-downs are discouraging and drain you of the energy you will need to make the changes necessary to lose weight. With body intelligence you will learn from your slips, develop strategies to avoid the circumstances that led to the slip, and give yourself a pat on the back every time you make a change for the better.

It's Not Fair That I Need to Diet

Another "should" statement. It would be nice if no one was born with a genetic predisposition to gain weight easily, but humans vary on many characteristics. It would also be nice if everyone was healthy, intelligent, and beautiful (or handsome), but that's not how it works. Considering all the possible inherited diseases, handicaps, and liabilities, a tendency to gain weight easily is not the worst possible burden.

I Never Reach My Goal

This is a mental filter. While it may be true that you haven't met your goal, it is quite likely that, at various times, you have changed some behaviors and lost weight. It is irrational to focus exclusively on your weight goal, which may have been unrealistic, and ignore the changes you have been able to make. To succeed at weight loss it will be necessary to feel good about positive changes you have made even when there isn't any immediate weight loss.

Since I've Failed at Dieting, I Have No Willpower

This is labeling. Using any of these phrases to describe yourself doesn't help you understand your difficulty with weight loss, nor does it suggest anything that you should do differently in the future. Instead of looking for a label that will provide a superficial explanation, it is more helpful to work on your body intelligence by examining the reasons for your eating, the way you view your body, and how you use it to determine what can be improved, and then gradually making the necessary changes.

How Much Would You Like to Lose?

To develop body intelligence it is necessary to discard the typical irrational dieting attitudes and replace them with more rational beliefs about weight loss. A good place to start is with your weight-loss goals. Each time you've tried to diet, you had a goal weight that you were hoping to reach. This goal might have been based on an "objective" standard, such as the ideal weight for your height that you found in a table of height and weight standards. Perhaps you were weighed hydrostatically (under water), the fat content of your body was determined, and a weight-reduction goal was based on these calculations. Or, your doctor consulted a chart and told you what you should weigh, or you used a formula to compute your Body-Mass Index (BMI) and decided how much you'd have to lose to fall into the normal weight category.

Although these methods are objective and usually are based on research data, they are not foolproof. For example, there have been scathing critiques of the methods used to accumulate the data used for the height and weight tables.

In addition to the objective standards, you probably have your own, personal weight-loss goals. Younger dieters may be tempted to set their goals based on the look of a movie star or rock singer that they idolize, while older dieters may have an image from their past that is used as a reference. For example, many women would be happy if they could fit into their wedding dress, while many guys fondly remember how they looked when they were playing sports in high school or college. There might be a specific dress or pants size that is associated with better feelings about your body, and your goal is to be able to wear that size clothing again.

Sometimes a weight goal may be based on the advice, or even the demands, from parents, spouses, or friends. Holly, a twenty-eight-year-old dental assistant, had recently divorced Doug, her drug-dependent husband. Shortly after filing for divorce, her mother pulled her aside, and in a confidential tone, told her that she needed to lose twenty pounds before she started dating again. Since Holly was feeling self-conscious about her weight, and her mother had been right when she warned her not to marry Doug, Holly started a diet to lose the twenty pounds. Tracy, a thirty-one-year-old teacher, is another example of someone who is trying to lose weight to please someone else. She is married to Rod, a thirty-year-old stockbroker. Tracy weighed 175 pounds and wanted to lose 35 pounds. When I asked her how she decided on that goal, she reluctantly admitted that it was Rod's idea. She was going to diet so he would be proud of her when they went to business functions together. Both Holly and Tracy are going to be disappointed. A desire to please others is not sufficient motivation to make the changes necessary for permanent weight loss.

The Benefits of Reaching Your Goals

Regardless of the source of your dieting goals, you had hopes and expectations for how your life would improve once you succeeded.

Let's examine those expectations. If you could fit into that dress (or pants) how would your life be different? Most dieters expect major changes in their daily lives once they have reached their goal weight. Look at the list below and check the benefits you expect when you've reached your goal:

❑ 1. I will be more physically attractive.
❑ 2. I will be able to wear smaller clothing and have a wider variety of clothing to choose from.
❑ 3. My health and fitness will be improved.
❑ 4. I will have more opportunity to play sports and participate in leisure activities.
❑ 5. I will have better opportunities at work.
❑ 6. I will have a better social life.
❑ 7. My self-esteem and self-confidence will improve.
❑ 8. My personal relationships will improve.

After you've checked the anticipated benefits from weight loss, go back over the list to see how many of them actually depend on losing weight. Clearly number 2, wearing smaller clothing, requires weight loss. Given the cultural emphasis on slenderness, you could argue that it is necessary to lose weight to enhance your appearance (number 1), but this is only partially true. (Chapter 7 will deal with this issue in more detail.) Likewise, improvements in health and fitness (number 3) are more likely following weight loss, but there can be some progress before there is significant weight loss.

It is widely assumed that having an "ideal body" will increase attractiveness, professional development, wealth, and happiness. If you checked any of numbers 4–8, recognize that while these are worthwhile goals, they aren't dependent on weight loss. For example, if you checked number 4, ask yourself if losing weight is really necessary before you can play some sports or become involved in other activities. You probably couldn't play full-court basketball at your current weight, but could you play volleyball, bowl, or swim? While you might be reluctant to participate because of self-consciousness about your body, it is possible that you could lose weight and still feel awkward, or you could reduce your self-consciousness regardless of your weight (see Chapter 8). If you checked number 8, ask yourself if you know any overweight people who have rewarding personal relationships. Do you know any slender people who have difficulty with their relationships? When you examine the evidence, you will find that successful relationships have very little to do with weight. If there is conflict revolving around your weight, it is likely that there are more basic issues in the relationship that are not being discussed.

Julie was a twenty-nine-year-old salesperson at a small-market radio station. Although she had two long-term relationships, Julie had never married and was currently unattached. Since high school she had been struggling with her weight and had a history of many failed diets and weight-loss programs. She described her weight-reduction goals and the benefits she expected when she finally reached her goal weight:

> *If I can just get down to 140 [her current weight was about 160], I won't be so self-conscious. When I go out with my girlfriends, I don't dance because I worry that I'd look gross out on the dance floor. If I weighed 140, I'd have the confidence to dance and maybe I'd meet a nice guy. At 140 I'll be able to wear cute clothes and go swimming in the summer. Also, if I were thinner, I think I'd get a better response when I try to sell a new account.*

Julie had high expectations for weight loss. Frequently it seemed that much of her life was "on hold"; she was waiting until she reached her goal before she would dance, swim, buy new clothes, or try anything new.

How many activities have you postponed until you reach a certain weight? In your notebook, write in activities that you would like to do but feel that you can't do until you've reached your weight goal.

The Disadvantages of Postponing Your Life

Postponing pleasurable activities until you reach an arbitrary weight goal is self-defeating, and when you think about it, frequently it's kind of silly. If Julie lost fifteen pounds, she wouldn't have reached her goal so she'd still be too self-conscious to dance, but if she lost twenty pounds would the self-consciousness magically disappear? It's unlikely that anyone else would be concerned about or even notice the five-pound difference! Instead of worrying about an arbitrary goal, it would make more sense to work on her uneasy feelings about dancing in public regardless of weight.

Research suggests that, similar to Julie, overweight college students report fewer pleasurable activities in their lives compared to normal weight students. This is counterproductive since weight control requires effort. One study found that positive experiences can restore the energy required to maintain self-control when tempted by goodies such as cookies and chocolate. Having fun can increase the motivation and energy needed to make this effort. Once her self-consciousness was overcome, Julie found that she enjoyed swimming and dancing even though she hadn't reached her weight goal.

Look at your list of postponed activities. Ask yourself whether it is the weight that prevents you from participating in the activity, or is it your feelings about the weight? If you are honest with yourself, you'll find that most often, it's your feelings that are holding you back. The sidebar, "Clothes Shopping," offers a few suggestions for one of the most frequently postponed pleasurable activities: buying new clothes.

Great Expectations Versus Intelligent Expectations

Having unrealistic expectations can undermine any weight-loss effort, yet many diets make wildly improbable promises. For example, one ad for South Beach Diet Online completely ignores the genetic determinants of weight, proclaiming, "We'll help you reach your target weight—whatever it is." When I went to the website and indicated that my goal was to lose 400 pounds, I was encouraged to sign up.

According to Dr. Janet Polivy and Peter Herman, two of the most prolific researchers on dieting, the reason most dieters fail

> . . . *is that they try to do more than they can realistically do, and even those who do manage to achieve their targets (temporarily or permanently) do not experience the sort of widespread personal and social improvements that they expected or hoped for.*

CLOTHES SHOPPING

One dilemma you may have confronted revolves around buying clothes. Regardless of weight, you'd like to dress fashionably and look good. Also, many women (and some men) enjoy clothes shopping. The problem with buying clothes that fit at your current weight is that it feels like you are admitting that you're never going to lose weight. If you should lose the weight, then the money you spent on the larger clothing was wasted. On the other hand, if you postpone buying clothes until you reach your weight goal, you are stuck wearing clothing that you no longer find attractive and you miss the fun of shopping for new clothes. Although there is no perfect solution, one option is to minimize your purchase of new clothes, but allow yourself to shop for shoes and accessories that are still going to be useful after you've lost weight. You can enjoy the shopping experience and change your look with the new shoes, scarves, purses, jewelry, and hair clips.

Some of Julie's unsuccessful diets had resulted in weight loss that fell short of her goal. As she lost weight, she became discouraged because many of the anticipated benefits did not miraculously appear as the numbers on the scale decreased. For example, with one diet she lost twelve pounds and was approaching her goal, but she still felt self-conscious when dancing or wearing a swimsuit. One of the reasons she gave up dieting was the expected benefits of weight loss didn't materialize. If her expectations had been more realistic, she could have been pleased with the twelve-pound weight loss, worked on becoming more self-confident, and maintained the weight loss rather than giving up and regaining the weight.

It is important to clarify your expectations so that you can separate the goals that require weight loss from those that can be accomplished even if your weight doesn't change. Review your list of activities that you've postponed, and consider if weight loss really is essential for all of them. Try to get started on some of these activities now regardless of your weight. Start with the least difficult and see what happens.

Ideal Versus Real Versus Tolerable Weight Loss

If you were going to start a weight-loss program, what would you hope to weigh at the end of the program? In your notebook, write your:

- Dream weight (if you could weigh anything you wanted)
- Happy weight (not ideal, but you would be happy to achieve)
- Acceptable weight (you wouldn't be happy, but you could accept this weight)
- Disappointed weight (less than your current weight, but you would be disappointed if it was your final weight)

Researchers at the University of Pennsylvania asked sixty obese women (their average weight was 218 pounds) these questions before starting a diet and exercise program. Although they lost an average of thirty-six pounds, none reached their dream weight and only 9 percent reached their happy weight. While thirty-eight participants had achieved a significant loss of weight after twenty-four weeks, few of the participants were satisfied, and many were frustrated and disappointed. At the end of the program, participants reported that their weight losses, although disappointing, had more positive physical and psychological effects than they had anticipated. Even though they still wanted to lose more weight, they reported significant improvements in their health, strength, and fitness. They felt they were more attractive, had an improved sex life, felt more comfortable in social situations, were more assertive, and had greater self-confidence. The implications of these findings for you are clear: a small weight reduction, even if it leaves you considerably heavier than your ideal, can have important physical and psychological benefits.

Are you skeptical about the benefits of small weight losses? If you could reach the disappointed weight you identified above, would you see this as a meaningless change? The participants in the Pennsylvania study were equally skeptical. Before they started treatment they were asked to rate the anticipated benefits if they only reached their disappointed weight. On average, the participants predicted that small weight reductions wouldn't have any great benefits, yet once they achieved these reductions they found many benefits. You might be pleasantly surprised to see how your life improves when you reach your "disappointed" weight.

Your Realistic Goal Weight

Examine the goal weights you identified above in light of these findings. It may be unlikely that you will reach your dream or happy weight goal, but you will find that there are more benefits from modest weight reduction than you now expect. It you are doubtful, try to suspend judgment until you have finished working on the body image issues in Chapters 7 and 8. This may not be easy. For many people, it is difficult to give up long-held ideas of what they "should" weigh.

Body intelligence implies a rational perspective on your weight and what you can realistically expect to accomplish. Although the height and weight tables—or their successor, the BMI charts—offer guidance about the healthiest weight, you shouldn't immediately settle on that number for your goal. While that weight might be ideal it might be unrealistic for you, depending on your genetics. It is also possible that you could lose weight, reach your desired BMI, and still be dissatisfied with the proportions of your body since the location of fat deposits is genetically determined. Instead of deriving your goals from tables of ideal weights based on studies of large groups of people, your goals should focus on your unique weight history. There is no value in setting a goal that you are unlikely to reach, or will find impossible to maintain. Instead you can set a realistic goal weight that you will be able to maintain indefinitely. Although it may not be ideal, you will decrease your health risks and improve your appearance. According to Dr. George Blackburn, a noted obesity researcher at Beth Israel Deaconess Medical Center in Boston,

> *Modest weight loss (5–10 percent of initial body weight) . . . improves the metabolic disorder associated with obesity by reducing insulin, blood pressure, fatty acids, and triglycerides. It also reverses insulin resistance, protects against certain cancers, and improves or reverses obesity-related comorbidities, including osteoarthritis, diabetes, and cardiovascular disease. This improvement occurs even if you are still overweight.*

Here are some guidelines to help you determine a weight-loss goal that is realistic for you. Remember that this is your initial goal. If you reach the goal easily, and can maintain it comfortably, there is nothing to prevent you from setting a new, lower goal weight. But for now, we want to identify a weight that you can reasonably expect to reach and maintain.

- If I lost 10 percent of my current weight, I would weigh _____ pounds.
- If I lost 5 percent of my current weight, I would weigh _____ pounds.
- Since I was 21, the lowest weight I have been able to comfortably maintain, when I wasn't sick, for at least one year is _____ pounds.

Stop for a few minutes and consider a realistic goal using your answers to the three statements above as guidelines. For most people, a 5 to 10 percent reduction in weight is a good starting goal. When you consider the lowest adult weight that you've been able to maintain for a year, you can adjust your goal up or down. Using your answers to these statements, decide on a weight goal and write this goal in your notebook.

Weight Control Readiness

If I told you that I was leaving tomorrow to drive from my California home to visit relatives in Florida, only I was a little worried because my twenty-year-old car was making funny noises each time I changed gears, the tires were bald, and sometimes I had difficulty getting the car started, what would your advice to me be? If you are going to start a weight-control program and you are starting a new job, moving to a new house, getting married (or divorced), dealing with a drug or alcohol problem, or grieving over a recent death in the family, what do you think is likely to happen? The lesson from both examples is that you don't want to start a lengthy journey when there are preexisting problems that are likely to prevent you from arriving at your destination. On the other hand, you can spend so much time preparing your car or getting ready to lose weight that you never get started. Life is never perfectly tranquil, so how do you know when it is a good time to start? Here are some questions you can ask yourself to help decide.

1. *Are you going through any major life transitions, or will you be in the near future?* If you are going through a divorce, having serious financial problems, or having other major stressors, it would be wise to postpone weight loss until your life is more settled.

2. *Are you suffering from a serious medical problem or mental illness?* While mild depression is not unusual, a serious mood disorder or mental illness will interfere with weight loss. It would be better to seek treatment for the disorder first, and then work on your weight.

3. *Do you have a drug or alcohol problem?* Aside from the extra calories in alcoholic beverages, any substance that reduces your ability to make rational decisions and exercise control will prevent weight loss.

4. *Is your living situation relatively stable?* Are you planning any lengthy trips in the near future? Remodeling your kitchen? Changing your work schedule? You will need some structure and routine in order to succeed at weight loss. It might be better to wait a few weeks until your situation is more settled before starting.

5. *Are you willing to devote some time and energy to making gradual changes in your relationship to food and your body?* Your previous weight-loss attempts were unsuccessful, or resulted in only temporary weight loss. There is no point in repeating this pattern. You can't get different results by doing the same thing that didn't work the last time! Are you willing to try something new, even if it feels unfamiliar to you?

If you answered no to questions 1–3 and yes to 4 and 5, there is no reason not to start on a realistic weight-control program.

If you've accepted a nondieting mentality regarding weight control, have a weight-reduction goal that makes sense for you, even if it isn't an ideal weight based on contemporary standards, and have determined that there are no significant roadblocks that would prevent you from getting started, it's time to look at your eating. While continuing to work on emotional eating and external eating, we can examine other aspects of your eating without imposing the artificial constraints of a diet. To do this it will be necessary to collect data.

Data for Body Intelligence

Do you remember the first time you heard yourself on an audio- or a videotape recording? Were you surprised to hear frequent speech disfluencies such as "um" or "uh"? Or, maybe you found that you used little phrases such as "you know" or "like" ("It was, like, so cold out, you know") repeatedly. These speaking habits don't register in our consciousness. We only become aware of them when there is an objective recording of our speech. The same is true for eating.

Regardless of your weight, some of your eating doesn't register in your consciousness even though the food has the same caloric value with or without awareness. For example, it is unlikely that you make a mental note of the caloric values of the peanut butter that you licked off the knife when making a sandwich for your kids or the tablespoon of spaghetti sauce you ate from the pot to see if it needed salt. If you pick up the dishes after your kids have finished eating, do the leftovers you nibbled so that "they don't go to waste" register as eating? If you don't eat a whole cookie, just a few broken pieces at the bottom of the bag, do the calories still count? Research has shown that when asked, overweight people typically underestimate their caloric intake by 30 to 50 percent, while normal weight folks underestimate how much they eat by 20 percent. A recent study showed that professional dietitians underestimated their own caloric consumption by 10 percent. If dietitians lose track of their eating, what hope is there for the rest of us? It would be shortsighted of us to put effort into changing the eating habits you are aware of while continuing other eating that occurs without awareness. It's necessary to be fully aware of what you are eating in order to be able to increase body intelligence.

Recall that in Chapter 4 you used a three-by-five card to record your emotional eating. You will use the same basic outline for this assignment only this time you will record *all* of your eating. This includes meals and snacks that are not triggered by any emotions. Before you dismiss this assignment as impractical or too difficult, let me reassure you that you will only need to do it for two weeks, you won't have to meticulously weigh everything you eat or compute its caloric value. As with your Emotional Eating Records, it is important to do your recording as soon as possible after eating rather than waiting until the end of the day and trying to remember everything you ate. If you are eating with other people nearby, it is reasonable to postpone the recording until you have privacy. It is not necessary for anyone else to know about or discuss what you ate or didn't eat. Since you won't be sharing this information with anyone else, there is no point in forgetting or fudging on this assignment.

Using a three-by-five note card or your notebook, make the following headings:

Time	Food/ Amount	Excess?	Location/People/ Circumstances

In the first column record the time you were eating. The type of food and the amount goes in the second column. In the "Excess" column make a check when you feel that you ate more of a food than you should have, or if you felt that your eating was out of control. Finally, in the "Location/People/Circumstances" column make a note of where you were and anything that may have contributed to your eating including people, emotions, specific external cues, or any other factors that will help you identify patterns of eating.

The typical responses I get when I present this assignment are moans, groans, and all sorts of reasons why it would be difficult or impossible to do. After a week, there are fewer complaints. It wasn't so hard to do, and almost everybody learned something new about their eating. It may help to know that several studies have demonstrated that people who carefully self-monitor lose significantly more weight than those who don't and failure to monitor eating is a predictor of failure to lose weight. When you monitor your eating you become aware of your patterns, you learn what needs to be changed, you will feel encouraged as you see changes, and, most important, with increased awareness comes the opportunity to make decisions about what you are going to eat. This is the heart of body intelligence: knowing what you are doing with food and making rational choices based on that knowledge. Finally, as you succeed in losing weight, knowing how to self-monitor will become your security blanket. When it seems that you are "losing it" and starting to regain the weight, resuming self-monitoring will enable you to find out what's not working, make the necessary changes, and continue making progress.

CHAPTER 6

EATING IS FUN

As you follow the guidelines in Chapters 3 and 4, you should be making some progress controlling both external eating and emotional eating. As you continue decreasing this type of eating for extrinsic reasons, we can focus on eating for intrinsic reasons: to provide necessary nourishment and because eating favorite foods is fun.

In contrast to the typical dieting mentality that prohibits many of your favorite foods and leaves you feeling guilty when you inevitably violate the prohibition, with body intelligence it is perfectly acceptable to eat foods solely for the enjoyment that they provide—so long as you follow a few guidelines that will help you enjoy the experience without guilt. You can have foods just because you enjoy them and still successfully regulate your weight.

If you've set a realistic weight goal and determined that you are ready to work on weight regulation, you will want to develop a strategy for eating. Unlike a diet with lists of acceptable and forbidden foods, we will use the information gathered from your Eating Records to separately consider each of the three aspects of eating:

- *What to eat:* how to make reasonable food choices that include your favorite foods
- *How much to eat:* the amount of food that will leave you feeling satisfied while losing weight
- *Where and when you will eat:* how to organize the structure and circumstances of your eating to make unnecessary eating less likely

In addition, we will consider how to get social support to help maintain your motivation.

Listed below are seven statements. Rate each statement by circling the appropriate number; assign a rating of 1 for Always, 2 for Usually, 3 for Sometimes, 4 for Rarely, and 5 for Never or Not at All.

1. I avoid eating fried foods.

      1   2   3   4   5

2. I avoid using butter on my food.

      1   2   3   4   5

3. I eat dessert.

      1   2   3   4   5

4. I enjoy eating sweets.

      1   2   3   4   5

5. I avoid buying ready-to-eat foods (cookies and crackers).

      1   2   3   4   5

6. I avoid eating junk food.

      1   2   3   4   5

7. I buy foods that I like regardless of their fat and calorie content.

      1   2   3   4   5

This is the Avoidance of Fattening Foods Scale.* To get your score, reverse your rating on items 3, 4, and 7 so that a 1 becomes a 5, a 2 becomes a 4, and vice versa (a rating of 3 doesn't change). Next, add up your ratings. Use the following table to interpret your score.

---

*C. F. Smith, D. A. Williamson, L. G. Womble, J. Johnson, and L. E. Burke, (2000). Psychometric development of a multidimensional measure of weight-related attitudes and behaviors. *Eating and Weight Disorders, 5,* 73–86.

Avoidance of Fattening Foods Score

	Women	Men
No or minimal avoidance	6.9	4.9
Low avoidance	12.7	10.5
Average avoidance	18.5	16.1
Above average avoidance	24.3	21.7
High avoidance	30.1	27.3

As its name suggests, this scale measures avoidance of fattening foods. Higher scores on this scale have been associated with greater weight loss for women participating in a twenty-week treatment program. If you have a high score it is likely that you do a good job avoiding fattening foods, but to lose weight you may also need to work on reducing the amount that you eat and organizing your eating to decrease unnecessary eating.

If you have a low score, you will need to develop a strategy for avoiding or minimizing, *but not prohibiting*, fattening foods. Regardless of your score, a list of "bad" forbidden foods won't increase body intelligence and is unlikely to be successful in the long run. Instead, by following the suggestions in the next section you can learn how to allow for a limited consumption of your favorite foods. To start, review a week's worth of your Eating Records. In your notebook, list the three or four high-calorie, fattening foods that you eat most often.

Go back to your Eating Records. Did you put a check in the "Excess" column when you were eating these fattening foods? If so, you will need to pay particular attention to the strategies for reducing portion size described later in this chapter. Also look at the "Location/People/Circumstances" column. Do you eat these fattening foods anytime and anyplace or are there some situations that are more likely to trigger your eating? For example, are you more likely to eat snack foods when your kids are snacking, or do you have ice cream when you eat lunch with a coworker? In your notebook, list any pattern of locations, people, or situations that seem to be associated with your consumption of the fattening foods.

Give some thought to altering these patterns. Later in this chapter eating in restaurants and at social events will be discussed, but the number of possible circumstances that could contribute to your eating is too great to discuss each one. Instead, review Chapter 3 to see how you can modify the external cues to minimize eating in these situations.

Eating Favorite Foods

If the fattening foods you previously listed in your notebook were among your favorites, you should not try to eliminate them. Regardless of your weight, there is no shame in enjoying foods just for their taste. Forbidding any food only increases its desirability so that eventually the craving becomes irresistible, resulting in overeating or even an eating binge. Eating intelligently includes planning for indulgences so that they do not disrupt your weight-control efforts. Even if you want to lose a significant amount of weight, you should not be deprived of one of life's pleasures.

GUILT-FREE CHOCOLATE

Here are a few ways of satisfying your craving for chocolate without doing significant damage (but not when you're hungry!).

➤ Instead of chocolate chip cookies or milk chocolate, eat a piece of dark chocolate. It has more flavor and fewer calories.

➤ Instead of chocolate ice cream, have a chocolate fudge bar (80 calories) or a half-cup of nonfat chocolate frozen yogurt (100 calories) with a half-cup of sliced strawberries (20 calories).

➤ Make a chocolate float with a half-cup of nonfat chocolate yogurt and diet soda.

➤ Some low-calorie chocolate puddings have 120 calories per serving.

➤ Chocolate sprinkles (jimmies) have about twenty calories per teaspoon. Sprinkle some on low-fat yogurt. A Chocolate Crunch popcorn cake has 60 calories. Necco Chocolate Wafers have 5 calories each.

If you're female, chocolate is probably on the top of your list, while for males pizza, chips, or other salty snacks are most popular. One study showed that you could indulge your yen for chocolate while *decreasing* the strength of your chocolate craving. The researchers found that eating chocolate when hungry increased future cravings but eating chocolate fifteen minutes after finishing a meal lessened later desire for chocolate. Although the researchers did not look at other frequently craved foods, it is likely that the same principle holds for most treats that are high in calories and fat. The secret is to never eat the chocolate (or other craved food) while you're hungry. Enjoy the treat after dinner or at other times when you are not hungry. A few suggestions for enjoying chocolate without guilt are presented in the sidebar, "Guilt-Free Chocolate."

Plan to integrate each of your favorite foods into your weekly eating. First, if you can enjoy the food guilt-free, how often would you

---

SHOPPING FOR INCONVENIENCE

Fattening foods are not prohibited, but they're not encouraged either. Since you have just planned your eating of several of your favorite foods, how will you ensure that you don't eat them at unplanned times? Also, what about those still fattening, but slightly less favorite foods? The best defense against unplanned consumption of fattening foods is to make them inconvenient. You can start by not buying them when you are food shopping. For example, if Oreos are one of your favorites, don't keep any in the house. When you are ready to have your scheduled treat, go out and buy some specifically for that purpose, but make sure you buy a single serving package, not the family size pack. If your roommate, spouse, or children absolutely insist that they have ready access to cookies, buy cookies that they like but you don't. If that isn't possible, buy several single serving packages and label them with the names of the intended recipients, so that you won't be tempted. The frequency of unplanned eating will decrease as its inconvenience increases.

like to eat it? Every day, twice a week, or on special occasions? You might be surprised to find that once it's not forbidden you would be happy with less than you think. Next, plan where and when you can eat it so that you won't be hungry and you won't be distracted or focusing on anything other than enjoying the food. Finally, how can you allow for the extra calories in your treat? Will you be satisfied with a smaller portion, a low-calorie variation of the food, or can you compensate by reducing consumption of some other foods? For each of your favorite foods, write in your notebook:

- How often you will eat it?
- Where and when you will eat it?
- How you will plan for the extra calories?

How Much Is for Dinner?

For each of the following seven statements circle the appropriate number: 1 for Always, 2 for Usually, 3 for Sometimes, 4 for Rarely, and 5 for Never or Not at All.

1. I eat less than most people would in a similar situation.

    1   2   3   4   5

2. I eat much more than the average person because I constantly snack on foods throughout the day.

    1   2   3   4   5

3. I leave food on my plate.

    1   2   3   4   5

4. I love food too much to watch what I eat.

    1   2   3   4   5

5. I rapidly eat a large amount of food in a short period of time.

    1   2   3   4   5

6. When I smell delicious food, I feel hungry even if I have just eaten.

    1   2   3   4   5

7. Some foods taste so good that I eat more even when I am no longer hungry.

    1   2   3   4   5

This scale measures tendencies to overeat.* As you would expect, research shows that lower scores are associated with success at weight loss. To get your score, reverse your rating for items 1 and 3 so that a rating of 1 becomes a 5, a 2 becomes a 4, and so on. Add up your ratings. Check the following table to interpret your score.

Tendencies to Overeat Score

	Women	Men
No or minimal overeating	28.6	30.4
Low overeating	24.3	25.9
Average overeating	20.0	21.4
Above average overeating	15.7	16.9
High overeating	11.4	12.4

If you tend to overeat, how did this habit get started? When you were a child, were you ever told that you were a "big boy" (or girl) because you ate a lot of food? Some men still take pride in the large amounts of food they can consume (on average, men score higher on the Overeating Scale). Bill, a sixty-two-year-old retired dentist, recalls his father bragging about the number of times he went back for more food when the family went to an all-you-can-eat buffet restaurant. Now, almost fifty years later, he describes himself with some pride as a "big eater" although he recognizes that most of his eating has nothing to do with hunger. Bill is less proud of the forty extra pounds he carries but assumes that he would go hungry if he ate less.

*C. F. Smith, D. A. Williamson, L. G. Womble, J. Johnson, and L. E. Burke, (2000). Psychometric development of a multidimensional measure of weight-related attitudes and behaviors. *Eating and Weight Disorders, 5,* 73–86.

Getting Full with Less

If you associate dieting with hunger or are just concerned that cutting back on your eating would leave you feeling unsatisfied, you shouldn't worry because calories don't count in satisfying your hunger. The amount of food you eat will determine whether you are hungry or satisfied *regardless of the caloric content of the food that you're eating*. In other words, you can be more satisfied and lose weight by eating larger portions of less dense (fewer calories for the same size portion) foods instead of a smaller portion of more dense food. If you've found that dieting always leaves you feeling hungry, eating less dense foods can help you lose weight without this discomfort.

According to Dr. Barbara Rolls, Professor of Nutrition at Penn State and author of *The Volumetrics Weight-Control Plan*, for 100 calories you can have one-quarter cup of raisins, or for the same 100 calories you can have almost two cups of grapes. If you choose the grapes, you will be less hungry than if you choose the raisins. Since raisins are just dried grapes, the difference is water. When you drink water by itself it is unlikely to make you feel full, but when water is a significant part of the food you are consuming you will get full on fewer calories. Fruits, vegetables, stews, cooked grains, lean meats, fish, poultry, and soup have high water content, so they tend to be filling even though they are less dense. Likewise, foods high in fiber such as whole grains and beans are filling without adding a lot of calories. An additional benefit of high-fiber diets is a lower incidence of constipation and colon cancer. In contrast, high-fat foods, such as butter, full-fat salad dressings, and most desserts, are dense because fat has twice as many calories per serving as carbohydrates or proteins. Many dry foods like pretzels and crackers, even if they are low fat or fat free, are also dense. Five pretzel sticks have about twenty-five calories but won't make a dent on your hunger. A whole tomato would be more filling and has the same number of calories.

One study demonstrated the value of low-density foods, especially when they are served at the beginning of a meal. Thirty-three women ate lunches consisting of a salad, followed twenty minutes later by a pasta main course. During the seven-week study, the density of the salad was varied and the amount of pasta consumed was unobtrusively measured. When the women ate a large portion of low-density salad, there was a 10 percent decrease in total calories consumed.

How hard would it be to plan to serve a large portion of a low-density salad or soup as a first course (*The Volumetrics Weight-Control Plan* has twelve soup recipes and twelve salad recipes) and wait a few minutes before starting the rest of the dinner? Remember, you don't have to give up all high-density foods, just make sure that you have healthy servings of low-density food before you have smaller portions of the high-density foods.

One advantage of this approach is that, unlike diets that restrict the foods you can eat, it encourages you to *add* foods to your diet. Put fruit on your cereal, include apple slices in your chicken salad, place salsa on your chicken or fish, add vegetables to your marinara sauce, put eggplant in your lasagna, and add veggies to your shish kabob skewers. By adding low-density foods you will become full sooner and eat less of the high-density food. For a more detailed description of this approach that includes low-density recipes see Dr. Rolls's book.

Supersize That?

The idea that eating a large amount of food is an accomplishment has been taken to the limit by Takeru Kobayashi and more than three thousand of his colleagues. Kobayashi is the ultimate "big eater." A twenty-five-year-old from Japan, he holds the world record for eating 50.5 hot dogs and buns in twelve minutes (that's 15,600 calories and more than one thousand grams of fat). He is the winner of the Nathan's Famous Hot Dog Eating Contest, an event "sanctioned" by the International Federation of Competitive Eating, which oversees 150 similar contests. But you don't have to try to be a competitive eater, or even an ordinary big eater to do major damage to your weight-control efforts. Eating too much has become a commonplace occurrence.

When you place your order at a fast-food drive-up window, you'll be encouraged to order a larger portion of the foods you want. The practice of supersizing has spread from restaurants so that the portions served in meals at home are also getting bigger. A study comparing average portion size in 1996 with 1977 portions found that homemade cheeseburgers were 25 percent larger and contained an additional 136 calories, Mexican food servings increased by 133 calories, and desserts by 55 calories. According to a study reported by the Centers for Disease Control and Prevention, American women are eating 300 more calories each day than they did twenty years ago. Men are consuming 168 additional calories.

What happened during the last twenty years to make us believe that we needed all this extra food to make us feel full? Some of the credit goes to a business executive who was trying to increase sales of soda and popcorn in movie theaters. People wouldn't buy more than one bag of popcorn, even when he offered two-for-one deals. Apparently eating two bags of popcorn seemed piggish, but when he offered a single jumbo popcorn serving or an extra large soda it became more acceptable to consume huge quantities of food.

Most people consuming all of their extra large drinks and supersized fries assume that they must be hungry and need the larger portions. Research suggests that any reported hunger is based on external cues, mostly seeing the food in front of you, rather than on any physiological signal that more food is required. A 2004 University of Illinois study demonstrated that people ate more just because they had larger portions. Dr. Brian Wansink had students come to his laboratory to participate in a taste test of tomato soup. Some of the students had trick soup bowls rigged with hidden tubes that kept the bowls full. These students ate 40 percent more soup. Apparently their eating was determined by the presence of food in front of them rather than any internal hunger cues.

In another study Dr. Wansink demonstrated that large portions lead to increased eating even when the food wasn't very good. Moviegoers were given stale, two-week-old popcorn. Half of the moviegoers got a regular-sized container, while half got jumbo buckets. The moviegoers reported that the popcorn tasted terrible, but those with the jumbo buckets ate 33 percent more anyway, even though they didn't like what they were eating. What these findings suggest is that if you can be persuaded to buy a larger quantity of food, perhaps because it seems like a "good deal" or because you're afraid that you'll be hungry later, you'll eat the whole thing even if you aren't hungry and it doesn't taste very good.

Ruth was a fifty-two-year-old retired schoolteacher who weighed 160 pounds and loved ice cream bars. Since this was her favorite treat, I was not going to tell her she should give them up. Instead I suggested that she limit her intake to one per day, rather than the three she usually ate. I encouraged her to make ice cream eating a "pure" experience. She should not do anything else while eating, focus all her attention on the sensory qualities of eating, and pause for two minutes after each ice cream bar before starting the next. At the following session she told me that most days she was satisfied with one ice cream because, during the pause, "I became involved in something else and forgot about it."

Organizing Your Eating

For most people, eating is not haphazard. Review the Eating Records you completed when you were working on Chapter 5. It's likely you'll find a pattern of two or three meals a day with well-defined snacks, such as a coffee break, and several instances of unplanned nibbling. Some of your eating is the result of a cultural pattern (noon is lunchtime) or lessons learned in childhood ("Eat your breakfast" or "Don't eat now, you'll ruin your appetite"). To eat intelligently, it's essential to examine your patterns. The overriding principle for organizing your eating is that *you should never be very hungry!* Hunger is more than just an unpleasant experience. When you are hungry you are likely to be irritable and tired, have difficulty concentrating, and be preoccupied with food and thinking about your next meal. When you finally have your meal, it is likely that you will lose some of the control you usually have. You will eat more rapidly, eat a larger amount of food, and be less concerned about the type of food you are eating. Moreover, when you do finally stop, you may feel bloated and uncomfortable. This episode of uncontrolled eating is likely to leave you feeling guilty, demoralized, and pessimistic about your chances for losing weight. It's essential to organize your eating to avoid hunger. Let's start at the beginning, with breakfast.

CONTROLLING PORTION SIZE

If you observe carefully you're likely to find that you eat more than you need. There are several steps you can take to reduce the size of your portions without being hungry or feeling deprived.

First, and most obvious, is to emphatically say *"no"* when asked, "Supersize that?" If you just can't pass up a "bargain," bring along a friend, order the larger size, and split it between the two of you. Otherwise, remind yourself that the regular portion will satisfy your physical hunger. Several studies have demonstrated that when you eat a food until you're no longer hungry, it stops tasting good. The extra food in the jumbo size wouldn't have provided any additional enjoyment; it would have just left you feeling bloated and angry with yourself, so you shouldn't feel deprived when declining jumbo portions.

Second, recognize that controlling portion size requires that you read the labels carefully to avoid being misled. For example, a snack package of Grandma's Homestyle Chocolate Chip Cookies has 200 calories, nine grams of fat, and twenty-eight grams of carbohydrates per serving, but if you read the label carefully, you'll find that a serving is only one of the two cookies in the package. More than likely you'll eat both cookies, so you'll consume twice as many calories, grams of fat, and grams of carbohydrates.

Sam, a forty-six-year-old engineer who had lost twenty pounds, learned that the price of continuing weight loss was eternal vigilance. Having avoided desserts for most of the week, he decided to stop at a convenience market after dinner to indulge his love of ice cream. He was doing everything right: he had eaten sensibly so he could allow himself a treat, he had finished dinner so he wasn't hungry, he wasn't using the ice cream to soothe any emotional turmoil, and he was planning on giving the ice cream the attention it deserved to get the maximum enjoyment from it. He spent a few minutes in front of the freezer case examining its contents before choosing an ice cream sandwich made with two cookies. He did some mental calculations and decided that he could afford the 295 calories listed on the label. When he got home he noticed that the serving size was "½ sandwich." The sandwich was perfectly round; there were no notches, dotted lines on the wrapping, or anything else to suggest that it should be cut in half. Sam struggled for a minute before deciding that he couldn't afford 590 calories, cut it in half, and put one half in his freezer before enjoying the other half.

Check the label on a package of pasta. The caloric values are for a two-ounce serving yet most recipes call for at least four ounces and restaurants may serve seven or eight ounces. You have to read the nutrition labels very carefully.

Third, slow the pace of eating. One study found that eating slowly was associated with greater weight loss for women in a weight-control program. When you're eating take smaller bites, put the knife and fork down frequently, talk more (remember, it's not polite to talk with your mouth full!), and stop eating for a minute in the middle of the meal, while there is still food on your plate. Don't distract yourself by reading or watching TV while you're eating. Pay attention to what you're eating. Notice the texture and temperature of the food and see if you can identify any spices that were used. If you focus on your eating, it's likely that you will be satisfied with smaller quantities of food.

Finally, review your Eating Records paying particular attention to the "Excess" column. While overeating is a general tendency that occurs in many situations, see if there are any particular "Times," "Foods," or "Location/People/Circumstances" associated with the checks in the "Excess" column. If you find any circumstances that make overeating more likely, you can plan to substitute low-density (high-fiber, high-water content) foods when you are in that situation.

Mom Was Right

Review your Eating Records. In the last week, how many days did you have breakfast? It may seem illogical, but breakfast, which is the easiest meal to skip, may be the most essential for controlling your weight. One study of almost three thousand young adults followed for ten years, found that people who ate breakfast two or fewer times a week were twice as likely to be obese compared to those who ate breakfast daily. The breakfast eaters also had less likelihood of developing insulin resistance syndrome (a precursor to diabetes). The benefits were greatest among those who had whole grain cereals instead of refined cereals or bacon and eggs for breakfast. Another study of sixteen thousand people found that the thinnest people ate hot cereal for breakfast while people who ate dairy products or eggs, meat, and potatoes were fatter. *But* the people who skipped breakfast weighed the most. Both studies point to the benefits of fiber found in hot and cold whole grain cereals. Also it's likely that starting the day with a regular meal helps set the pattern for controlling eating throughout the day. If lunch is your first meal, more than twelve hours will have passed since your last meal, you will be hungry, eat rapidly, and have less control over your eating.

If you've habitually skipped breakfast you may have difficulty making it part of your morning routine. The sidebar "Relearning Breakfast" presents a few suggestions to help.

RELEARNING BREAKFAST

Especially if your mornings are hectic and rushed, and you aren't hungry, the idea of adding several minutes to eat a meal that you don't want seems ridiculous. If you really aren't hungry first thing in the morning, don't try to force yourself to eat. Instead, plan on taking a break after you get to work. If you prepare the night before, you can take a plastic container filled with high-fiber cereal (or a packet of instant oatmeal), a banana, and a small container of low-fat milk and have your breakfast while your coworkers are having their coffee and donuts.

Check your Eating Records to find the number and usual times of your meals and snacks:

- What is your eating schedule like after breakfast?
- Do you have lunch regularly at noon, or is it more random?
- Do you snack in the afternoon, have an early dinner, or have a snack before bedtime?
- Do you have a small lunch and large dinner or vice versa?

Heather was a twenty-three-year-old, habitually dieting college student who initially resisted my suggestion that she monitor her eating. Rather than acknowledge that she was embarrassed about her eating, she attributed her reluctance to keeping an Eating Record to "not having enough time" or simply "forgetting." After several weeks she felt trusting enough to keep track of her eating. Her records showed a pattern of haphazard snacking, punctuated by frequent binges. Typically, she skipped breakfast because she wasn't hungry. She didn't have lunch because she was in class, or too busy, but instead bought chips and a soda from vending machines. By mid-afternoon or late afternoon she would go to the student cafeteria with a friend and have a slice of pizza or nachos. When her roommates were having dinner, she rarely joined them because she wasn't hungry. Later in the evening, however, she would binge, usually by going to the drive-thru window at a fast-food restaurant and then eating while sitting in her car.

Heather's "dieting" had several unintended consequences: skipping meals increased her hunger, making it harder for her to control her eating when she finally did eat. Without the structure of regular meals and planned snacks, it was harder to keep track of how much she actually ate. She was always disappointed that she hadn't lost weight despite missing meals. When she established some structure to her eating, she was gradually able to regain control over her eating and the frequency of her binges decreased.

Despite what you may have read in diet books, there is no single pattern of meals and snacks that is likely to lead to weight loss. In England they routinely have a small meal in the middle of the afternoon (tea time), and in France it is common to have dinner after 9 P.M. In many

Latin American countries, they traditionally have the main meal at noon followed by a siesta. The specifics of your structure are less important than having a structure that will minimize hunger and provide guideposts that will help you evaluate your eating for the day. Until she completed the Eating Records, Heather rarely knew how much she had consumed because her eating had been so disorganized.

Snacking isn't bad. Although some diets suggest that you have frequent small meals rather than three larger ones, the frequency of eating is unrelated to weight. What is important is the caloric content of the snack and its effect on later appetite.

The best rule for snacking is to have a snack anytime that you're hungry *but* limit your snacks to fruits, vegetables, or plain nuts. Although it may seem illogical, most snack foods are too energy dense to be used for snacking. If you are craving goodies such as chocolate, potato chips, or cookies, you should deal with them as treats or as cravings not as snacks. Snacks are just for when you're hungry so you should use low-density foods to reduce the hunger and save the goodies for a time when you're not hungry.

Restaurants, Holidays, and Social Events

Many people who have been successful in organizing their eating and controlling portion size have difficulty when they are eating outside of the home. In addition to eating in restaurants, Thanksgiving, Christmas, birthdays, anniversaries, going away parties, bar mitzvahs, wakes, weddings, and other celebrations are challenging because you have less control over the type and amount of food available to you and the circumstances of your eating. These environments aren't supportive of your attempts to control your eating. Typically eating is a major focus of the proceedings. After all, what is Thanksgiving without a turkey and stuffing or a birthday without a cake? The other people around you are eating a lot, so if you don't participate fully you might feel that you are missing the spirit of the occasion or that you are putting a damper on their enjoyment. Combine the atmosphere encouraging overeating with a little alcohol and, despite your best intentions, you are eating too much.

THE MOST FATTENING FOOD

Alcohol provides seven calories per gram, making it more fattening than protein or carbs (four calories per gram) but less fattening than fat (nine calories per gram) so strictly speaking, it isn't the most fattening food. However, when you eat fatty foods you will feel full and the feeling will stay with you for a while. Drinking alcohol does not reduce hunger, so you will still need to eat whatever else it takes to satisfy your stomach. The calories from alcohol will be added to the calories you would have consumed normally. Since your body has no way of storing alcohol, your digestive system works on the alcohol first and stores the other nutrients as fat. If you're having some cheese with your wine, it's likely that you'll be wearing the cheese as fat before too long! But if you're having a mixed drink (the kind with the cute umbrellas), you won't need to eat *anything* to get fat to accumulate. The sugar in the mixed drink will do the trick.

In addition to the metabolic properties of alcohol, the psychological effects of drinking will have a real impact on your weight regulation efforts. Alcohol is disinhibiting, so the controls on eating that you've set for yourself will be abandoned when you've had a few drinks. This was demonstrated in two studies of ice-cream eating. Women on a diet ate more ice cream after drinking, while nondieting women did not. If alcohol is dangerous to your weight-loss efforts, should you give up drinking? If you enjoy drinking and are a moderate drinker (one drink per day for women, two per day for men), you shouldn't have to give it up. Remember, you're not on a diet and shouldn't feel deprived. Instead, plan your drinking:

➤ Avoid high-calorie mixed drinks, choosing instead white wine (80 calories) or light beer (100 calories)

➤ Avoid drinking before a meal, since alcohol can increase your appetite

➤ Avoid alcohol-food pairings such as beer and pretzels or wine and cheese, have your wine or beer with the meal rather than with snacks

Out-of-home eating presents challenges, but they are not insur-
mountable. The basic principle: although you don't control the restaurant or party environment, with a little planning you can reduce the
temptations. You can also increase your resolve by telling your spouse
or companion what you are going to eat and what you are going to avoid
before you get to the restaurant or social event. In addition:

- If you are going to a fast-food restaurant, check fatcalories.com
  before you go so you can make an informed decision before
  ordering.
- Avoid restaurants that offer all-you-can-eat buffets, serve mostly
  fried foods, or don't allow substitutions or modifications of items
  on the menu.
- When you're eating with a companion, consider ordering two
  salads and one entrée that you will split.
- Ask the waiter to bring you a "doggie bag" before you start eating
  and divide the food into a reasonable portion, which you will eat,
  and the excess, which you will take home.
- Ask the waiter to take away the bread.
- Be careful with salads. The vegetables are low-density foods, but
  the dressing, croutons, and cheeses in the salads are not. Skip the
  croutons, order the dressing on the side, and dip your fork into the
  dressing before each bite.

Dinner parties, holiday celebrations, and other social events offer
similar challenges, try the following suggestions to maintain your
control.

- At cocktail parties keep a glass of sparkling water in your hand. If
  you are feeling awkward or uncomfortable, you can sip rather than
  nibble on hors d'oeuvres.
- At a house party, stay in the room with the least food and keep
  your back to the table with the food.
- Plan ahead and be ready to respond to social pressure. Who is
  going to encourage you to have seconds and what will you say to
  them?

Finally, the most obvious, but frequently overlooked remedy for extra calories consumed in restaurants and social events is to *eat less at your next meal.* With the typical dieting mentality, overeating at a party is likely to result in the "what the hell, I've already blown it" mentality that provides a rationale for more eating. With body intelligence, there is recognition that when you overeat you won't require as much food later on. For example, if you've had a large midday meal, you can have a light supper before going to bed.

Eating in a Vacuum

Most diets tell you what you should and shouldn't eat as though your eating occurred in a vacuum. In the real world it's likely that you do most of your eating with other people. Even if you ate all your meals by yourself, friends and family will offer comments ("Oh, you've lost weight") and opinions ("You shouldn't wear that; it makes you look fat") about your eating and weight. It's not surprising that other people can have an impact on what you eat and how you feel about your weight-loss efforts.

Try to recall your previous diets. Did other people try to influence your eating directly, or did you ever have the feeling that you were getting mixed messages from others? Sometimes, spouses, friends, or parents will seem to be supportive, "helpfully" reminding you of your commitment to a diet, but then behave in a clearly unsupportive way. Consider the following examples.

- Suzanne was a thirty-eight-year-old mother of three teenage boys. Her husband, Jeff, had a physically demanding job with the local utility company. Although Jeff was pleased when she joined a weight-loss program, none of the males in the house were pleased when she prepared low-fat meals and neglected to bring home the usual assortment of cookies, ice cream, and chips when she went shopping. The frequent complaints and looks of disappointment made Suzanne feel guilty so, after three weeks, she resumed her usual shopping and eating habits and dropped out of the program.

- Sisters Erica and Donna were in their early thirties. Both were married, had kids, and weighed an extra twenty-five to thirty pounds. When they got together or talked on the phone the conversation often focused on the latest diet, low-carbohydrate or low-calorie recipes they were trying, the inevitable dieting slips, and an almost daily comparison of scale readings. For several years, both had minor successes but the typical five- to ten-pound weight loss was quickly regained. When Erica joined an aerobics dance class and went three times per week, she was enthusiastic and tried unsuccessfully to convince Donna to join. After several months Erica continued to be enthusiastic about her aerobics and was maintaining a fifteen-pound weight loss, but she noticed that Donna sometimes referred to her as the "Aerobics Queen" at family get-togethers and frequently made sarcastic comments when the topic of weight or exercise came up.

- Frank and Marjorie were a married couple in their forties. Marjorie was overweight when they married eighteen years earlier. Frank frequently expressed disappointment that Marjorie never succeeded in losing weight despite her dieting and his "helpful" reminders that she needed to stick to her diet. After several weeks in the hospital program I was conducting, she had lost ten pounds and was past the point where she would usually get discouraged. Frank started complaining that, because of the meetings and the exercise classes, she was gone too often. He started bringing home chocolates for her and, at least once, encouraged her to have seconds when they were having dinner at a friend's house.

These three examples illustrate a frequently overlooked truth about weight loss: if you have been fat for some time, other people may have difficulty adjusting to your new eating and exercise behaviors and may be uncomfortable with the weight loss that follows. Usually this is not the result of maliciousness; your spouse, family, and friends may truly want what's best for you, but they may be threatened by the changes you have made.

In the first example, Suzanne's husband and sons were upset because her new eating habits were inconvenient for them. They were accustomed to having goodies readily available whenever they wanted instead of having to plan to get their treats outside of the home. Donna's reaction to Erica's enthusiasm for aerobic dance is more complex. Since they had a history of commiserating with each other over their inability to lose weight, Erica's success caused Donna to feel jealous and a little inadequate since she was reluctant to be as active as her sister. Rather than confront these feelings directly, Donna's sarcasm and ridicule were attempts to disrupt Erica's efforts so that they would again be equally unsuccessful in losing weight. Frank was simply scared. He had gained weight and was self-conscious about his appearance. As long as Marjorie was fat, he felt safe because other men wouldn't be attracted to her, and even if they were, she would be lacking self-confidence. He thought that if she lost weight he might not be good enough for her so he did what he could to ensure that she stayed heavy.

Consider the people who are close to you: your spouse or partner, siblings, mother and father, friends, and coworkers. Include anyone who might be inconvenienced, who might be jealous if you succeeded, or who would feel an implicit pressure to change because you have changed. Also, think about how your weight has become a factor in your relationships. If others were accustomed to thinking about you as overweight, would their interactions with you change if you lost weight? Would they see you differently and have to treat you differently? In your notebook, list the names of those people who *might* be affected by any change in your weight or eating habits. If these people are important to you, and you want to maintain the relationship, you need to develop a plan to remove the eating/weight issues from your interactions with them.

First, recognize the underlying truth: *you are in charge of your body. Unless you request advice, what you eat and what you weigh is your business.* You can help your family make alternate arrangements if you stop bringing home potato chips, and you should consult with them to plan convenient times for your exercise sessions, but *you do not need to justify your decision to change your eating and exercise patterns.*

For each of the people you've listed in your notebook, recall the type of comments that they typically make about your eating or weight. Is it a "humorous" comment, well-intentioned advice, a complaint, or a question that puts you on the defensive? Spend a few minutes thinking about a response that you can make that isn't rude but lets the other person know that you don't want to discuss the matter. Your comment could be humorous, "I'm allergic to ice cream. Whenever I eat it I break out in fat." Or, it could be serious, "I feel like I'm getting mixed messages from you. You tell me you want me to lose weight but then offer me seconds." Or, you can politely refuse to discuss the issue by changing the topic or turning the question around without answering it, "Why would you want to know that?" For each of the people you've listed above, plan a response to a typical comment and write it in your notebook.

It may take a few repetitions, but soon even the most stubborn inquisitor will learn that you are not going to allow yourself to be diverted from your weight-control strategies.

There's Strength in Numbers

Although some people may try to sabotage your efforts, others can be a great help. Groups like Overeaters Anonymous, Take Off Pounds Sensibly (TOPS), and Weight Watchers can provide mutual support and encouragement for participants, although not everyone is comfortable talking about their weight with a group of strangers. Online programs such as *e-Diets* and various Internet chat groups can provide support without the need to attend meetings, but, since you never meet these people, you may miss some of the benefits of personal contact. Also, when things are not going well, it's easy to minimize the difficulty you're having if you're just typing on a keyboard and there's no one to call you on it.

Ideally, the most helpful support can come from people who are important in your life—your friends and family. One study demonstrated that participants in a weight-loss program who were recruited with three friends or family members were more likely to stay in treatment and maintain their weight loss after treatment ended. The treatment included assignments intended to increase social support so that losing weight wasn't such a solitary activity. For example, participants called each other between meetings to offer support. They also worked on assignments in teams, then the results were reported to the whole group.

The implications are clear: working with a partner who also wants to lose weight can be a great help in maintaining your motivation. Sharing your successes and getting support will keep you going after the initial enthusiasm wears off. A partner can also help by gently confronting you when you're tempted to make an excuse or a rationalization for failing to follow through on a planned change. When you are feeling discouraged, knowing that you will disappoint your partner if you give up will help you keep going.

Think about the people you know who are struggling with their weight. Identify someone with a positive outlook, who would be pleased to see you succeed, and talk with that person about becoming your weight-loss partner. Your partner doesn't need to be a family member or close friend. You can even choose a partner you like but don't know that well. Watch your relationship deepen as you work on this goal together.

Change Is a Process

Are you feeling overwhelmed by all the planning you have to do and changes you have to make to eat intelligently? Maybe you've tried a few of the suggestions before and gave up without seeing any significant weight loss. Before you decide that you're going to have to lead a life of unintelligent eating, give some thought to the process by which change takes place. Although you might know of people who decided one day to throw away their cigarettes and never took another puff, changing a long-standing habit is rarely so straightforward. Especially with eating behaviors, change is a gradual process that takes place over time following a predictable pattern. Dr. James Prochaska, a University of Rhode Island psychologist, and his colleagues have identified five stages of change:

- *Precontemplation.* You don't think about changing. You may be in denial ("It's not going to happen to me") or just have given up because you feel that change is impossible.
- *Contemplation.* You are thinking about the change but haven't done anything yet. You have mixed feelings—"I know I should exercise (pro), but I don't have the time and I hate to sweat" (con).

- *Preparation.* You may try a small change or experiment with some of the behaviors necessary for change. For example, on one visit to a fast-food restaurant you order a grilled chicken sandwich instead of a hamburger and fries.
- *Action.* You are making a determined, consistent effort to promote the desired change. For example, you limit your ice-cream eating to a fudge bar three times a week.
- *Maintenance and relapse prevention.* The new behaviors become routine rather than effortful changes. There are "slips," but they are caught early on and reversed.

If you have read this far in this book, you are probably at the contemplation or preparation stage or going back and forth between the two stages. To move into the action stage it will help to:

- *Take small steps.* If you are having difficulty eating breakfast, start by having breakfast two days a week and then gradually increase the frequency.
- *Reward successes.* Make deals or contracts with yourself. "If I limit myself to one glass of wine with the meal, I'll go to the movies with a friend tomorrow."
- *Collaborate with a weight-loss partner.* Tell your partner a specific behavior you are trying to change to get support and encouragement.

Remember, change is rarely straightforward and uncomplicated. It is more likely that you will cycle through contemplation, preparation, and action several times. To keep from getting discouraged reread the "Dieting Attitudes" section in Chapter 5 and keep at it until you get to the maintenance stage.

Eating Really Is Fun

With body intelligence there is no need to struggle and experience the feeling that you're being deprived of one of life's pleasures. With planning and attention you can still enjoy eating while you control your weight. Remember, you shouldn't try to eliminate your favorite foods. You should plan to eat them intelligently:

- Eat high-density treats when you're not hungry.
- Buy treats in single-serving packages.
- Start your meals with low-density foods.
- Read the labels to determine portion size and avoid anything supersized.
- Take your time eating and make it an enjoyable experience.
- Plan your eating to avoid being hungry.
- Eat a high-fiber breakfast.
- Drink alcohol in moderation, with meals rather than with snacks.
- Plan eating at restaurants and social events to control portion size and minimize unnecessary nibbling.
- Avoid discussing your eating and weight with people who are not supportive.
- Plan ahead so that holidays, vacations, and life changes don't disrupt the progress that you are making.

CHAPTER 7

MIRROR, MIRROR ON THE WALL

When you look at a mirror what do you see? Does it make you sad, frustrated, angry, or even disgusted? Do you avoid mirrors so that you don't have to experience these negative feelings and thoughts? When I asked these questions to a weight-control group I was leading, I got several different answers that shared a common underlying theme: shame about having a body that varied from the widely accepted notion of desirable. Anne, a 160-pound teacher, said she doesn't have a full-length mirror in her house. She described her shock when she saw her reflection in a store window as she was walking by. She was upset and made a mental note to stay farther away from windows unless there was something specific that she wanted to look at. Melodie, a 145-pound, twenty-eight-year-old mother of two young children, described her strategy for avoiding the unpleasantness of seeing herself. Whenever she was confronted with a mirror, she focused on a facial feature and kept herself busy with an internal dialogue about makeup alternatives. She distracted herself with thoughts about different shades of mascara instead of focusing on her body. Tiffany, a twenty-year-old college student, didn't like the wall of mirrors in the dance studio she attended. Although she wasn't fat, she always tried to position herself in front of a mirror that had a minor distortion that she thought made her look thinner.

Anne, Melodie, and Tiffany are not unusual; most women and many men are dissatisfied with their bodies. In this chapter we will explore your feelings about your body and uncover the implicit beliefs that underlie these feelings. Although body image is neglected in almost all diet books and weight-loss programs, it is an indispensable component of body intelligence. From a traditional dieting perspective, your feelings about your body are irrelevant. All that matters is that you avoid carbs, calories, or fats. If you just follow the diet, you'll lose weight. The assumption is that once you reach your goal you'll be happy and automatically like your body. This isn't always true. Often dieters who have lost weight are still dissatisfied with their bodies, lose their motivation to continue dieting, and regain the weight that they worked so hard to lose. In contrast, body intelligence specifically includes developing a healthy body image. Understanding how you experience your body; developing positive, realistic thoughts and feelings about it; and treating it with respect are essential to maintain the motivation that is required for long-term weight regulation. To get started, think of a single word or phrase that you would use to describe your body.

Next, put a check mark next to each statement that is true for you.

❑ 1. I am dissatisfied with the shape of my body.
❑ 2. When people see me, they think I'm too fat.
❑ 3. I am ashamed of my body when I am naked with my partner.
❑ 4. I am unhappy with the dimples on my flesh.
❑ 5. My flesh isn't firm enough.
❑ 6. Sitting on a bus, train, theater, or plane seat I have sometimes felt that I take up too much room.
❑ 7. I avoid mirrors because I don't want to see how big I've become.
❑ 8. One part of my body (for example, stomach, thighs, bottom) is too large for the rest of my body.
❑ 9. After eating I look noticeably fatter.
❑ 10. I hate that my fat jiggles when I walk or run.
❑ 11. When I meet someone I hold my stomach in.
❑ 12. I am careful to choose clothing that will hide my body's flaws.
❑ 13. I avoid dancing, swimming, or any activity that will draw attention to my body.
❑ 14. I try to avoid having my picture taken.
❑ 15. I have missed a class reunion or other social event because I didn't like the way I looked.

Although this is not a scientifically validated test, your answers to these questions will help you assess your body image. Body image is the "mental picture" you have of your body. It is comprised of the following three parts:

- Your subjective thoughts and feelings about your body or body parts—which are probably too negative
- The experience of your body, including your perception of the size of your body—which is probably exaggerated
- Anxiety you experience about your body and the behaviors that you do or avoid doing because of your discomfort with your body—which probably are unnecessarily restrictive

Thinking About Your Body

Start with the single word or phrase you used to describe your body. Was it a put-down (*gross, disgusting, ugly*) or was it neutral (*healthy*) or positive (*attractive, sexy*)? Next consider your responses to the first five statements. How many of these negative thoughts and feelings did you endorse? If your responses indicate a painful dissatisfaction with your body, you might take some slight comfort knowing that you have plenty of company. Surveys of *Psychology Today* magazine readers have found that the percentage of American women dissatisfied with their appearance has doubled in the years between the first survey in 1972 and the most recent survey conducted in 1997. In the 1997 survey, 56 percent of the women and 43 percent of the men reported being dissatisfied with their overall appearance. Seventy-one percent of the women were dissatisfied with their abdomen, and 61 percent didn't like their hips and upper thighs. A similar survey of college women found 91 percent dissatisfied with their bodies. These surveys of magazine readers and college students included many women who weren't overweight, yet they were still dissatisfied with their bodies. *You don't have to be fat to hate your body!*

Even though body dissatisfaction is very common, it is not healthy. Several studies of women in weight-loss programs have demonstrated that body dissatisfaction is associated with lower self-esteem and depressive symptoms. The degree of dissatisfaction is not related to the number of pounds of excess weight. Moderately overweight women are just as dissatisfied as women who are severely obese. Hating your body has become so common that it is viewed as "normal" for American women although it is less common among African-American women who tend to be more satisfied with their bodies. If you used a negative term to describe your body and agreed with the negative statements, you will need to work on improving your body image regardless of your current weight.

Perceiving Your Body

Your body, regardless of its size and shape, is a tangible, physical reality. You know how tall it is, how much it weighs, and the dimensions of various body parts. Because you have objective measures of your body, it is reasonable to expect that your mental image of your body is equally objective. This is rarely the case, especially if you are overweight.

Look at your responses to statements 6–10. These statements deal with your subjective experience of your body, especially its size. If you agreed with some or all of them, you see your body as too big. Although it is hard to disagree with your perceptions, consider the possibility that what you are seeing is not a perfect reflection of reality. An extreme example of perception disagreeing with reality is the "phantom limb." Some people who have had an arm or leg amputated will report pain or itching in the limb that is no longer there. The amputee's experience of itching or pain isn't realistic but that's what he or she feels. It is possible that, when you look in the mirror and see yourself as too fat, your perception won't be entirely accurate either.

Research suggests that overweight people frequently misjudge the size of their body. Compared with the nonobese, obese people are three times as likely to *overestimate* their body size and their estimates are an average of 6 to 12 percent greater than their actual size. If you have been struggling with your weight, it's likely that you see yourself as larger than you really are when you look in the mirror. Similar to Anne and Melodie, you may have developed strategies to avoid having to look at reflections of your body, so you never have an opportunity to see if your perceptions are accurate. On the other hand, if you frequently look in the mirror you may focus your attention on the part of your body that is most distressing to you and not get an accurate impression of your overall appearance. Janice, a participant in a college women's body image group, was amazed when the group did an exercise intended to increase the accuracy of their body perceptions. The women took turns tracing each other's bodies while lying on large pieces of plain wrapping paper. Janice discovered her outline was not nearly as large as she had expected.

You know that you'd like to be less fat but until you have objective evidence, consider the likelihood that your perception of your body may not be accurate. Chapter 8 will describe exercises to help you develop a more realistic and healthier body image, but for now it makes sense to suspend judgment. When you look in the mirror you can remind yourself that your perceptions may not be correct.

Avoiding Your Body

Checking any of the last five statements in the previous list suggests that you change your behavior because of your body image. It is true that if you are very heavy, your body will limit some of your physical activities (see Chapter 9), but it is more likely that your body image, rather than your body itself, is what's keeping you from doing things you would otherwise enjoy. Having a negative body image can make you feel bad and interfere with enjoyable activities. For example, one study found that sexually active college women who were self-conscious about their bodies had orgasms 42 percent of the time while less self-conscious women reported orgasms 73 percent of the time. In addition to everyday examples such as changing your posture or dressing to hide body flaws, your body image may be responsible for your feeling embarrassed in social situations or passing up opportunities at work.

Give some thought to how your behavior is affected by your negative body image.

- Do you avoid social events, dancing, getting a physical exam, weighing yourself, swimming, playing sports, or wearing fitting clothing?
- What do you do to try to hide your body?
- Do you hold your stomach in when other people are nearby?
- Do you make jokes about your weight or body to reduce your self-consciousness?
- Have you given up opportunities because you felt limited by your weight?

In your notebook, list the activities you have avoided and the behaviors you have changed because of your body dissatisfaction.

Review this list. Body image matters to you because most of these limitations were a result of how you thought about your weight. Very few, if any, of these behaviors were physically impossible because of excess fat. When you change your thinking about your body, you'll be able to participate without being self-conscious. Chapter 8 presents methods for improving your body image regardless of weight.

Why Body Image Matters

Aside from the fact that a negative body image is a downer and interferes with your participating in activities that you would enjoy, research suggests that having a healthy, realistic body image is associated with greater success losing weight. This might seem paradoxical. It would be reasonable to ask, "If you like your body, won't you be satisfied with your weight and not be motivated to lose weight?" Although this seems logical, it doesn't appear to be true. A study of obese women in a program designed to enhance body image found that they did not gain weight after their body image and self-esteem improved. In my work I have found that overweight people who have a healthy body image and are free of the dieting mentality have more energy to devote to making the changes necessary for permanent weight control.

Sara, a thirty-eight-year-old financial planner participating in a body intelligence group I was leading, is a good example. Although she was only twenty pounds overweight (BMI of 28), she was very self-conscious about her body and avoided many social and recreational activities that she would have enjoyed. After doing some of the body image exercises in Chapter 8, her preoccupation with her "flaws" decreased and she spent more time doing things with other people. She joined a softball team at work, went out dancing with friends, and generally felt more confident socializing. Although she felt better about her body, her desire to lose weight did not decrease. Instead, participating in activities that she had been avoiding was energizing. She had more motivation to follow through on the lifestyle changes presented in other parts of the program; she was more physically active and lost weight.

Once you've lost weight a healthy body image will increase the likelihood that you will be able to maintain that loss. Several studies suggest that weight loss, by itself, may not improve body image. Bariatric surgery patients having had significant weight losses may still be dissatisfied with their bodies. One study of formerly overweight people found that they were just as dissatisfied with their bodies as people who were currently overweight. Disliking your body can become a habit. Even after losing weight, you might still be unhappy with your thinner body. Instead of being preoccupied with fat, you might be dissatisfied with your stretch marks, wrinkles, the shape of your nose, or some other less-than-perfect feature.

Body Image and Weight Goals

Weight loss by itself is no guarantee of improved body image so you might as well work on body image now, whatever your weight is. Recall from Chapter 5 all the expectations that typically go along with unrealistic weight-loss goals. When you dieted in the past, you may have still been dissatisfied with your body after you lost the weight. Give some thought to your last two serious attempts to lose weight regardless of if it was a program you joined or a diet that you made a sincere effort to follow. What happened? Were you pleased with the results, or were you dissatisfied because some part of your body didn't live up to your expectations even though you'd lost weight? If you were disappointed in the outcome, what happened? Most likely, you asked yourself something like, "If I made the effort and I don't like the results, why continue making the effort?" The typical response is to give up on your diet, regain the weight, feel like a failure, and be more discouraged about your body.

Toni, a forty-eight-year-old mother of two college students, was very unhappy about her body. For most of her adult life, she had been told, "You have such a pretty face, if only. . . ." The well-meaning advice always suggested that she needed to do something about her 190-pound body. Bill, her husband, was a successful attorney and avid weekend bicyclist. Over the years, he had suggested that they ride together, offering to go at a slow pace and turn around when she got tired. Toni usually declined with the rationale that she didn't want to make Bill ride slowly so she could keep up. She was too embarrassed to admit that a more powerful deterrent to bicycling was her worry about how her backside would look when it was perched on the small bicycle seat. For similar reasons, she avoided dancing and swimming when they went on their annual cruise and turned down invitations to go clothes shopping with her friends.

Toni was an on-again, off-again dieter. She'd had her greatest success with a low-carbohydrate diet, losing thirty pounds. Although she was thrilled to have lost the thirty pounds, Toni still was unhappy with her body. At 160 pounds she disliked it every bit as much as she did when it was 190 pounds. She still felt too fat to ride a bike, go dancing, or shop for clothes; nothing had changed despite her efforts. After reaching a discouraging plateau, she gave in to her cravings for pasta and the sourdough bread she loved.

Review the body image statements you've checked and look at the list of activities you avoid because of your weight. If you have been hampered by a negative body image, it would be helpful to improve your body image now, before losing weight. You will have more motivation while you are working on your weight, and when you reach your goal and are in the maintenance stage, you won't be disappointed and tempted to give up. Chapter 8 will present specific methods for improving your body image, but before you start it will help to understand how our culture makes it difficult to develop a healthy body image.

Barriers to a Better Body Image

Chapter 2 briefly described the origins of body image. It might be helpful here to have a better understanding of the social forces contributing to attitudes about fat.

Usually overweight people try to lose weight to improve their health, fitness, and appearance. Although most discussion among dieters tends to focus on health, the reality is that appearance is a more potent motivation for weight loss. Even obese patients with significant health problems who are seeking bariatric surgery are primarily motivated by a desire to look better. Why is "looking good" so important? Could it be that you're just being vain by focusing so much attention on your looks?

The Perfect Body

According to Dr. Kelly Brownell, a Yale University psychologist and one of the preeminent obesity and eating disorders researchers,

> *. . . having a desirable body signals the outside world that the individual is in control. It shows control over impulses to eat and to be inactive, and reflects hard work, ambition, and desire.*

It is assumed that having the perfect body brings with it success, happiness, and loving relationships. The reality is that being physically attractive is a mixed blessing. Halle Berry, arguably one of the most beautiful contemporary movie stars, said:

> *Beauty? Let me tell you something—being thought of as a beautiful woman has spared me nothing in life. No heartache, no trouble. Love has been difficult. Beauty is essentially meaningless and it is always transitory.*

Most of us can recall the disappointment and hurt of losing out to a more attractive rival in high school or college. Yet women who were attractive in college rate themselves as less satisfied with their lives when they are middle aged. Children and adolescents who are valued for their looks may seek out superficial relationships in which they continue to be valued for their appearance. These relationships will become less satisfactory as they age and become less attractive.

Being physically attractive is often equated with being sexually desirable and having a fulfilling sex life. While appearance plays a role in attracting a partner, it has little to do with sexuality. Most people are average looking with average bodies yet they find a mate and enjoy their sexuality. If physical beauty were a prerequisite to finding a loving relationship or a sexual partner, the human race would have died out thousands of years ago.

Discrimination and Stigma

Even if you're not striving for the perfect body, controlling your weight is still important to avoid the stigma and discrimination associated with obesity. Discrimination against fat people is the last acceptable form of prejudice. It is not polite, and it may be illegal to discriminate against or make derogatory comments about racial or ethnic minorities, gays, and people with disabilities. In contrast, there is no official protection against discrimination toward the obese in such areas as employment, medical care, and education. The stigma typically associated with being obese is based on the assumption that obesity results from internal, controllable causes, typically a lack of willpower or self-discipline. These vague, overly generalized terms serve as a justification for jokes, rude comments, and unwanted advice intended "for her (his) own good." Of course, this rationale completely ignores the significant genetic determinants of weight and the environmental forces that make weight gain more probable. The stigma is not equally divided among fat people; it is worse for women.

Girl Fat Versus Boy Fat

In the animal kingdom it is usually the male of the species that sports the colorful plumage that enables him to attract a suitable mate. Humans are atypical. For our species the female is supposed to be pretty in order to find a husband. In Western culture, men are valued for their accomplishments, their physical strength, the wealth and possessions they have accumulated, their intellect, and, then, for their appearance. Traditionally, women are valued for their appearance regardless of their accomplishments.

A psychology intern I was supervising provided several examples of the importance of weight. Before starting her M.S. program she was a counselor at a franchised weight-loss center located in the financial district of San Francisco. Most of her clients were professional women: accountants, lawyers, and corporate executives. Typically the clients were immaculately groomed, wore expensive clothes, and conducted themselves in a professional manner suggesting competence and self-confidence. Many of the women were quite attractive, however, the air of self-confidence evaporated once they started discussing the difficulties they were having with their weight. In spite of their career success, most of these women felt thoroughly incompetent when dealing with their weight. How could a few pounds, or a losing struggle over a rich dessert, undermine the well-being of these intelligent, competent, successful women?

A heterosexual male can be proud of his body even if he doesn't look like a weight lifter or a *GQ* model (this is less true for gay males). In contrast, a female is likely to feel some shame when she doesn't measure up to the media ideal. It has been suggested that the difference in the importance of being thin is responsible for the higher rate of depression among women. This difference was illustrated a few years ago when I was shopping for a shirt in a department store. Nearby a six-foot, 250-pound man announced to the salesclerk, in a voice loud enough for everyone nearby to hear, "I want to see *men's* pants, I don't want pants for boys." It would be hard to imagine similar circumstances where a woman would loudly draw attention to her inability to fit into the clothing being offered.

For most of recorded history, the rounded female form was idealized because it reflected the woman's reproductive power. Even today in much of the Arab world obese women are more desirable as wives. In the U.S. fat was stylish and sexy until the advent of the flappers in the 1920s. As a career became more important and motherhood was less significant in defining a woman's identity, the rounded form lost its allure. According to psychologist Rita Freedman:

Slimness became a sign of emancipation, a symbol of nonreproductive sexuality and independence. The accent shifted to looking like a playgirl rather than an earth mother.

Unfortunately, the idealized slender physique is unrealistic for most women, and, for many, it would be unhealthy even if it were attainable. For example, one study of 240 women who were *Playboy* centerfolds from 1978 to 1998 found that their average Body-Mass Index (BMI) was 18. This is classified as underweight, and more than 75 percent of the playmates weighed 85 percent of their ideal weight. Weighing 85 percent of expected body weight is one of the criteria for anorexia nervosa! A *People* magazine cover story showed before and after pictures of twelve movie and television stars who had lost weight and quoted a Hollywood trainer: "Maybe too thin actresses are not clinically anorexic but they definitely have disordered eating habits." In contrast, Marilyn Monroe, *Playboy*'s first centerfold and the reigning sex goddess of the 1950s and early 1960s, weighed between 118 and 135 pounds. She had a BMI of 19.6 (in the normal weight range) at her thinnest.

Hopefully as knowledge about the genetics of obesity becomes more widespread, the stigma associated with weight will decrease and the definition of female beauty will be less restrictive. There are some early signs that the idealization of the scrawny female form may be on the decline. Movies such as *My Big Fat Greek Wedding* and *Real Women Have Curves*, media efforts such as the "body love" issue of *Glamour* magazine, and the success of Curves, a fitness program that encourages heavier women to participate, may be indications of a trend toward increased acceptance of larger bodies. But even if there is continuing progress, you can't afford to wait until everyone agrees that protruding ribs and collarbones are unattractive. You need to improve your body image now, regardless of other people's views of beauty. Chapter 8 helps you do this.

CHAPTER 8

THE MIRROR IS YOUR FRIEND

Even after reading Chapter 7 you may be skeptical about liking your body before losing weight. If you have your doubts, you don't need to accept my assurances. After all, I've never seen your body while you are intimately acquainted with it. Instead, you can maintain your skepticism so long as you make a good effort to do the assignments suggested in this chapter. Keep in mind that hating your body is not helpful. You can like your body and still lose weight.

To learn to like your body it is necessary to identify the specific negative thoughts you have about it. I'm sure there is some variation of the "I'm too fat" theme in your thinking, but what are the other, more specific disparaging thoughts about your body? For example, Toni, the forty-eight-year-old married to Bill the attorney/bicyclist from Chapter 7, was convinced that anyone riding by in a car would automatically focus their attention on her rear and be "disgusted" because it was bigger than the bicycle seat. For Toni, this thought was a given. Even though she had never seen a picture of what she looked like on a bike and had never checked to see how many motorists were actually looking at her as they drove by, she never questioned her belief that people would be disgusted. Anne, the teacher who avoided full-length mirrors, was particularly self-conscious about her abdomen. In addition to holding her stomach in when she was around others, she avoided dating because she was sure that any potential sexual partner would be "grossed out" by her rounded midsection.

Monitoring Your Body Image

For the next week, keep track of your thinking about your body. Use your notebook or three-by-five note cards to make a Body Image Record that you will keep with you at all times. Make three columns: "Trigger," "Thoughts/Feelings," and "Action." The trigger is any stimulus that makes you think about your body. It could be passing a mirror, seeing an old dress hanging in your closet, hearing people talk about a diet, or anything else that draws your attention to your body. Examples of thoughts about your body that you would write in the second column include: "I'm too fat" or "I'll never fit into that dress" or "They'll be grossed out by my thighs." Also note the feeling, typically sadness, anxiety, guilt, or shame that accompanies this thought. In the "Action" column, write what, if anything, you do in response to the thoughts and feelings. It might be you look away from the mirror, hold your stomach in, or change your clothes. The action might also be to not do something that you would have liked to do. For example, if you wanted to go swimming but thought "I'd look fat in a bathing suit" and then felt anxious until you decided not to go, you would write that in the third column.

Give the "Action" column careful thought. There may be some activities that you have avoided for so long that you no longer think about doing them. For example, you might assume that you're too fat to play softball so you don't even consider signing up for the team at work. Even though you're not thinking about it, the avoidance is a result of your body image and should be recorded in the third column. For example, this is what Toni wrote when Bill invited her to go bicycling with him:

Trigger	Thoughts/Feelings	Action
Bill asked me to go on a bike ride.	People will be disgusted. I'll be embarrassed.	Made an excuse for not going.

It may be difficult to keep track of your thoughts and feelings at first because many of them are so automatic that they don't register in your awareness. To make the process of recognizing automatic thoughts easier, identify the situations that you know make you especially uncomfortable about your body. In your notebook, list the frequently occurring situations (places, people, and activities) that are most likely to trigger negative thoughts and feelings about your body.

Once you've identified four situations, make sure you use your Body Image Record to record the thoughts/feelings and actions the next time you're in any of these situations. If, for example, you are likely to have negative thoughts when you pass by a full-length mirror in the lobby of your apartment building, plan to record your thoughts and actions when you're in the lobby. These situations that you've identified are just a starting point. Once you start monitoring your body image thinking, you will become aware of other situations that trigger these thoughts. During this week, don't try to change anything; the purpose of this exercise is just to become aware of your thinking and actions related to your body image.

Triggers

After you've monitored your thinking about your body for a week, review your Body Image Record to identify your patterns. Look at the first column to see if there are people, places, or situations, in addition to the four you've identified above, that trigger body image thoughts. You may be surprised to find that seeing one friend makes you more focused on your body than seeing other friends, or walking past a gym on your way to work triggers these thoughts. In your notebook, list the additional triggers you've identified after monitoring for a week.

Thoughts/Feelings

There are several common patterns of body image thoughts and feelings. The first is the mental filter (see the "Twisted Thinking" sidebar in Chapter 4 for a definition). If you see yourself in the mirror, does your attention immediately focus on a part of your body that you find unsatisfactory instead of looking at the whole picture? For example, do you instantly focus on your stomach and ignore your face, your clothing, and the rest of your body? A second common pattern is labeling or using emotionally charged words such as *ugly*, *gross*, or *disgusting* when you are thinking about a part of your body that you don't like. If you don't use these nasty words, do you use "humorous" terms that are still put-downs, such as *thunder thighs*, *bubble butt*, *beer belly*, or *love handles*? Regardless if you use negative or "humorous" terms, thinking about your body in this way is likely to make you feel sad, guilty, or angry with yourself, which will undermine your self-confidence. A third common thought pattern is jumping to conclusions or making predictions about the future based on your assessment of your body. For example, after thinking that your body is "gross" you might then conclude that no one would ever want to marry you, or that you will never advance at work because everyone is disgusted by your appearance. These predictions will lead to further discouragement and lower self-esteem.

In your notebook, write in body image thoughts you've had during the past week. In addition to mental filters, negative labels, and jumping to conclusions, you may find that you've had other types of negative thoughts about your body.

Actions

Now review the "Action" column on your Body Image Record. In addition to holding your stomach in, what did you do or not do because of your body image? Many people will avoid mirrors, but others will check compulsively, fretting about whatever body part they don't like.

- Did your body image affect your choice of clothing?
- Was there an outfit you would have liked to wear except you thought it made you look fat?
- Do you wear clothing that isn't appealing but you hope it will hide certain parts of your body?
- In the past week were there social or recreational activities you avoided because of your body image?

In your notebook, list the things you did or didn't do because of your thoughts about your body.

Your review and summarizing of a week's body image monitoring should reveal the power of your body image to control your thoughts, feelings, and behaviors. In order to maintain your motivation for weight control, improve your self-esteem and mood, and allow yourself to participate in enjoyable activities, it is necessary for you to improve your body image.

Taking Back Your Body Image

After reviewing the list of triggers you've identified from your week's recording, see if you can recall the first time in your life when you felt bad about your body in each of these situations.

- Do you remember an embarrassing experience, maybe in childhood or adolescence that made you painfully aware of the "defect" in your body?
- Did a classmate or friend tease you?
- Did a gym teacher or coach draw attention to you in a way that made you embarrassed about your body?
- When you started dating, did a potential date express disappointment about some aspect of your appearance?
- Were you physically or sexually abused, or raped?

Although it may be painful to recall these experiences, in your notebook write in the first name of the person and the comment or reaction that made you feel that your body was inadequate.

Now, give some thought to the impact these comments have had on you. When we did this exercise in a group I was leading, Brooke, a twenty-eight-year-old marketing executive, remembered a boy named Jeremy walking behind her in the hallway in junior high. He was joking with his friends when he saw Brooke and made pig noises and a rude comment about the size of her butt. Brooke was humiliated and decided that she needed to go on a diet. When I questioned her about her current feelings about Jeremy, her mood lightened as she looked back on her junior high experiences from an adult perspective. After some discussion, she decided that a fourteen-year-old schoolboy with his own shortcomings shouldn't be the final judge of the acceptability of her body.

Review your list of people and painful experiences. From an adult perspective, try to understand the motivations of the person who made the comments or put you in an uncomfortable situation. If it was a parent or other authority figure, were they transmitting their insecurities about their own body to you? Adults who are unhappy with their bodies sometimes become overinvolved with the weight and eating of their children. Could they have been angry with you for some other reason but chose to criticize your body rather than dealing directly with whatever was bothering them? If it was a sibling, friend, classmate, or other peer that made a hurtful comment, were they showing off for friends (like Jeremy) at your expense? Were they jealous of your success or accomplishments and trying to make themselves feel better by making you feel worse? Perhaps they were just feeling awkward around you and didn't know what to say, so they made a "joke" to decrease their own discomfort.

When you have a clear picture in your mind of the early experience(s) that made you self-conscious and you have some understanding of the motivation of the other people involved, you can revise your current feelings about this incident. Looking back, what would you like to have said to the person commenting on your body? When I asked Brooke, she thought for a moment, smiled, and said, "You know Jeremy had pimples. I could have just told him he should be worried about his complexion instead of looking at my butt." After our conversation, Brooke wasn't immediately content with the size of her rear but she did feel less shame about it, which was the beginning of an improved body image.

Now that you are an adult, do you want to give this person so much power over how you feel? In your notebook, write the first name of the person and an adult response to the hurtful comment or action they made years ago.

If the initial embarrassment about your body was not the result of a single person's comment, you can still review the circumstances from an adult perspective to reduce the bad feelings. For example, Amber, a thirty-two-year-old music teacher, remembered a softball game when she was playing outfield on her junior high team. Running to catch a fly ball she slipped on the wet grass and landed on her rear. For the rest of the game she was concerned that the wet stain on her pants drew everyone's attention to her rear. As an adult looking back, she recognized that she would have been embarrassed about slipping and missing the ball even if she had a skinny butt. Developing adolescents are usually self-conscious whenever attention is directed to their bodies regardless of their weight.

Although early experiences can be especially painful, there is no reason that they need to have a lasting impact. You aren't a child or a teenager anymore. You are more secure and have a better sense of your identity than you did when you were in school. Reviewing these experiences from an adult perspective can help you decrease the emotional responses that resulted from the incident and help you see things more clearly in the future.

Cleaning Up Your Thinking

In evaluating your thoughts and feelings about your body, it's important to first determine how much of your body dissatisfaction is caused by disappointments in other areas of your life. If things aren't going well you may focus on your body rather than the more complex problems that are troubling you.

Maryann, a forty-one-year-old photographer, was feeling "stuck" in her relationship with Patrick. They had been living together for more than a year. She wanted to have children, but Patrick couldn't commit to getting married or becoming a father. Maryann didn't want to break off the relationship, but she was becoming increasingly frustrated. As her frustration grew she became more preoccupied with her body and spent more time unhappily staring at the mirror wondering if Patrick would be more committed if she lost weight.

Review the thoughts/feelings you recorded during the past week. Ask yourself if some of the dissatisfaction with your body might be the result of some other, more complicated problem in your life. If you find that there are other issues that increase your body dissatisfaction, it would help to separate the two, work on the important problem, and put less emphasis on your body.

Mental Filters

In reviewing your thoughts/feelings during the past week, did you find that you tend to focus your attention on the parts of your body that you think are too big, too small, or unattractive? If so, the first goal will be to have you give equal attention to more desirable features. In your notebook, make a two-column list. In the first column list the two parts or features of your body that cause the most dissatisfaction. In the second column list the two parts of your body or features that are the most attractive.

In the next week, make a deliberate effort to think about the attractive features of your body each time you think about the "flawed" body parts. For example, if you're in the habit of brooding about your abdomen, remind yourself of your pretty eyes each time you have unhappy stomach thoughts. While this may seem forced and unnatural in the beginning (especially if you are not accustomed to having any nice thoughts about your body), with repetition it will become more comfortable. Eventually, you will develop a more realistic view of your body, focusing on both its positive and negative aspects.

Check Your Words

Pay attention to the words you use to describe yourself. The goal is not to have you ignore or minimize the body parts that you are dissatisfied with, but rather to develop a more factual, less emotional description of them. It is difficult to develop a healthy body image if you are using emotionally laden words like *gross* or *disgusting* to describe part of your body. Likewise, it's hard to like yourself if you think of part of yourself in these terms. Instead, get in the habit of describing body parts in more neutral terms even when you are dissatisfied with their size or shape. For example, you could say you have a round stomach or a big stomach; both are accurate, objective descriptions. Other descriptive terms you could use to describe body parts include: *large, heavy, dimpled, protruding,* or *sagging.* You are not denying the reality of the size or shape of a part of your body; you are just describing it in more neutral terms so that it doesn't undermine a healthy body image.

Think about the two body features you've identified as causing the most dissatisfaction. In your notebook, write an accurate but emotionally neutral description of these body parts. Make a deliberate effort to clean up your terminology. Whenever you catch yourself thinking or saying a judgmental description, stop and correct yourself. Substitute an accurate, but neutral term.

Looking in the Mirror

The next step may be a little more difficult. When no one else is at home, find a full-length mirror, stand in front (fully clothed), look at your reflection focusing on the first unsatisfactory body part, and, out loud, describe it using the neutral term you wrote in above. Focusing your attention in this way may make you feel anxious, embarrassed, or ashamed, but it is unlikely to cause any real harm. When you do this several times, the bad feelings will decrease. Eventually, you'll be able to look at that part of your body and describe it without feeling uncomfortable. Your body image will improve as you stop feeling bad about the less-than-perfect parts of your body.

Repeat this exercise for the second body part you listed. Repeat the neutral description out loud several times while focusing on the reflection. This exercise should only take a few minutes, so you can repeat it once a day until it becomes boring. When it is thoroughly tiresome you have succeeded. You can think about and look at these body parts without feeling bad.

After becoming comfortable with your body when you are by yourself, the final step is to become comfortable when other people are nearby. This requires the help of a trusted friend. Don't choose a parent or spouse, but someone of the same gender who you consider a noncompetitive friend. Explain that you are trying to become less self-conscious about your body and you need someone to help. If it appears that they don't understand what you are trying to accomplish, or if they don't take your request seriously, change the topic and look for someone else to help you with this assignment. On the other hand, if the friend expresses interest or curiosity, ask them to observe while you point out parts of your body that you feel dissatisfied with. Then, fully clothed, have your friend look at the body parts as you describe them with neutral terms. Continue doing this until the tension decreases and you feel comfortable with your friend's attention focused on your body. When you can be relaxed knowing that others could be looking at your body, you'll find that your body image improves and there will be fewer enjoyable activities that you avoid.

With some uneasiness, Cindy asked her friend Carol to look at her thighs. After changing into shorts Cindy awkwardly started to discuss her large thighs. She was pleasantly surprised when, with a big smile, Carol pulled up her skirt and suggested that they compare. Laughing about dimpled flesh and varicose veins released the tension. Cindy felt less self-conscious just knowing that her friend wasn't repulsed by her thighs.

Controlling Runaway Implications

Go back and review the "Thoughts/Feelings" column again, only this time pick one thought and look for implications in your negative thinking about your body. For example, if you thought, *The dimples on my thighs are really ugly*, ask yourself what do you think will happen or what has happened to me because of having dimpled thighs? In your notebook, write exactly what you think will happen because that body part is unsatisfactory.

Recall from Chapter 7 that there is evidence of discrimination against fat people based on the rationale that any reasonable person could be slender if he or she just made the effort. Although you may have experienced discrimination based on your size, it's unlikely that you hear rude comments every day. What is a daily occurrence is the anti-fat rationale for discrimination that you've internalized. According to sociologist, Natalie Allon:

> *It is no wonder that with the many negative views about fat people, many fat persons are full of self-disparagement and self-hatred. They*

*are trebly disadvantaged: (1) because they are discriminated against,
(2) because they are made to feel that they deserve such discrimination,
and (3) because they come to accept their treatment as just.*

If you've internalized anti-fat prejudice, you are accepting at least
one of the common implications of weight: someone will reject me
because of my weight, or my weight is evidence of mental illness ("I'm
a neurotic food addict"), negative personality traits ("I'm weak and
lazy"), or moral weakness ("I can't resist temptation"). The following
are more rational interpretations of these assumptions.

- *Social rejection.* It is possible that someone might make a rude comment, embarrassing you in front of others, or not want to associate
  with you. Although these outcomes are possible, ask yourself how
  often will they happen. If you are feeling self-conscious about your
  thighs, there will be a tendency to assume that everyone else will be
  equally concerned about them. This is rarely true. Remember that
  body dissatisfaction is virtually universal among white American
  women so it is likely that any companion will be more focused on
  their own appearance than on your thighs. There might be an
  instance when you are confronted with an individual rude enough to
  make a comment, but they are likely to be immature, angry, or jealous. In any event, you won't want to let this person have so much
  influence over your feelings.
- *Mental illness.* Examine your thinking. Do you view your difficulty
  controlling your food cravings as an indication of an addictive personality, a neurosis, or other mental disorder? You may be surprised
  to learn that the official psychiatric diagnostic manual, DSM-IV-TR,
  includes anorexia nervosa and bulimia nervosa under the eating disorders category but does not list obesity as a psychiatric disorder or
  addiction. Furthermore, research suggests that, with the exception
  of binge eating, which is associated with depression, obesity by itself
  is not associated with any type of mental illness.
- *Negative personality traits.* Do you assume that you are unworthy
  because your less-than-perfect body demonstrates a deep-seated per-

sonality defect? Although you don't have a mental illness, perhaps your undesirable personality traits (lazy?, weak?, stupid?, low self-esteem?) are responsible for your weight? Again, research does not find any consistent set of personality traits related to obesity. You may or may not be lazy, weak, and so on, but it is unlikely that your weight is a reflection of any of these characteristics. You may need to occasionally remind yourself that your weight and body shape are determined by genetics and body intelligence, but there is no evidence that they are related to personality traits.

- *Moral weakness.* Perhaps, instead of a mental illness or personality trait, you think that your weight is a result of a moral deficiency. After all, gluttony is a sin and the immorality of weight gain is implicit in many of the words used by dieters. If you have "cheated" on your diet by eating "forbidden" or "illegal" foods (especially "sinfully" rich desserts), then your excess weight is visible proof of your transgressions. Among some religious fundamentalists, dieting is seen as a variation of the struggle to resist temptation and attain virtue and salvation. Even if you accept this framework, it would be difficult to understand why some people are genetically programmed to have a more difficult struggle while a lucky few can achieve salvation with minimal effort.

If you recognize the social rejection, mental illness, negative personality traits, or immorality themes in your thinking about your body, the next step is to develop disputing thoughts that you can use to counteract the irrational thinking. I've pointed out a few irrational assumptions in these negative thoughts, but you should develop your own, personalized disputing thoughts. For example, if you think that your body is evidence of your laziness, you could remind yourself of instances when you had a difficult or unpleasant task that you didn't want to do but you did it anyway.

Carolyn was a thirty-one-year-old working mother of two young boys. One night she had to stay up until 3 A.M. to take care of nine-year-old Josh, who had a terrible cough. When the alarm rang the next morning, she made herself get out of bed and go to work. Yet, because her BMI was 29 and she didn't like her body, she thought she must be lazy.

This is irrational. If she was truly lazy she would have called in sick and spent the day catching up on her sleep.

In your notebook, write two realistic thoughts that dispute the unrealistic ideas you've had about your body.

Although it will take careful attention and repetition, try to catch the negative thoughts you have about your body and substitute the more rational thoughts. If you are alone, it is helpful to say the rational thoughts out loud.

Check Checking

Although some people avoid scales and mirrors, others feel compelled to check how they look or ask for reassurance frequently. For example, before going out, do you try on several blouses and look in the mirror to see which does the best job of hiding your stomach? Do you ask your spouse, "Does this make me look fat?" If you are a frequent checker, ask yourself if this activity is helpful. When I explored this issue with Carolyn, the thirty-one-year-old working mom, she recognized that her mood had a major influence on her body dissatisfaction. If she was unhappy for any reason, she was more dissatisfied with the way she looked. Ask yourself if you feel better after repeatedly looking in the mirror. Is checking your appearance accomplishing anything?

Usually checking or asking for reassurance is counterproductive because it focuses your attention on the parts of your body that you don't like while you ignore the parts that you like better. Since it's unlikely that there will be a dramatic change in your hips or stomach since the last time you checked, you will just be reminding yourself of your dissatisfaction. This will be discouraging and decrease your motivation to develop new eating habits. Instead of persisting with this unhelpful ritual you can limit your checking. If you weigh yourself often, try to decrease the frequency. Usually weighing once a week is best since more frequent weighing may result in preoccupation with trivial fluctuations that can be distracting. After you get dressed, limit yourself to one brief glance in the mirror—but look at your whole body in the mirror, not just the part that you dislike. Make sure you give equal attention to your good features and then move on. Don't go back to the mirror or ask others for reassurance.

Acting As If You Like Your Body

Once you start disputing some of the irrational thoughts you have about your body, it will become easier to do some of the activities that you have been avoiding. Go back to your list of six things that you did or didn't do because of your view of your body. Rank them in terms of difficulty with 1 being the easiest and 6 being the most difficult. For example, standing upright without holding your stomach in might be the easiest activity on your list while dancing at a party or lying on the beach in a swimsuit with a group of friends might be the most difficult. Your assignment is to do these activities starting with the easiest and progressing through your list. If you find yourself feeling anxious or full of dread or repeatedly putting off an activity, examine your thinking about it. Undoubtedly you will find a runaway implication in your thinking. You will need to make an extra effort to remind yourself of the rational disputing thoughts you've identified previously to decrease your discomfort with this assignment.

The final exercise might be a little scary since it requires that you go out of your way to draw attention to your body. For example, instead of wearing baggy clothes you could wear a form-fitting outfit or tuck your blouse in rather than letting it hang loose. Go for a walk wearing shorts. The goal is not to become an exhibitionistic show-off but rather to make yourself comfortable with your body even when you know that other people are around. When you get comfortable doing this you could go shopping for clothes, try something on, and ask the salesclerk how it looks on you. You might not get a truthful answer, but it doesn't matter. The point of asking is to be relaxed when you know other people are looking at you. If this assignment seems impossible, you will need to do some more work on your thinking. When you have disputed the implications of being overweight and can comfortably describe your body in accurate, neutral terms, it won't be so painful to have other people noticing your body.

Liking What You See in the Mirror

Transforming your body image is not a short-term project. Recall from Chapter 7 that even after weight loss many people still feel fat. Although it may not seem as important as changing your eating habits, improving your body image is an essential component of body intelligence because it is necessary for long-term weight regulation. To improve your body image:

- Keep a Body Image Record to monitor your thoughts, feelings, and actions.
- When you look in the mirror, consider the whole image rather than focusing exclusively on less satisfactory parts of your body.
- Get in the habit of using neutral terms to describe unsatisfactory parts of your body.
- Start doing enjoyable activities that you had been avoiding because of concerns about your appearance.
- Examine your thinking about weight and challenge irrational assumptions.
- Become comfortable with parts of your body that are less than perfect.

The third component of body intelligence, using your body intelligently, has a reciprocal relationship with body image. As your body image improves, your willingness to get involved in physical activity will increase. As you become more physically active, your body image will improve further. In the next chapter, we'll explore why it has been so difficult to be physically active and how to turn that around.

CHAPTER 9

ALL PAIN, NO GAIN: WHY YOU REALLY HATE TO EXERCISE

Whenever I mention the "E" word in a body intelligence group I'm leading, some of the participants will laugh nervously and squirm in their seats. I know that they're expecting a sermon exhorting them to do activities that they don't want to do. Usually they are mentally preparing lists of reasons why they haven't been more active and thinking of all the circumstances that would prevent them from becoming more active. Only after I've reassured them that I didn't think they were lazy and I wasn't going to make them feel guilty for being sedentary do they relax and start to consider their feelings about their bodies and physical activity. Getting past the defensiveness about exercise is necessary to develop a realistic plan for the third component of body intelligence: comfortable, routine physical activity.

If you have been struggling with your weight for some time, you've probably had similar experiences when you've been encouraged to exercise. Even reading about exercise now might be making you feel a little uncomfortable. If the whole idea stirs up uneasy feelings we will need to understand, and then overcome, the uneasiness. Some of the discomfort can be traced back to experiences in childhood and adolescence, but first let's consider your experiences as an adult trying to exercise to lose weight. It is important to know what exercise can and can't accomplish so your expectations are realistic. It's equally important to understand how your earlier experiences caused you to feel estranged from your body and uncomfortable using it. When this has

Physical Activity Connected with Your Job

1. Time on job spent sitting:

Practically all	(0)
More than half	(1)
About half	(2)
Less than half	(3)
Almost none	(4)

2. Time on job spent walking:

Almost none	(0)
Less than half	(1)
About half	(2)
More than half	(3)
Practically all	(4)

3. Walking to get to and from work:

None or less than 1 block	(0)
1 or 2 blocks	(1)
3 or 4 blocks	(2)
5 to 9 blocks	(3)
10 to 19 blocks	(4)
20 to 39 blocks (1 mile, not 2)	(5)
40+ blocks (2+ miles)	(6)

4. Lifting or carrying heavy things:

Very infrequently or never	(0)
Sometimes	(3)
Frequently	(6)

5. Transportation to and from work:

None	(0)
Car and/or bus and/or railroad and/or ferry	(1)
Subway	(2)
Subway and one or more other modes of transportation	(3)

6. Hours on the job:

Less than 25	(1)
25–34	(2)
35–40	(3)
41–50	(4)
51+	(5)

Total_____

been accomplished, you will be able to develop an activity plan that fits into your life and makes you feel good.

To get a rough idea of your activity level, circle the best response to the items here and on the next page about your physical activity on and

Physical Activity Off the Job

	Frequently	Sometimes	Very Infrequently/ Never
Take walks in good weather	2	1	0
Work around house or apartment	2	1	0
Do gardening in spring or summer	2	1	0
Take part in sports (active ball game other than golf or bowling)	4	3	0
Other physical activity	3	2	0
Total_____			

off the job. This is the H.I.P. Physical Activity Questionnaire* developed for an insurance company to estimate work and leisure physical activity.

To get your scores for physical activity on the job, add the numbers in parentheses next to the responses you circled for each item. For the leisure activity score, add the numbers you circled. Use the chart below to interpret your scores.

If you scored in the Inactive or Moderately Inactive ranges, you have plenty of company. According to a national survey conducted in 2000, 72 percent of American women and 64 percent of men don't get regular exercise. There are a few exceptions. For example, Amish farmers who work their fields with horse-drawn plows engage in fifty-two hours of vigorous labor each week (and aren't obese), but most of the rest of us don't get much exercise at work. Likewise, many outdoor recreational activities have been mechanized so that they no longer count for exer-

	Activity on the Job	Leisure Activity
Inactive	1–10	0–1
Moderately Inactive	11–14	2–3
Moderately Active	15–18	4–5
Most active	19–28	6–10

*S. Shapiro, E. Weinblatt, C. W. Frank, and R. V. Sager. The H.I.P. study of incidence and prognosis of coronary heart disease. Reprinted from *Journal of Chronic Diseases*, 18, 527–558. Copyright ©1965 with permission from Elsevier.

cise. Snowmobiles often have replaced cross-country skis, steering an ATV takes the place of hiking, and golfers ride around on their carts rather than walking the eighteen holes. For most Americans, a regular routine doesn't include much physical activity.

What Are Your Reasons?

I've listed eight of the most commonly cited reasons for not exercising below. Look at the list and put a check mark next to the reasons that explain your reluctance to exercise.

❑ 1. I tried to exercise but I didn't lose any weight.
❑ 2. I don't have the time.
❑ 3. I'm too lazy.
❑ 4. If I exercise I'll get hungry and eat more.
❑ 5. I hate to sweat.
❑ 6. I am in pain after exercising.
❑ 7. Exercising is boring.
❑ 8. I work so hard on my job that I don't have any energy left for exercise.

A study of middle-aged adults who had quit exercise programs found that lack of motivation (which included boredom and laziness, numbers 3 and 7 above) and difficulty with time management (number 2) accounted for half of the dropouts. Let's look at the logic behind the eight rationalizations above and explore some additional, less obvious reasons for being uncomfortable with exercise. As with eating intelligently and developing an intelligent body image, the first step toward using your body intelligently is to understand your current habits and patterns.

• If you've tried to lose weight by exercising, it's not surprising that it didn't work. According to Drs. Steven Blair and Elizabeth Leermakers of The Cooper Institute for Aerobics Research in Dallas, "Physical activity alone produces only modest weight loss." The bad news is that a Big Mac has 600 calories and a medium Coke has 210. If you burn 325 calories per hour walking at four miles per hour, you'll need to take a two-and-a-half hour, ten-mile hike to work off that unplanned stop at McDonald's. Based on these figures you could reasonably conclude that exercise is impractical because it requires too much effort for minimal or no results, but this would be short-sighted. Over time, small changes in activity can have significant results. A recent Mayo Clinic study found that obese individuals sat an average of two hours more per day compared to lean individuals. The lean individuals used an extra 350 calories per day by not sitting as much. If a 175-pound woman walks an additional ten minutes each day and nothing else changes, she will lose more than five pounds in a year. Although you won't see any immediate effects, increased physical activity will also lift your mood making it easier to regulate your eating. Since physical activity is absolutely necessary for weight-loss maintenance, it is an essential part of your body intelligence plan.

- If you "don't have the time," ask yourself if everything that you do is more important than your health. Consider that many busy people have found the time. Both Presidents Bush and President Clinton ran while serving in the White House. According to George W. Bush, "If the President of the United States can make the time, anyone can." Since all of the important things that you need to do are dependent upon being healthy, spending thirty minutes a day being active is a good investment of time. When you review your daily activities you can rearrange your schedule to fit exercise in. Chapter 10 will help you do this.

- Thinking about yourself as "too lazy" is circular reasoning that doesn't adequately explain the legitimate negative feelings you have about exercise. For example, if I asked you "Why don't you exercise?" You would answer, "Because I'm lazy." If I then asked, "How do you know you are lazy?" You'd probably answer, "Because I don't exercise." Laziness is just attaching a negative label to your discomfort with physical activity. This is unfortunate since there is a good reason for not liking exercise. Any physical activity is more difficult for you than it would be for someone who is carrying around less body mass. The extra weight means that any physical activity will be more difficult and you'll get tired sooner. Labeling yourself as lazy doesn't help to understand your reluctance to exercise nor does it provide any help in overcoming it.

- Logically, you would expect that when you exercise you use more energy so your appetite would increase and you would eat more. The best evidence suggests that food intake does not increase after exercise, and for some people appetite decreases after activity. Likewise when an active person becomes sedentary, it is unlikely that they will automatically reduce their eating. Instead he or she will go on eating as much as they did before when they were active. There isn't much of a relationship between the amount of activity you do and the amount of food you will eat.

- Hating to sweat, feeling pain after exercising, being concerned about your heart pounding, or being out of breath are negative associations you may have had with your past attempts to exercise. These feelings are consistent with a long-standing pattern of feeling estranged from your body. We will explore this in more detail later in this chapter.

- Some exercise routines are repetitious and boring, but it would be irrational to assume that you couldn't find a routine that is more interesting, and perhaps fun. Even if the routine you chose involves repetition, with a little planning you can make it less boring.

- If you have a demanding job, put in long hours, or work in a stressful environment, you will feel fatigued at the end of the day. But thinking hard or being stressed doesn't substitute for physical activity. If you've been working at a desk, you won't have used any more energy than if you had been home relaxing in your easy chair. At the end of a long day, you won't feel like being active, but if you can push yourself to get started, you will feel better and have more energy when you've finished than you had before you started.

Why Bother?

If you review your past weight-loss efforts, you'll probably find that they focused on what you ate, not on how much you exercised. If you did try some type of exercise you probably gave up because it didn't result in any weight loss (see number 1 above). Since you hear repeated exhortations to exercise to lose weight, it is reasonable for you to be frustrated and confused. Did you do it wrong? Did you quit too soon? Did exercising just increase your appetite, causing you to eat more?

Fat, Muscle, and Resting Metabolism

While exercise may not produce dramatic weight losses, it can still produce fat losses. In one recent study overweight women who exercised but didn't diet had a significant reduction in their waist circumference even though their weight was unchanged. In addition, exercise has beneficial effects—including an increase in energy level—that, over the long run, make it essential for permanent weight control. During the time you are exercising, you will burn more fat and your metabolism will increase as much as twenty times from its resting rate. When you've finished exercising and you're just taking it easy, you could burn as many as 130 additional calories depending on the intensity and the length of your workout.

Your resting metabolic rate is the energy, expressed in calories, your body uses to maintain itself when you aren't doing anything. Your muscle tissue uses more calories than your fat tissue even when you are resting. If you lose weight by dieting alone, up to one-quarter of weight you lose will be muscle, not fat. Since it takes more calories to maintain muscle tissue than fat tissue, you will lower your resting metabolic rate by losing muscle. In other words, dieting without exercising can be self-defeating! On the other hand, if you exercise, even if you're not pumping iron, you will minimize the muscle loss and increase the number of calories your body uses to maintain itself. As you get stronger you will use more calories doing the regular activities in your daily routine.

Exercising will help reduce the frustration that you may have felt when you've been dieting and your weight plateaus. When you're still following the diet but the scale stubbornly refuses to budge it's likely that you'll get discouraged. Instead, when you become more active you will offset the decline in resting metabolism caused by dieting so you should continue to lose weight.

Maintaining Losses

If you are still doubtful about your need to increase physical activity, consider that, even if adding an activity routine did not produce any weight loss, without exercise, it is unlikely that you could maintain any weight you had lost by dieting alone. One study compared obese women who lost weight and then regained the weight with equally heavy women who lost weight and kept it off. Ninety percent of the losers who maintained their losses reported exercising three times a week for thirty minutes or more while only 34 percent of the losers who regained weight exercised regularly. In another study, 1,047 people who had lost an average of sixty-four pounds and maintained that loss for an average of six years averaged an hour a day of physical activity. A *Consumer Reports* survey found that 81 percent of successful losers (a 10 percent or more weight loss maintained for at least one year) exercised at least three times a week. The more than eight thousand successful losers mentioned exercise more than any other weight-loss method. These studies have important implications for your efforts to regulate your weight. It is unlikely that you will be able to maintain any weight you lose by diet alone. If you are going to make the effort to lose weight, it is essential to be active to maintain your weight loss.

Fringe Benefits

Exercise has psychological benefits, including decreasing depression, improving mood, and enhancing self-esteem. These benefits don't depend on the type or intensity of the activity. It can be aerobic or non-aerobic, and there are benefits even if the activity isn't intense enough to improve cardiovascular fitness. If you are skeptical, try this little experiment proposed by Dr. Robert Thayer, an expert on mood regulation. When you are sitting around feeling tired, and maybe a little depressed, rate your energy on a seven-point scale with 7 representing your most energetic mood and 1 your least energetic, most lethargic mood. After you've rated your energy level, force yourself to get up and take a brisk walk for ten minutes. When you get back, rate your energy on the seven-point scale again and see if you aren't feeling more energetic. You might also find that if you had been tempted to snack before when you were feeling tired the urge has decreased. Being active will lift your mood and make you feel better about yourself. When you increase your activity you'll find that your body image will improve and you will have more motivation to follow through on making changes in your eating behaviors.

Gwen, a fifty-three-year-old married civil servant, provides a good example of the indirect benefits of increased activity. Over ten years she had made many attempts to lose twenty pounds but was never success-ful. Her physician prodded her to join my program at a local hospital, but she was deeply skeptical and let me know that she held out little hope. Reluctantly, she agreed to participate in the "Aerobics for Begin-ners" class that was part of the program. At the end of the program six months later she had maintained a fifteen-pound weight loss. At our last meeting she told me that the aerobics was the key to her success. For the first time, she felt comfortable exercising, found that she actually enjoyed the aerobic dancing, and started to feel more connected to her body. With the improvement in mood and body image, she felt that she had more energy to devote to changing her eating habits and felt less struggle with the new behaviors. She was clear that without the aero-bics class our program would have just been another failure for her.

Health Benefits

The human body was designed for movement. When physical activity consists mostly of going from a bed to a car seat to a desk chair to a recliner and then back to bed, the body is destined to malfunction. Health statistics show that inactivity is hard on your body; there are an estimated 250,000 deaths attributable to inactivity each year. The most common cause of death in the United States, coronary disease, is clearly linked to weight. One study compared the health status of London dou-ble-decker bus drivers with the health of the conductors on the same buses. The drivers sat all day while the conductors walked up and down the stairs collecting fares. Not surprisingly, the conductors had lower rates of heart disease; and when they did suffer heart attacks, conduc-tors were more likely to survive.

In addition to heart disease, diabetes, some cancers, osteoarthritis of the knees and hips, gallstones, pulmonary dysfunction, sleep apnea, menstrual irregularities, and various reproductive problems in women are associated with excess body weight. There is also some less conclusive evidence linking asthma, gastroesophageal reflux disorder, and impaired wound healing to being overweight. Exercise not only helps to prevent illness, it may increase the likelihood of surviving a potentially fatal disease. A recent study of women diagnosed with breast cancer found that moderate exercise decreased their chance of dying between 20 and 50 percent. According to a recent *Newsweek* article, "Medical science has yet to produce a treatment that can match the benefits of moderate exercise." If a pharmaceutical company had discovered and patented exercise, we'd be seeing advertisements touting its miraculous benefits and demanding that our health insurance cover this new treatment. Instead many people who could benefit ignore this "miracle" treatment. Why would someone who is concerned about his or her health, who goes to the dentist for regular checkups, brings their pets to the veterinarian at the first sign of a problem, and has the oil changed in their car on schedule avoid a simple routine that confers so many benefits? If a consistent plan to increase activity would help you gradually lose some of your excess weight, avoid the weight that you would have gained as you get older, decrease a variety of health risks, improve your mood and self-concept, and help maintain your motivation to make the other changes necessary for permanent weight control, why is it so difficult?

Being Estranged from Your Body

If you recognized any of the eight rationalizations for not exercising from the list above, you probably know that, while there is some validity to your objections, there are other less obvious reasons why you resist being more active.

Heather was a thirty-eight-year-old who was referred to me by her physician after repeated unsuccessful attempts to lose weight. With some justification, she endorsed almost all of the rationalizations for not exercising. She was a self-employed attorney and single mother of two children so time was at a premium. Given her hectic and unpredictable schedule, she felt she could not commit to a regular exercise program. Several years earlier, she had partially successful back surgery so she was justifiably concerned about doing anything that would exacerbate her pain. When I questioned her about her history with exercise she said she had tried before but gave up because "it didn't do any good." She didn't lose weight, and she hated to sweat and be out of breath.

Although many of her reasons for not exercising had a logical basis, several underlying themes for her reluctance emerged as I got to know Heather better. Having a history of poor body image, Heather felt detached from her body. She thought of her body as an unpleasant reality that unfortunately was attached to the "real me." Her personality, her intellect, her maternal feelings, and all the other intangible qualities were who she really was; the body was just the means for getting around.

As a child Heather was comfortable with her body. Although her parents sometimes described her as "chubby," they also thought that she was a "tomboy" because she spent as much time with the neighborhood boys playing ball as she did with the girls playing with dolls. This changed in junior high school. She developed before most of her classmates and started to feel self-conscious, especially around the boys who noticed her newly rounded form. She was less comfortable playing active games with boys and spent more time with girlfriends. Heather especially disliked gym class because she had to wear uniforms that accentuated her developing body. Over a period of several years, games, sports, and physical activity changed from being one of the more enjoyable parts of Heather's day to chores that had to be endured in gym class. In the process, the pleasure of using her body was lost.

As Heather's understanding of the reasons for her discomfort increased, she recognized that many of her adolescent concerns were no longer applicable. She didn't need to wear a gym uniform or worry about rude comments from teenage boys. Although she wasn't interested in starting a formal exercise program at a gym, she regained some of the joy of using her body. She signed up for a ballroom dancing class at the adult education center and rediscovered the fun of playing softball.

Give some thought to your experience. Remember that there is a genetic basis for *some* aspects of physical activity. You may have inherited a tendency to be less active than your classmates were. In addition to your genetic code, your childhood experience may have set you up for later inactivity. For example, your parents might not have modeled active behaviors or encouraged you to be active. You may not have had support for participating in athletics or team sports. Genetics and parents just lay the groundwork for inactivity and being estranged from your body. Experiences with your peers and the larger society are at least as important. Your body intelligence will increase as you understand how you lost the natural joy of being active and start to find pleasure in using your body.

If you hated gym class, you're not alone. Oprah Winfrey recalled, "I had always avoided gym class whenever I could. I sat it out or dreaded participating." Before you had a gym class was there a time when you were naturally active? Did you run, swim, ride your bike, skate, dance, or play sports just for fun, without feeling like you were making a special effort? If you remember being more active, what changed? Obviously you're not in school anymore so you don't have your afternoons free to go out and play, but what else has changed? How did you lose the natural joy in using your body?

To help you answer this question for yourself, I've listed some of the common negative experiences that can contribute to a feeling of estrangement from one's own body.

- Did you feel embarrassed when you did poorly in a sport? For example, when you struck out or didn't catch a ball.
- Were sports associated with social rejection? Were you the last one picked when teams were chosen, or did classmates ridicule your performance?
- Did participation in an activity make you uncomfortable because the clothing drew attention to your body? For example, were you self-conscious wearing leotards, a swimming suit, or gym shorts?
- Were you embarrassed because you couldn't keep up with your peers? On a group hike, for instance, did the others have to wait for you while you stopped to catch your breath?

- Were you nervous because you were the center of attention and everyone was watching you? For example, were you nervous if you had to take a foul shot when playing basketball, knowing that all eyes in the gym were focused on you?
- Did you feel clumsy or uncoordinated because you couldn't do what everyone else was doing? Did you have trouble getting the rhythm when jumping rope with other girls or keeping the basketball when taking it down court?
- Did a gym teacher, coach, or other important adult embarrass you by criticizing your performance in front of a group?

Any of these experiences could make you reluctant to try the activity again. If you saw sports or physical activities as a failure experience, you might distance yourself from such activities and invest yourself in other pursuits. Instead of thinking of yourself as a good baseball player or dancer or swimmer, you might have emphasized your intellect or musical or artistic abilities. These are attributes you valued, while physical activities were viewed as unpleasant failed experiences. You saw yourself as smart or popular, a musician, or an artist but also nonathletic and perhaps clumsy, weak, and lazy.

The Consequences of Being Estranged from Your Body

When you talk to athletes, runners, or avid bicyclists, you might hear the phrase "work up a sweat" used positively. For example, Jill, a twenty-eight-year-old graduate student, didn't feel satisfied with a bicycle ride around the neighborhood because the ground was flat and the frequent stop signs made it impossible to build up speed. She was happier riding up and down the nearby hills and was genuinely pleased when her clothes were soaked with perspiration. In contrast, when the topic of sweat comes up in a conversation with someone who is estranged from his or her body, it is usually described as an unpleasant experience as in "I hate to sweat" or unhappily, "I got all sweaty."

The same differences are found with attitudes toward other physical effects of exercise. Ron, a fifty-five-year-old professor, describes the sensations in his muscles after a workout in the gym as "burn" or "feeling tight" and is pleased because he views these sensations as evidence that he is getting stronger. His friend Stan, also a professor in his midfifties, signed up at the same gym but dropped out after a month. Part of the reason Stan gave up was that the sensations from stressing his muscles were unfamiliar and he interpreted them as being painful. He stated that lifting weights made his muscles "hurt."

When people who are comfortable with their bodies start gasping for breath, they know they need to slow down or cut back. When people who are estranged from their bodies are breathing too hard, they become scared, perhaps afraid of suffocating. When you are comfortable with your body you interpret small increases in heart rate as evidence that you are making your heart stronger. When you are estranged from your body, the same sensations are frightening and might make you think that you are having a heart attack.

To become comfortable with exercise, it is necessary to become reacquainted with your body and the sensations it gives off when it is being used. Instead of interpreting these sensations negatively or unrealistically, you can learn to recognize them, think logically about them, and find pleasure in the bodily feedback you are getting. Literally, you are getting intelligence from your body.

Let's start with sweat. If you're female you may have learned that ladies don't perspire, much less sweat. Even if you weren't brought up with an extensive list of ladylike and unladylike behaviors, you may still associate sweating with being anxious (before an important interview, for example), or being hot and sticky on a muggy summer day. Most women, regardless of weight, can recall feeling uncomfortable because there were sweat stains on the blouses they were wearing. Sweating because you are anxious or because it is hot and humid is a different experience from sweating because you are exercising. When you have planned to go to an aerobics class, a bike ride, or a brisk walk, you will dress appropriately. Since you will be wearing a T-shirt or sweatshirt you don't need to worry about ruining a good blouse or running up a dry-cleaning bill to remove the sweat stains. Most likely, you will take a shower after exercising so you don't need to worry about sweat ruining your appearance. If sweat dripping off your forehead makes you uncomfortable, you can wear a sweatband.

There is nothing intrinsically bad about sweating. It's your interpretation of what sweating means that makes it uncomfortable. But you can change your thinking, and recognize that sweating is useful. When the sweat on your skin evaporates, it cools the skin, helping to maintain an optimal temperature for your body. Sweat is comprised mostly of water with salt and a few other chemicals. Bacteria and yeasts on the skin, rather than the sweat itself, cause the odor you associate with sweat, so if you really can't stand the smell, you might try washing before you exercise. When you are working up a sweat, remind yourself that the sweat is tangible evidence that you are strengthening your heart, increasing your metabolism, and decreasing a variety of health risks. You can take pride in and perhaps actually enjoy sweating!

Overcoming Inertia

As you learn to like your body, you will find it easier to enjoy using it. Despite its imperfections you will get more satisfaction from meeting physical challenges, even if the challenge is only to walk around the block. You can develop a routine so that you don't need to agonize over when and where you'll exercise or feel that you'd be "wasting time" if you took a walk. You can revise your self-concept so that, instead of being lazy or nonathletic, you see yourself as active and fit even if you haven't reached your weight goal. To do this you have to get over the inertia that keeps you stuck. Chapter 10 will show you how to do this.

CHAPTER 10

THE JOYS OF SWEAT

In Chapter 9, Heather, Gwen, Ron, and Oprah were able to overcome their early experience with exercise, break out of the inertia, and become active. With an intelligent approach to exercise, you can, too— but don't go out and try to run a marathon or buy the most expensive membership at the neighborhood gym. Instead, recognize that you're likely to feel conflicted. You know that you need to exercise to help lose weight and maintain the loss; you know that there are real health benefits to becoming more active; you understand that many of the reasons you've had for not being active are just rationalizations; and you understand some of the issues that have made the whole idea so unpleasant for you. *But you still don't feel like doing anything!*

Before you retreat into the laziness rationale, a more intelligent approach is to recognize that change is a process that evolves over time. Dramatic resolutions or flashes of insight by themselves are unlikely to produce lasting habits. Recall from Chapter 6 that change is a process that evolves as you go through the predictable stages: precontemplation, contemplation, preparation, action, and maintenance. You will increase your activity by identifying your current stage and making small steps to advance to the next stage.

Stages of Change

If you are in the precontemplation stage, you don't have any plans to become more active in the foreseeable future. You've read Chapter 9 so you know the reasons why you should be more active, but you have your doubts that you can do it. You might be afraid that you'd fail at any exercise program, so you'd rather not think about it. It's also possible that you're not thinking about being active because you're being pressured by your family or your physician. They've been bugging you to exercise, and you just don't feel like being told what to do. Maybe, if they back off, you'll think about it sometime in the future, but right now you have no plans to exercise.

Lucy, a thirty-six-year-old medical secretary, was in the precontemplation stage. She had a rocky relationship with Mike, her thirty-nine-year-old husband. One of his frequent complaints was that she needed to exercise to lose weight. She knew that she should be more active but didn't want to give him a "victory" in their ongoing conflict. I suggested that he already had won this conflict since she was just responding to his demands rather than making up her own mind. Instead of continuing to resist, she was able to move into the contemplation stage when she decided to develop a plan that was comfortable for her—while ignoring Mike's negative comments.

If you've been resisting pressure to get more active, stop to consider how self-defeating this is. Admittedly, few adults like to be told what to do, but if you are refusing to do something because of pressure from others, they are still controlling you. You free yourself when you make the decision regardless of what others say.

When you're in the contemplation stage, you are seriously thinking about becoming more active. People in this stage usually plan on making changes in the next six months, but sometimes they continue to think about it for two or more years without actually starting. Paul, a sixty-two-year-old retired contractor in my hospital program, confessed that he had called for information a year earlier, but when he found out that there was an aerobics component, he decided to postpone joining. It took him eleven months to get through the contemplation stage. He knew that he needed to be more active. He wanted to participate in the program and frequently thought about joining, but it took almost a year before he was ready. If you're in the contemplation stage, you're ambivalent. You know the advantages of exercise and think that you should be more active, but you're also aware of the personal costs and possible disappointments so you hesitate to get started.

In the preparation stage you have made some tentative steps toward reaching your activity goals, but you haven't established a consistent pattern. Maybe you decided to become more active by walking. So, you went for a walk one day but then forgot about it until the next week. Or, maybe you made a New Year's resolution and went to the gym a few times before dropping out. The preparation stage is characterized by on-and-off attempts to change the target behavior. Since one study found that about half of the participants in exercise programs quit in the first six months, it appears that many people never get beyond the preparation stage.

In the action stage you are consistently meeting your goal. This stage requires the most effort. Regardless if the goal is a daily walk or going to the gym three times a week, it will be necessary to use a variety of methods to maintain the behavior with some consistency. Several strategies for maintaining your motivation are presented later in this chapter.

After six months in which the goal has been accomplished with consistency, you enter the maintenance stage. During this stage the amount of effort required to accomplish the goal is lessened. Vigilance is still required to ensure that you don't relapse (returning to the contemplation or preparation stage). For example, you know that it would be tempting to "forget" your exercise routine after a vacation so you make plans to ensure that you resume when the vacation is over. Usually it takes a minimum of five years in the maintenance stage before it is safe to conclude that there is no risk of relapse.

If you have been inactive for years, you shouldn't despair but rather recognize that you are in the precontemplation or contemplation stage. This does not mean that you are predestined to a life of sedentary nonactivity, but rather that any attempt to increase your activity needs to take into account your current stage. Frequently the difficulty in moving on to the next stage can be traced back to problems with setting goals. If you were a smoker, setting your goal would be easy. Regardless of your height, weight, gender, number of years smoking, or any other characteristics, your goal would be to completely stop smoking. With exercise it's not so simple. While "being more active" is a worthwhile goal, there isn't a single activity that fits everyone, even if everyone had the same weight-loss target. With body intelligence you'll move to the next stage by developing a goal that takes into account your individual circumstances and preferences.

Exercise Versus Activity

I've been using the terms *exercise* and *activity* or *physical activity* interchangeably. To establish tangible, measurable goals it's necessary to distinguish between formal exercise and increased activity. Formal exercise is a period of time that is specifically intended to increase exertion. Running, weight lifting, an aerobics dance class, or lap swimming are examples of formal exercise. Activity, on the other hand, involves exertion and might be just as vigorous as formal exercise, but the intent is to do something other than exercising. For example, if you swing a nine-pound splitting maul to split logs into wood for your fireplace, you will be using more calories than you would if you were swimming laps and you will be building muscle, but it would be an activity since the primary goal is to make firewood, not to exercise.

If you're in either the contemplation or preparation stage it's likely that the goal you're thinking about involves an exercise program. You might be thinking of joining a gym or signing up for an aerobics class or some other formal exercise program. This is a worthwhile goal but it may not be suitable for everyone. Many people recognize the benefits of exercise described in Chapter 9 and are motivated to start a formal exercise program, but when they think about the costs in time, effort, and the risk of failure their motivation decreases. If you find yourself stuck, you can resolve this impasse by putting a formal exercise program on hold and instead making your goal to increase your daily activity. For most people, the simplest way of increasing activity is to walk more.

Walking

Although you won't see dramatic weight losses, you shouldn't minimize the long-term benefits of daily walking. One study of 600 people who lost an average of sixty-six pounds and maintained the weight loss for five years found that 78 percent were regular walkers, while aerobic dance was the second most popular type of exercise. Another study compared the outcomes of group exercise sessions using a treadmill in a clinic facility with a home-based walking program. Both groups participated in a yearlong weight management program and received equal support for exercising. After fifteen months, the home-based walkers had greater weight losses than the participants who exercised in the clinic facility. Several other studies have demonstrated that increasing routine, home-based activity is more likely to produce long-term weight maintenance than an organized aerobic exercise program.

The speed of your walking will depend on your fitness level when you get started. If you have been completely sedentary a brisk thirty-minute walk may be too uncomfortable for you. Instead, try a leisurely three miles per hour stroll for ten minutes three times per day. While you will burn more calories if you walked at a faster pace that can come later. What is important now is to start to move.

Monitoring Footsteps

To help move into the action stage, start by monitoring your footsteps. You'll need to get a pedometer (see the "Picking a Pedometer" sidebar) and keep an Activity Log. You can keep the Activity Log in your notebook or a piece of paper divided into three columns:

Date   **Number of Steps**   **Other Activities**

You don't need to carry the log with you, just keep it in a convenient place so that you can make your daily entry either at night before you go to bed or the first thing in the morning before you reset your pedometer. The "Date" and "Number of Steps" columns are self-explanatory while the "Other Activities" column requires some judgment. While counting steps is an approximate measure of activity, it doesn't include upper body movement. For example, if you wash your car the pedometer will record the steps you take while walking around the car and dragging the hose but it will not register all the swirling motions you make with your arms while washing and drying the car. If

PICKING A PEDOMETER

A pedometer is a small device that you wear clipped to your belt or waistband. It detects your body movements and counts your footsteps. More elaborate models will tell time, provide feedback on the distance you've walked, give an estimate of the number of calories you expended, and tell the time you spent walking. At least one model comes with an FM radio so you can listen to music while walking. Pedometers are inexpensive (typically $5–$30) and readily available at sporting goods stores or on the Internet (try pedometersusa.com or bodytronics.com).

To make sure all your steps are counted, wear the pedometer as close to your hip area as possible and make sure that it is parallel to the ground. Also, it's a good idea to tie the pedometer's clip to a belt loop so that you don't lose it when you sit down. Even if you are in the precontemplation stage and have no immediate plans to be more active, you'll find it interesting to see how your activity fluctuates from day to day.

you rake leaves in the yard, the pedometer won't measure your back-and-forth raking movements so you would note these activities in the "Other Activity" column on your log with the time spent: "washing the car—30 minutes;" "raking leaves—20 minutes;" or "volleyball—30 minutes."

After recording for two weeks review your Activity Log. Add up the total number of steps you recorded over the two weeks and divide by fourteen to get your daily average. Drs. Cooper, Fairburn, and Hawker, Oxford University researchers, suggest the following criteria to help evaluate your activity level:

Activity Level	Steps per Day
Very Low	less than 3,000 steps
Low	3,000–5,000 steps
Moderate	5,000–7,000 steps
High	more than 7,000 steps

Using these criteria, have you been less active than you thought you would be? According to one estimate, the average American takes fewer than four thousand steps per day. Do you find any patterns in your Activity Log? Do you take more steps on weekends or during the week? Looking back at the days when you were especially inactive and the days when you were significantly more active, what was the difference? For example, Liz, a forty-eight-year-old medical assistant, found that she walked less on a day when it was raining (1,055 steps) and more on a Saturday when she went shopping with a friend (5,467 steps), but her average was still less than 2,000 steps per day. Checking the "Other Activities" column Liz found that she was inactive except for vacuuming her apartment on both Sundays.

Adding Footsteps

After you've determined your daily average, your goal will be to gradually increase the number of daily steps you take. A reasonable goal is to increase the daily number of steps by 20 percent. Multiply your daily average from above by 1.2. This is your daily goal for the next week. Each week, multiply your daily average by 1.2 until you get to a daily average of ten thousand steps or more.

Once you've set your goal, you can review your daily routine to find opportunities for adding steps. Since the pedometer will keep a running total, you don't need to do all your walking in one session or keep track of the duration of lots of short walks. The "Adding Steps" sidebar on the next page lists painless ways to increase the number of steps you take each day.

Think about adding steps to your daily routine. Liz didn't have a pet, but she enjoyed playing with a neighbor's dog. Since she usually got home from work in the mid-afternoon she volunteered to walk the dog every afternoon. To increase her motivation to walk at work, Liz announced to her coworkers that she was going to make all her phone calls while walking around the office and take a walk during her break. She started paying attention to her routines and was always on the lookout for opportunities to add steps.

ADDING STEPS

➤ Pace while waiting for a bus or subway.
➤ Use a portable phone and walk around the room while making a call.
➤ Use stairs instead of elevators or escalators.
➤ Park on the far side of the parking lot when shopping.
➤ If you're watching TV, get up and walk during commercials.
➤ Take a little walk during lunch or breaks at work.
➤ Don't pay at the pump or use a drive-up window at a restaurant or bank. Walk into the building instead.
➤ Walk the dog more often.
➤ Take a one- to four-minute walk each hour at work (for example, use a watercooler on a different floor).
➤ Go for a walk with a child.
➤ Take out the trash frequently.
➤ Get off the bus or subway one stop before your usual stop and walk the rest of the way.
➤ Don't accumulate items at the foot of the stairs, make a separate trip for each item.
➤ Walk your children to school, if you take them to a soccer or Little League game after school, walk around the field while you watch them play.
➤ Fly a kite.
➤ At home or work, use a bathroom on a different floor.
➤ Walk to your coworkers' offices instead of e-mailing or calling them.

Adding Fun

Review the "Other Activities" column of your Activity Log. Although measuring "Other Activities" isn't as straightforward as measuring footsteps, you should have an idea about some of the physical activity you did in the past two weeks. Were most of the physical activities household chores, such as vacuuming and washing the car, or were there any

activities that you did just for fun? Did you play ball, dance, or row a
boat? If you have been estranged from your body, you may have forgotten how to use your body for the sole purpose of having fun. While
you are increasing your footsteps each day you can also start to find
enjoyment in using your body. For example, Heather, the thirty-eight-
year-old attorney we met in Chapter 9, lost the enjoyment of sports and
games as she went through puberty, but as an adult she was able to recon-
nect with her body and enjoy ballroom dancing and playing softball.

Give some thought to the sports, games, and physical activities you
used to enjoy.

- As a kid, did you like to ride a bike, jump rope, or roller skate?
- Even if you were sedentary as a child, what did you fantasize
  about?
- Did you ever pretend to be a major league ball player, an Olympic
  ice skater, or a ballet dancer?

Allow yourself to daydream, and see what kind of images pop into
your consciousness. At this point don't let reality censor your day-
dreams. Even if you're only five feet tall you can still fantasize about
playing professional basketball. Giving free rein to your imagination,
what would you like to do?

What's stopping you from trying? Even if you'll never make the
N.B.A., what would prevent you from shooting a few hoops? Remember, you don't have to join a team, keep score, or play a whole game.
You won't disappoint anyone if you miss the basket, you won't be the
center of attention, and you can stop when it's not fun anymore. If the
only thing stopping you is that you "don't have the time" to add a new
activity to your life, consider reducing the time spent with America's
favorite time-waster, the television.

Kill Your TV, Indulge Your Fantasy

You may have seen a bumper sticker that exhorts you to "Kill Your Television." In terms of physical fitness that may be too extreme. Rather

than killing it, you should only try to maim your television. According to one survey American men watch TV an average of twenty-nine hours per week and women average thirty-four hours per week; overweight people spend even more time watching. It's likely that you could take a few of those hours to indulge in your fantasy activity and still not miss your favorite program.

If you're in the habit of turning on the tube to relax and take your mind off the difficulties of the day, consider that, instead of relaxing, you may be adding another difficulty to your day. A study reported in the *Journal of the American Medical Association* found that for every two hours per day spent watching television there was a 23 percent increase in obesity and a 14 percent increase in the risk of type 2 diabetes.

Instead of sitting and watching, spend the time doing something that's fun. Take a ballroom dancing class at an adult education center, join a beginner's softball team, or learn kayaking, fencing, or carpentry. Just turn off the tube, get off the sofa, and move your body. Once you get past the initial inertia, you'll find it to be more fun than anything you would have watched.

To get started it will help to define short-term (next week) and long-term (next year) goals. Goals should specifically describe things that you will do and when you will do them, rather than general statements such as "I will exercise more." For example, a long-term goal might be to pitch nine innings in a softball game or take a kayaking trip up a nearby river by this time next year. A short-term goal could be to play catch with a friend for twenty minutes twice in the next week. Pick one of the activities you identified above, and write down your short-term and long-term goals for that activity. Keep track of your efforts in your Activity Log.

Formal Exercise

Although several studies cited earlier demonstrate that home-based activity is more likely to result in weight loss, probably because it requires less time, some people prefer the structure of a formal exercise program, typically at a gym or with an aerobic dance class. If you think that you'd do better in an exercise program, or if you'd like to combine it with increased activity, review the suggestions in the "Choosing a Gym or Exercise Program" sidebar.

CHOOSING A GYM OR EXERCISE PROGRAM

Make sure you carefully evaluate the gym or program before you sign up. Some things to consider:

➤ Is the facility close to your home or work? A lengthy commute will make it more likely that you won't go.
➤ Are the hours compatible with your schedule?
➤ Will you be comfortable there? Are some of the participants similar to you in age, background, and fitness level? If they are all huge weight lifters or petite women in designer leotards you might feel self-conscious and not want to go.
➤ Visit the facility when it's likely to be busy (during lunch hour or right after work). Are people waiting in line to use the machines or get into the class?
➤ Will you enjoy the aerobic activities they offer? If you like to swim, do they have a pool? If you prefer aerobic dance, step classes, or spinning, do you like the music they play? Can you choose between treadmills, stationary bicycles, Stairmasters, rowing, and ski machines?
➤ Do you know anyone who already belongs or who will join with you? Getting started will be easier if you see a familiar face.
➤ Is the staff competent, and will you be comfortable with them? Are they certified by an organization such as the American Council on Exercise or the American College of Sports Medicine? In the beginning you will need someone to show you how to use the equipment and monitor your progress.
➤ Avoid long contracts. Ask for a few trial sessions and then sign up on a month-to-month basis until you are sure it is the right facility for you.

Maintaining Your Motivation

Whether you're walking, playing a sport, or going to the gym, once you get started, you'll find your motivation is greater some days and less on other days. Usually people who have been active for some time find that activity and exercise are their own rewards. In contrast, people who have been sedentary don't look forward to activity and will need to develop strategies to keep them motivated. If you've been inactive you will need to develop your own reasons, rituals, or rewards for being active. These will help keep you going until you start to see yourself as someone who is an active person. Once you're over this hurdle and start to see yourself as an exerciser, you will be more inclined to seek out new opportunities to be active. Listed below are strategies to help keep you motivated. Review this list to evaluate which might be helpful for you, but keep in mind that you won't know until you try it.

- *Schedule your activity.* Decide when and where you will be active and write it in your appointment book. It's not necessary that your activity occur in one session. For example, you could walk for thirty minutes on a treadmill every morning before you take your shower or you could take a fifteen-minute walk during lunch at work and spend fifteen minutes dancing by yourself when you get home. For some people the hardest part of activity is debating with themselves about when they will feel like doing it. Once your routine has been established, you will spare yourself that aggravation.
- *Do your activity with a partner.* Knowing that your friend will be standing on the street corner waiting for you at 7:00 A.M. will help get you out of bed. Even if you don't need the added boost to get you started, doing an activity with a partner will make it more fun.
- *Write down your goals and keep a chart or graph.* Seeing tangible evidence of your progress feels good and serves as a reminder. If you think you might "forget," you can show your chart to a friend and ask him or her to review it each week.
- *Leave prompts or reminders to exercise.* For example, you could leave your walking shoes next to your bed, pack your gym bag and put it by the door, or put a Post-it note on your computer to remind yourself to walk during lunch.

- *Reward yourself for accomplishing small goals.* Especially when you're getting started, knowing that there's a payoff such as going to the movies on Friday because you walked every day will help to keep you motivated to follow your schedule.
- *Have a friend reward you.* When you get started give a friend small amounts of money, favorite CDs, or other possessions with instructions to give them back to you each week you meet your goals.
- *Make the activity more interesting.* If your daily walk becomes boring, get a Walkman with headphones and either listen to music, recorded books, or your favorite news-talk radio program. If you use a treadmill or stationary bicycle, set aside your favorite magazine and only read it when you are using the machine.
- *Punish yourself for noncompliance.* Use this only if the other methods fail. Write several checks for $5 payable to a political party or cause that you actively dislike. Give the checks to a friend with stamped, addressed envelopes and instruct your friend to mail a check each week you don't meet your goals. At the end of the week when you have met your goals, the two of you can enjoy tearing up that week's check.
- *Anticipate breaks in your routine.* Business trips, illnesses, vacations, and other changes in routine can interfere with your scheduled activities. It is easy for the temporary interruption to become a retreat to the contemplation stage. Plan ahead so that you will resume your activity as soon as the disruption is over.

Progressing Through the Stages of Change

Lewis is a fifty-two-year-old colleague whom I've known for almost twenty years. He is an excellent example of a sedentary individual who progressed through the stages of change, first for lifestyle activity and then for a formal exercise program. I remember when several of our mutual friends started running he emphatically stated that he wasn't interested. He confided that the most exercise he was getting was when he got off the sofa to get a second helping of ice cream. He acknowledged that he was thinking about doing something more active, but he just wasn't sure if there was anything that he would like doing. He remained in the contemplation stage for more than two years until his doctor told him that he needed to lose weight. Reluctantly he agreed to start walking. He lived on a country lane and would occasionally walk down to the creek after dinner, but frequently he would "forget."

Lewis stayed in the preparation stage until the next semester began. Rather than buy a decal for the parking lot near his office on campus, he decided to park on the street in an adjoining neighborhood. He would have to walk between five to seven blocks each way. After a week he decided that his walks were too much work, but it was too late to give up since all of the parking decals had been sold. After a few months, the daily walks became a habit. One day a friend saw Lewis walking and offered him a lift to his car. Without stopping to think, Lewis declined the offer. It occurred to him that he didn't want to give up his walk because it helped him make the transition from home to work and from work to home. On the way to work he mentally prepared for the day's activities. Walking on the way home he reviewed what he had accomplished and what he still needed to do.

Several years later Lewis's wife started taking aerobic dance classes at a health club. Lewis had no interest in dancing, but was curious about the weight machines. Although he usually made disparaging comments about "jocks," the idea of having more muscle definition appealed to him and the machines seemed less intimidating than free weights. He bought a trial membership. He was fortunate to have social support in the beginning. His wife encouraged him to go to the gym while she was in her aerobics class. Once he got there he usually found someone he knew to talk with when he was resting in between the machines. If there was no one to talk to, he would put on his headphones and listen to a news-talk program while doing his routine.

Lewis has been walking and working out for more than ten years. When I asked him if he enjoys working out, he responded:

I like my daily walk, but I can't say that I really enjoy working out. What keeps me going back to the gym is that I enjoy the effects of working out. I feel a sense of accomplishment and relaxation when I'm finished so I know that I have to go to get those good feelings. Sometimes I'm tempted to skip a session, and usually I can find a good reason that would justify missing it, but I know that I'd just be fooling myself, and I'd feel worse later. I have to remind myself that, even if I'm not in the mood now, I'll feel better afterward. Sometimes, when I'm feeling tired I'll give myself permission to use fewer machines, or use less weight, or do fewer repetitions on each machine, but once I get there I do my usual routine anyway. If I do miss a few sessions because I've been sick or away on vacation, my body feels heavy or sluggish even if I haven't gained any weight. Ten years ago I would have never thought that there would be a day when I actually look forward to going back to the gym.

Lewis's example illustrates how someone who has been sedentary can progress through the stages of change and learn to use his body intelligently. You can do likewise.

- Use a pedometer and activity log to monitor your daily footsteps.
- Look for ways to increase the number of steps in your daily activities.
- Instead of watching TV, spend the time doing a physical activity that is fun.
- Consider joining a gym or an aerobics class.
- Develop your own strategies for maintaining motivation.
- Plan ahead for inevitable breaks in your routine.

Remember that change occurs in stages but with persistence you will develop a consistent activity routine that makes you feel good and helps with long-term weight regulation.

CHAPTER 11

RAISING A CHILD WITH BODY INTELLIGENCE

T he focus of Chapter 2 was your childhood: the individual, social, and cultural forces that shaped your body intelligence. While reading that chapter you probably identified influence from your parents, your peers, and the larger culture that undermined your natural body intelligence. If you are a parent, it's only natural that you would want to shield your child from some of the influences that diminished your body intelligence. Unfortunately, it's not so simple. In addition to the changed environment confronting your child (how much time did you spend with a computer when you were a child?), in the last twenty years parents have become increasingly concerned about eating disorders. Consider Mrs. Arria's dilemma:*

> *For the past two years, I've been telling my ten-year-old daughter, Bri-ana, that she's not fat—a little overweight, yes, athletic, strong, even chunky—but not fat. Then in June, I received a letter from Cam-bridge's Public Health Department. It was a "health report card" and part of a plan to help parents in our city identify and help their over-weight or underweight children. I knew that Briana was the biggest girl in the fourth grade. She is 5 feet tall and weighs 128 pounds. What I didn't realize until I opened the letter and saw it staring me*

*S. Arria, and L. Welch. (2003, September 7). Balancing act. *New York Times*. Retrieved September 7, 2003, from nytimes.com.

in the face was that she is also in the 97th percentile based on her height and weight among girls her age. That number was like a kick in my stomach. Before that moment, I kept telling myself that it was a phase she would grow out of . . . I'd been living in total denial.

Briana was lucky. The "health report card" cut through Mrs. Arria's denial and made her realize that Briana was not just the heaviest girl in her class but was among the heaviest girls in the city. After recognizing the problem, Mrs. Arria made an appointment for Briana at the weight-loss clinic at a Boston hospital. Dealing with Briana's weight hasn't been easy for Mrs. Arria since she has weight issues of her own. She wants to make sure that Briana doesn't become obsessed with her weight.

Like Mrs. Arria, nearly a third of mothers responding to one survey did not recognize that their children were overweight. If you are not sure if your child is overweight or if you are worried about your child's eating, exercise, and weight, you're confronted with a very real dilemma. If you intervene and express concern or try to restrict your child's eating and encourage exercise, you run the risk of increasing conflict, self-consciousness, and a poor body image. This might encourage unhealthy eating behaviors that could eventually develop into an eating disorder. Alternatively, you could ignore your child's excessive eating and lack of activity and just hope that he or she will outgrow the weight. Let's examine the twin dangers of childhood obesity and eating disorders before outlining a strategy for developing body intelligence.

The Dangers of Childhood Obesity

Increased blood pressure, lipid levels, and glucose tolerance are risk factors for cardiovascular disease. Sixty percent of overweight children have at least one of these risk factors, while 20 percent have two or more. A recent study of more than five thousand children and adolescents found that the average systolic and diastolic blood pressure had significantly increased from 1988 to 2000. The researchers attributed this to the larger percentage of overweight children and adolescents and

IS YOUR CHILD TOO FAT?

Since a child's body fat changes as he or she matures, determining if a child is overweight or obese is more complicated than it is for adults. The Centers for Disease Control and Prevention (CDC) has growth charts that show Body-Mass Index (BMI) by age for boys and girls. Using these charts, a child in the 95th percentile is considered overweight while scores in the 85th to 94th percentiles indicate a risk for becoming overweight. These charts are available online at cdc.gov/growthcharts. To use the charts you'll have to calculate your child's BMI first by dividing your child's weight in pounds by height in inches. Then divide the resulting number by the child's height again. Multiply the new number by 703 and then refer to the charts to determine your child's percentile standing. For a calculator that does the computations for you, go to kidsnutrition.org/bodycomp/bmiz2.html.

   If your child is at or above the 85th percentile, he or she has plenty of company. Using CDC data, the National Health and Nutrition Examination Surveys found that the prevalence of being overweight in children and adolescents had doubled from 11 percent in the 1963–1970 surveys to 22 percent in the 1988–1994 surveys. In California, more than three million children are overweight—three times as many as there were in the late 1970s. Unfortunately, most of these children will not outgrow their childhood overweight. One study of 2,617 children with BMIs above the 95th percentile found that 77 percent of them became obese adults.

warn that they will have a greater risk of heart disease as adults. Other studies point to rapid increases in diabetes associated with childhood obesity. Type 2 diabetes used to be called adult-onset diabetes because it rarely occurred before middle age. In the last decade there has been a tenfold increase in the number of children diagnosed with type 2 diabetes. Almost all of these children were overweight. In the next ten to twenty years the researchers expect to see many of these children suffering from kidney failure, blindness, heart attacks, and amputations as a result of their diabetes.

The psychological consequences of childhood obesity can also be heartbreaking for parents. While these consequences are not as potentially lethal as diabetes or heart disease, they are more immediate. Prejudice against obese children is found in children as young as age six. In one study of kindergarteners, an overweight child was described as lazy, dirty, stupid, and ugly. Almost all obese adolescent girls surveyed reported having been verbally abused. College students rated embezzlers, cocaine users, shoplifters, and blind people as better marriage partners than an obese person. This discrimination is more distressing because the overweight child knows why he or she is being rejected and internalizes the negative stereotypes. A study in the Netherlands found that, for both boys and girls, overweight children rated themselves lower on measures of physical appearance, athletic skill, social acceptance, and global self-worth. Frequently the problem becomes self-perpetuating. The overweight child withdraws from social activities, is lonely, and uses food to console him- or herself.

No parent would want their child to suffer the medical and psychological consequences of obesity, but there are very real dangers associated with an excessive preoccupation with a child's weight and diet.

The Dangers of Childhood Eating Disorders

Anorexia nervosa is a serious mental disorder that typically affects adolescent girls and an increasing number of adolescent boys. The severe weight loss may require hospitalization to avoid the cardiovascular problems that are fatal in about 10 percent of the cases. Bulimia nervosa (binge eating followed by vomiting, laxative abuse, or some other attempt to compensate for the binge) is a less severe disorder but still can cause erosion of dental enamel, swollen salivary glands, and tearing of the esophagus. Many anorexics and bulimics were overweight as children. As adolescents they became preoccupied with dieting and developed a distorted body image. Frequently they report that their dieting started after parents, teachers, coaches, or physicians had made comments about their weight. Although there are many factors that can contribute to the development of an eating disorder, excessive parental concern about weight in childhood often plays an important role. For example, one retrospective study found that adult bulimic women reported their mothers were more likely to show excessive concern with their eating, weight, and shape when they were teenagers. Another study followed ninth-grade girls for four years and found that their mothers' excessive concerns about weight and shape were related to the girls' later disordered eating.

Body Intelligence Versus Dieting

By age eleven, more than 66 percent of American girls have tried to diet. Recall from Chapter 5 that, regardless of the current diet hype or whether a low-fat or low-carbohydrate diet is in favor, any type of dieting is an ineffective strategy for weight control. It may be even less effective for children and teens than it is for adults. One study tracking 153 girls from age five through nine found that higher levels of dieting, concern about weight, and body dissatisfaction were associated with greater weight gains, suggesting that attempts to diet may have the opposite effect of increasing weight.

Another study of ninth-grade girls followed for three years found that girls who dieted were more likely to gain weight than nondieters. While there are several possible explanations for these findings (for example, dieting may provoke binge eating or young people may see themselves as dieting when, in fact, they are not cutting back on their eating), it is clear that self-directed dieting is counterproductive for children and adolescents no matter what the reason. Although the Federal Drug Administration recently approved Xenical (orlistat), the weight-loss drug for use with children, it is only "moderately useful." Using the drug still requires that the child avoid such foods as pizza and french fries or suffer unpleasant side effects.

In contrast to dieting, a recent review of thirty-nine studies suggests that more systematic approaches to healthy eating, behavior change, and exercise (components of body intelligence) can produce long-term reductions in childhood obesity.

Samantha was a sixteen-year-old high school junior who weighed 150 pounds. Her weight had fluctuated from a low of 110 pounds at age twelve to 160 when she was fifteen. She told me of her extensive dieting history, which included being enrolled in Weight Watchers with her mother, experimenting with self-induced vomiting, trying various herbal supplements she bought at a health food store, and trying countless variations of low-fat or low-carbohydrate diets that she found in women's magazines. As she described a typical diet, an all too-common pattern emerged. She had always been a "big girl," but she said, "I just wanted to be little for once. I got a lot of attention every time I'd lose weight. People would tell me 'you look so good,' but I never could stick to my diet for very long."

Since there were few family meals there was little structure to Samantha's eating. When trying to follow a diet, she skipped breakfast and worked at ignoring her hunger during the day. But then she often misjudged the caloric content of the fast food and snacks that she had in the afternoon and evening. Her tendency to binge increased whenever she was on a particularly restrictive diet.

Samantha initially resisted my attempts to have her stop dieting, but her repeated failure to lose weight made her desperate enough to try life without diets. Although her family continued to eat haphazardly, we established a meal and snack structure for her and a plan for reasonable physical activity. As therapy progressed, her body image improved as she understood the role that her inherited build, her early physical maturation, and her mother's lifelong struggle with weight played in her feelings about her body. With increased body intelligence she found that she could comfortably maintain a weight of 140 pounds, and at that weight, she still felt good and got plenty of attention from the boys.

If dieting doesn't work, how do you help your child regulate his or her weight? As with adults, children and teenagers need to develop the three components of body intelligence: becoming aware of the whys of their eating so that they can reduce unnecessary eating; developing a healthy, realistic body image; and becoming comfortable with routine physical activity. As a parent your job is to help. Since much of the help you can provide involves your own increased body intelligence and requires your active participation, rather than just giving directions, both you and your child will benefit.

Eating Intelligently

Intelligent eating in childhood includes managing physical hunger so that your child doesn't become so hungry that he or she loses control when finally confronted with food. Intelligent eating also entails minimizing eating prompted by external stimuli as well as addressing the emotional upsets of childhood and adolescence without eating. Parents who are concerned about their child's eating and weight have available at least three general strategies to change their child's eating behavior: making prohibitions and admonitions, controlling the eating environment, and modeling healthy behaviors. Unfortunately, most parents rely excessively on the first strategy and tend to ignore the second and third.

Parental Prohibitions and Admonitions

Telling a child what to eat and what not to eat is the most widely used parental strategy. It is an effective approach for very young children since infants and toddlers won't try new foods without encouragement. Repeated prompts to "just try a little" may be necessary to expose your young child to unfamiliar foods, but as your child grows older verbal instructions will have less influence. If you need proof of the futility of trying to control the eating of older children and adolescents, remember all the instructions you got from your parents (see Chapter 2 for a list). How many times did you hear and then ignore something like, "Don't eat now, you'll spoil your appetite?" Research findings as well as your own childhood experiences suggest that, except for the very young, prohibitions and admonitions are ineffective and often counterproductive.

Controlling the Eating Environment

Until your child goes off to school or starts spending time at a friend's house, you will control the circumstances of his or her eating. If you followed the suggestions presented in the "Minimizing Visual Cues" sidebar in Chapter 3 your house should have fewer external cues that would prompt your child to eat. If you bypassed the suggestions because you "didn't have the time" or you thought it wasn't worth the effort, reread the chapter and make the changes for your child's benefit, if not for your own.

Similar to adults, children tend to like high-fat, high-sugar foods, but unlike adults they aren't as set in their preferences. Although it may take repeated exposure, you can help your child learn to like healthier foods. Allow your child to make decisions but structure the choices available to him or her. Recognize that there will still be instances of poor food choices or excessive eating, but over time, you are helping your child develop good eating habits. The "Creating a Healthy Eating Environment" sidebar presents some additional suggestions for controlling your child's eating environment.

CREATING A HEALTHY EATING ENVIRONMENT

If you've been following the guidelines presented in Chapter 6 you are well on your way to creating a healthy environment for your child. Here are some additional ideas:

➤ Structure your family's eating. Although hectic schedules can present challenges, do not give up on the idea of family dinners. Discourage eating on the run and random snacking. Instead establish routines for breakfast, lunch, dinner, and after-school snacks.

➤ Offer a choice of several high-fiber, low-sugar breakfast cereals with milk (skim or, if necessary, 1 percent) and fruit. Check the nutrition information on the box and avoid cereals that are high in sugar. Oatmeal, raisin bran, fat-free granola, Cheerios, and shredded wheat are good choices. If your child is used to sugary cereals, gradually mix in healthier cereals while reducing the proportion of the sweeter stuff.

➤ Don't try to forbid fast food or "junk food." Consider them as treats to be enjoyed occasionally but not in place of regular meals or snacks. If you need to keep cookies (a maximum of three grams of fat per serving; avoid partially hydrogenated oils) and desserts in the house, limit the number of choices and try to buy single serving packages so there is less temptation to overindulge. Substitute healthier choices whenever possible. A child offered nonfat frozen yogurt is unlikely to miss high-fat ice cream.

➤ Reduce the number of distractions while your child is eating. Turn off the television and discourage eating in front of the computer or video games.

➤ Minimize consumption of sugary sodas and fruit juices. The calories in soft drinks do nothing to provide nutrition or reduce hunger. While eating an apple or grapes reduces hunger, drinking apple or grape juice doesn't.

➤ Serve reasonably sized portions to your child. If he or she is still hungry, they can ask for seconds. If you misjudge and serve too much, either save the excess to eat later or throw it away. But don't encourage the child to eat food just to avoid wasting it.

➤ Don't use foods as rewards for eating other foods. If having dessert depends on eating vegetables, you are communicating that vegetables are less desirable, which may lead to the child disliking them.

➤ Don't offer your child food when he or she is feeling sad or upset. Similarly, don't use food as a reward for an accomplishment.

➤ Don't buy toys that glorify junk food. Instead buy a children's cookbook and make the recipes together.

➤ When introducing new, healthy foods, encourage your child to help in the kitchen preparing the food. If he or she refuses the new food, don't assume that they'll never like it. Try again another day.

➤ Monitor your child's school lunches. Three out of four school lunches have too much fat and not enough fruit and vegetables. Twenty percent of schools offer fast food in the lunchroom.

➤ Try to substitute small, inexpensive toys for candy at holiday celebrations. One study found that, when given a choice,

(continued)

> Halloween trick-or-treaters were just as likely to choose such toys as glow-in-the-dark plastic bugs as lollipops or candy.
>
> ➤ Let your children know that when they are eating away from home they get to choose what they will eat. You have no control anyway, and giving them permission will reduce the likelihood that they will lie to you about it. They may feel the need to have pizza or a Slurpee to fit in with their friends, so encourage your child to socialize with kids who don't overindulge in junk foods.

Modeling Healthy Behavior

When you tell a child, "Do as I say, not as I do," you can safely bet that he or she will ignore this advice and do as you do, not as you say. If he or she is a teenager, the admonition to "avoid the mistakes I've made" usually falls on deaf ears and may provoke accusations of hypocrisy. Brian, a thirty-three-year-old contractor, recalls his mother telling him, "Brian, don't gobble your food." He also remembers that his father would come home at 5:00 and they would eat quickly so that his father could get to his second job by 6:00. More than twenty years later, Brian still eats rapidly despite his mother's scolding. If you're going to promote intelligent eating, you'll have to "walk the walk" rather than just talk about it.

In addition to the guidelines presented in Chapter 6, here are some suggestions for modeling healthy eating behavior.

Christine, a forty-nine-year-old insurance executive, is the mother of three grown daughters in their twenties. Although the older two were concerned about losing weight after their pregnancies, none have had serious weight issues. Christine explained,

My girls never dieted, even when all their friends were trying different diets. Although two of them were a little heavy in elementary school, it wasn't an issue because they were active and they had good eating habits. Probably the most important thing was that we never had cookies, chips, or candy in the house. Every so often, one of the girls

DOING AS I DO

➤ Make dinner and other mealtimes pleasant. Save discussions of poor report cards, misbehavior, and other stressful topics for another time.

➤ Sample different fruits and vegetables until you find several that you enjoy; then let your child see you choosing these foods.

➤ If you've been served a large portion of food, leave some on the plate.

➤ Limit yourself to no more than one dessert per day. If you are offered dessert with lunch, politely decline the offer.

➤ When your children see television ads for candy, sweetened cereals, or fast foods, let them know why you think the ads are deceptive or manipulative.

➤ Relax and enjoy eating well! Even when you are self-monitoring, you don't need to obsessively brood about the caloric content of everything you eat.

➤ Maintain your cool. Despite your best efforts, whether your child is a toddler or a high school senior, he or she will test your patience by developing novel methods of challenging the nutritional wisdom you are trying to impart. Do not get upset, take this personally, or turn it into a power struggle. Coping is part of the job description for parents. Count to ten and try again tomorrow.

would help me bake cookies, but that was a special treat. If they wanted a snack they could have raisins, cheese, or fruit. They liked snacks that were bite-sized, so I cut up an apple when they came home from school. Since they didn't fill up on junk food, they were hungry by dinnertime and ate what they were served, including the vegetables. They still like vegetables and fruit and don't eat a lot of junk foods. I was a little worried because my oldest daughter's husband grew up with cookies for snacks and dessert after meals, but she's got him eating his cookies with lunch at work so that they don't keep any in the house.

Viewing the Body Intelligently

While some parents may not recognize their child's weight problems, you are concerned if your child gains too much weight. The problem is that you don't want your concern to make your child ashamed of his or her body, undermining their self-esteem. Recall from Chapter 7 that a poor body image is associated with depression and lower self-esteem, and often causes adults to avoid activities that they would have enjoyed if they were less uncomfortable with their bodies. Perhaps you've already noticed your child being self-conscious and passing up activities and social situations because of a poor body image. As with adults, a poor body image will make weight loss more difficult for children since inactivity and social withdrawal may lead to increased eating.

If your child hasn't started school yet, he or she probably still likes his or her body despite the "baby fat." By the time your child reaches elementary school, he or she will be exposed to innumerable messages that will undermine this comfort with his or her body. When you add peer pressure and more time spent with TV and the media, it becomes increasingly difficult for your child to have a healthy body image. Although helping your child see his or her body intelligently is easier in the early years, you still are an important influence, regardless of your child's age.

Before you try to help your child develop a healthy body image, examine how you feel about having a child who isn't slender. Try to separate realistic concern about childhood obesity from judgments that your child's fat is unattractive, or from concerns about what other people will think about you when they see that your child is overweight. Even if you don't make any direct comments, your child will pick up on your uneasiness and will feel badly for making you uncomfortable. It might help to separate your struggle with weight from your feelings about your child's physique. With your increased awareness of body intelligence, there is no reason that your child will have to repeat your unhappy experiences. You can help develop your child's body intelligence with the same loving attitude as you have when helping develop your child's academic intelligence.

Modeling is just as important for body image as it is for eating. Even if you are a long way from reaching your weight goal, your child should not hear you make disparaging comments about your body or see you avoid activities because you don't like your body. In a 2002 *New York Times* article, Dr. Dianne Neumark-Sztainer—a researcher at the University of Minnesota School of Public Health—warned, "It's so common to say, 'Oh, I look so fat in this outfit,' but if you say that, then your kids are going to say it also." Instead, let your child occasionally hear you express pride in your appearance when you are nicely dressed and satisfaction when you do something physical. If someone compliments you on your appearance, accept the compliment gracefully instead of disagreeing or making a reference to the number of pounds you still need to lose. As long as it's genuine, it's not boastful to like the way your new hairstyle or outfit looks. In addition to modeling a healthy body image, there are specific things you can do to help your child. The "Enhancing Your Child's Body Image" sidebar has some practical suggestions for parents. Some are more applicable to one sex or the other, but most can be adapted to use with either boys or girls.

Wendy was a thirty-eight-year-old divorced pharmacist raising Karen, her ten-year-old daughter. Karen seemed upset one night so Wendy asked her if she was feeling sad. Karen replied, "School sucks," and went on to describe how she had been ignored while Heather, her thinner friend, got all the attention from the boys at a class party. Karen went on to resolve to give up carbs so she could lose weight and be thinner like Heather. Wendy acknowledged that feeling ignored was a "real bummer." But she also explained:

> *You shouldn't get too upset about one party. You can't compare yourself to Heather, or anyone else for that matter. Wherever you go there will be someone prettier than you and someone less pretty; someone taller and someone shorter, someone fatter and someone thinner, but you're the only one just like you and there will be people who like you for being yourself. If you spend all your time comparing yourself to other people, it will just make you sad, and that will make it harder for other people to get to know you.*

ENHANCING YOUR CHILD'S BODY IMAGE

Children, even rebellious teenagers who think their parents are hopelessly "out of it," can be influenced by information from their parents. Although your child might not give you the satisfaction of knowing that you are getting through to them, you should persist nonetheless. Here are a few suggestions:

➤ Whenever possible let your child choose what he or she will wear. If the outfit is clearly inappropriate, compromise and let him or her wear the least outrageous part of it. Although you don't want to overemphasize appearance, there is nothing wrong with complimenting your child when he or she looks especially nice.

➤ Help your child develop media literacy. Discuss movie, TV, and rock stars who are unrealistically thin and all the illusions necessary to create the desired appearance for movies or magazine pictures. Explain the economic motivations of advertisers promising to make you thinner or better looking.

➤ Discuss the changes that will come with puberty well before they are expected (some girls start as early as eight or nine years old). Early puberty can be difficult for girls who may misinterpret the changes to their body as evidence that they are getting fat.

➤ Explain the genetic aspects of body shape and size. Your child may be concerned that he or she will inherit an undesirable feature similar to a family member. Help the child recognize that he or she may have only limited control over the expression of genetically determined characteristics but, regardless, the world would be incredibly dull if everyone looked the same.

➤ Encourage friendships with peers who are less concerned with body size and appearance. Especially for girls, having friends who are preoccupied with appearance, weight, and dieting makes it more likely that she will be dissatisfied with her body. Instead of hanging out at friends' houses discussing clothes and makeup, encourage your daughter to participate in team sports but be cautious about ballet, cheerleading, gymnastics, or other activities that can overemphasize slenderness.

➤ Be careful about the terminology you use when describing your child. Words such as *tomboy*, *sissy*, or *weakling* can be harmful.

➤ Don't criticize or comment on other people's eating, weight, or shape in the presence of your child.

➤ Have a discussion with teenagers in which you describe a younger child who is preoccupied with trying to lose weight. Ask your teenager for specific things to say to the younger child to help him or her accept their own body. One study of female college students found a reduction in idealization of thinness and body dissatisfaction following a similar procedure.

When you are helping your child eat intelligently the effects are observable; you can see changes in his or her eating. When you help your child view his or her body intelligently, there are fewer obvious signs that you are succeeding. Even though you may not see the effects of your efforts immediately, you can take comfort from knowing that you are counteracting some of the cultural influences that make children dissatisfied with their bodies and you are helping to make long-term weight regulation more likely.

Using the Body Intelligently

Roger, a forty-eight-year-old musician, weighs 220 pounds. He remembers weekends as a child when his father would wake up at 5:30 on Sunday morning so he could get a spot at the local golf course. After playing nine holes, his father would come home at about the same time as Roger was getting up. They would have breakfast, and Roger's father would then take a nap after telling his son to "go outside and get some fresh air." But Roger preferred to watch cartoons. As an adult, Roger still prefers watching television to being active. His doctor wanted him to exercise, but each time he joined a gym, signed up for a team, or just resolved to get active the good intentions faded after a few weeks. If Roger's dad had taken him golfing, played softball, gone for a hike, or participated in almost any physical activity with him, it's quite likely that Roger's weight would be less than 220 pounds.

As with intelligent eating, you can't expect to teach your child to use his or her body intelligently by telling them what to do, even if the directions are more specific than "go outside and get some fresh air." To be effective, you have to arrange the activity environment and model active behavior.

Before you get started, examine your attitudes toward activity in general, and sports in particular. Recall from Chapter 9 that you may feel estranged from your body. Hopefully you have made progress in revising some attitudes about physical exertion. For some parents it will also be important to examine, and perhaps change, attitudes toward sports. For example, if you dismiss professional sports as unimportant and classify athletes as "dumb jocks," it will make it more difficult for your child to get fully involved in sports activities. While you don't need to become an avid fan of a sports team, it would help if you were able to communicate reasonable respect for the accomplishments of the athletes. Also, examine your attitude toward your child's gym classes. A vigorous gym class can lower blood pressure and body fat. Try to set aside any negative experiences you may have had in your gym classes. Express interest in your child's gym class in the same way that you would ask about their other classes.

Arranging the Activity Environment

Not so many years ago a child's environment would naturally require him or her to be active in the course of a normal childhood routine. Children would walk or ride their bikes to school, jump rope or play tag before class and during recess, go to gym class several times a week, and then go out and play after coming home from school. Currently, television, computers, and countless labor-saving devices, combined with cutbacks in physical education in school and realistic concerns about children's safety when left alone outside, have combined to make the environment less conducive to activity. Now it seems that children's natural state is to be sedentary and out of shape. A recent statewide assessment of California children in grades five, seven, and nine found that 75 percent failed to meet the standards for six basic physical fitness categories.

It will require a deliberate effort to get your child to be more active. To start, review your child's physical environment. Probably the single most helpful environmental change you can make is to remove the television from your child's bedroom. Chapter 2 presented considerable evidence demonstrating the harmful effects television can have on a child's developing body image, eating, and activity habits. Joseph Piscatella, author of *Fat-Proof Your Child*, summarized much of the research:

> . . . *excessive television viewing increases the risk of childhood obesity, keeps kids from exercising, increases their stress, decreases their metabolism, causes them to crave junk food, contributes to high cholesterol, and bears much responsibility for the lost art of family communication. Would you hire a babysitter with such a résumé?*

Although some parents might want to raise their children without any TV, for most families this isn't realistic. The sidebar, "Taming Television," has some suggestions for minimizing the negative impact of TV on your child.

If setting limits on television is a significant change for your children, you can expect complaints about being bored, or hear that "there's nothing to do." You need not feel guilty or be concerned that you're being unreasonable. Children were able to find things to do before the advent of TV. It may take a little boredom to motivate them to find new, and more active pursuits, but they soon will.

Limiting screen time is important, but it is not the only environmental change you can make to increase you child's activity. Many of

TAMING TELEVISION

Television can serve as a babysitter, giving you a much-needed break. It can be entertaining and occasionally educational, but as a parent it is necessary to maintain some control over TV viewing. Recognize that you won't have control when you're not home or when your child is at a friend's house, but just because you don't have complete control doesn't mean you should abandon all attempts to limit TV viewing.

➤ Set a daily limit for screen time, which includes TV, computers, video games, DVDs, and videos. Excluding computer use for homework, two hours a day is a reasonable limit for most kids.

➤ Take the television set out of your child's bedroom. When your child wants to be alone in their room, he or she can find something else to do.

➤ Have your child identify specific programs he or she wants to watch rather than allowing aimless surfing.

➤ Discuss the programs he or she has watched. You may not have much control over the content of the programs your child watches, but you can influence the lessons he or she takes away from the programs and commercials.

the suggestions for "Adding Steps" that were presented in Chapter 10 can be used with your children. Some additional tips to increase activity are presented in the sidebar "Creating an Environment for Activity."

Modeling Healthy Activity

If you are still working on increasing your daily step count, you might feel that it is hypocritical to be encouraging your child to be more active. You don't need to be an athlete to effectively encourage your child's activity, but you do need to be active yourself. Studies of four- to seven-year-olds demonstrate that kids who had physically active parents were almost six times as likely to be active compared with kids who

CREATING AN ENVIRONMENT FOR ACTIVITY

➤ For toddlers, minimize the amount of time spent in restrictive environments such as playpens.

➤ Buy toys and games that require movement. Avoid toys that can be used while sitting.

➤ Designate an area in the house and another outside where running, jumping, and, if possible, throwing a whiffle ball are permitted.

➤ Keep a Frisbee in the car. Rather than sit in the car while your partner shops, find a park and toss the Frisbee with your child for a few minutes.

➤ If your child isn't too out of shape, encourage him or her to try out for a cross-country team. Compared with football, basketball, or baseball, it requires less coordination and there should be less competition to get on the team.

had sedentary parents. The sidebar, "Getting Physical," has activities that you can do with your child that will get both of you moving and adding to your daily step count. You will be demonstrating that being active is a normal part of daily life, and it can be fun.

There is ample evidence that intelligent eating and activity and a healthy body image acquired in childhood have long-term benefits. With planning and some effort, you can help your child maintain his or her body intelligence despite the influence of popular culture. You can:

- Use BMI charts for children to determine if he or she is overweight.
- Establish routines for family meals and snacks while discouraging dieting.
- Limit prompting or prohibiting foods to younger children; offer choices of healthy foods to older children and teens.
- Avoid using foods as rewards or consolations and reduce external eating cues at home.
- Model intelligent eating, body image, and activity.

GETTING PHYSICAL

You can help your child get into the habit of being active by providing opportunities for activity at different times of the day in different circumstances. It is important to be sensitive to your child's likes and dislikes so you can encourage enjoyable activities, and, hopefully, participate in many of them. Here are a few suggestions:

➤ Walk or ride bikes to school with your child.

➤ On a windy day, go fly a kite; on a cold day, ice skate; on a hot day, swim or put lawn sprinklers out for you and your children to run through.

➤ Plant a garden with your child.

➤ Sign up for charity walks or community cleanups with your child.

➤ Have your child help rake leaves, shovel snow, and wash the car.

➤ Bring home a hula-hoop or jump rope as a surprise gift for your child.

➤ Buy an aerobics video and do the dance routines with your child (but don't count it as screen time).

➤ Get a backpack, walk to the neighborhood market, and do your shopping with your child.

➤ Help your child make a fitness video with his or her friends and then do the routine with them.

➤ For other creative ideas check the fitnessmom.com website.

- Limit TV viewing and discuss food advertisements and unrealistic standards of beauty with your child.
- Buy toys and games that require movement.
- Participate in physical activities with your child.

The next chapter will show how you can help start changing the culture so that in the future developing and maintaining body intelligence will require less planning and effort.

CHAPTER 12

THE CULTURE OF BODY INTELLIGENCE

Throughout the discussion of intelligent eating, body image, and physical activity, I have suggested methods to help you and your children overcome the influence of television and the media, fast food, advertising, and labor-saving devices that interfere with the normal development of body intelligence. While each of us needs to follow an individual program, wouldn't it be nice if you didn't feel like you were fighting every step of the way? The purpose of this chapter is to offer suggestions so that the larger environment would be more supportive of developing body intelligence.

If you are pessimistic about the likelihood of a change in culture, consider what has happened to our attitudes about smoking. Thirty years ago the Marlboro man was the epitome of masculine virility, and smoking was smart and sophisticated for non-cowboys. Who would have guessed then that people would come to shun smokers because of concern about the effects of secondhand smoke and that lighting up would be illegal in most public buildings? In the span of several decades, smoking has been transformed from a sign of sophistication to evidence of a nasty addiction. This change wasn't an accident. Starting with the Surgeon General's 1964 report identifying the health risks and continuing with public education and legislation making smoking more expensive and difficult, the number of smokers has declined. Or consider seat belts. Few cars were equipped with them until the 1960s, and when they were introduced they were rarely used. A $25 million seat belt advertising campaign—combined with laws requiring their use and frequent media reports noting that seat belts save lives—has increased seat belt use to 79 percent.

In 2003, the Surgeon General started a campaign to control the childhood obesity epidemic. It's too early to tell if this campaign will be successful, but it's not too early to start our own campaigns. While you can't go out and change American culture this week, there are small changes on a local level that you can encourage, as well as national policies that you can support that will help make body intelligence easier for your kids and future generations. Probably the best place to start to change the culture is in the neighborhood school.

Intelligent Schools

Unfortunately, most schools are not helping to combat the childhood obesity epidemic. Food companies actively court youth because kids between age four and twelve have $30 billion of their own money to spend and influence their parents' spending of an additional $600 billion. Despite your best efforts to promote body intelligence at home, when your child gets to school he or she may be confronted with well-financed efforts to garner those dollars. The food industry will market their products in school with television ads for junk foods, textbooks that use the brand names of candies in examples, high-calorie sodas in vending machines, and fast food in the cafeteria.

For example, Channel One is a for-profit television network shown in twelve thousand schools with eight million adolescent viewers. Sixty-nine percent of the commercials broadcast are for fast food, candy, sodas, and snack foods. According to the Centers for Disease Control and Prevention (CDC), 98 percent of American high school students can buy fast food, soda, candy bars, and other fattening foods without leaving their schools. One survey of 200 schools in twenty-four states found that 75 percent of the drinks and 85 percent of the snacks sold in school vending machines had little nutritional value. Of the 9,723 vending machine slots counted, only 26 offered a fruit or vegetable. The

CDC estimates that about 20 percent of the nation's schools offer brand-name fast foods in their cafeterias.

Many schools willingly invite the participation of fast-food, soda, and snack food companies for a simple reason: it helps pay the bills. Channel One provides free video equipment to schools who use its programming. Candy sales often finance field trips, extracurricular clubs, and athletic teams. More than five thousand schools have fast-food outlets in their lunchrooms. School districts receive royalties from the vending machine and fast-food companies that sell their wares in the cafeteria. For example, in 1998 the Colorado Springs school district was paid several million dollars to sell only Coca Cola. Fearing that sales quotas wouldn't be met, an administrator sent a letter urging principals to move the vending machines so they would be accessible to students throughout the day. While it is clear that schools benefit from the money, video equipment, and other inducements offered by promoters of fattening foods, are the benefits worth the likely costs?

Schools can help increase body intelligence. Psychologists at the University of Wales, Bangor, noted that fewer than 4 percent of British children age four to six ate the recommended five servings of fruits and vegetables per day. They developed a creative "Food Dudes" video, which had four slightly older cartoon children battling the "Junk Punks" who were intent on destroying all the fruits and vegetables on earth so that humans would be deprived of their "Life Force" foods. In addition to six short episodes shown in class, the program included Food Dude stickers, pens, and erasers used to reward students for trying the target foods as well as encouraging letters from the Food Dudes. Although the whole program lasted for only sixteen days, fruit and vegetable consumption more than doubled and the gains were still present four months after the program ended. One of the studies demonstrated that the increase in fruit and vegetable consumption was accompanied by a decrease in consumption of chocolate, potato chips, and the usual snack foods. The researchers suggest that their program motivates children to try the target foods, and, after repeated exposure, they learn to enjoy them so the videos and rewards are no longer necessary. More information about this program is available at fooddudes.co.uk.

What You Can Do

Do you know what kinds of food the schools in your community sell to students? If there are no restrictions on junk foods and drinks, you could start lobbying local school officials and state legislators to ban foods that don't meet minimal nutritional standards. Although kids enjoy fast food, colas, and snacks, you shouldn't conclude that they would dislike more healthy alternatives. In January 2003, Ed Wilkins, the San Francisco school board's director of student nutrition, introduced a policy that food sold at the school has to contain less than 30 percent of its calories from fat (less than 10 percent from saturated fat) and less than 35 percent from sugar. The food must also meet minimal standards for vitamin, mineral, protein, and fiber content. French fries, soda, Gatorade, hot dogs, chips, and all battered and fried foods were banished from the cafeteria. Although food sales declined at first, they quickly rebounded. Wilkins is also introducing a salad bar in elementary schools. He reports, "Kids love it—it's like a field trip, somehow." He is planning a "grab-and-go" breakfast for kids who skip breakfast at home.

In most communities the first step would be to talk to the school principal and dietitian about your concerns. A 2002 *Newsweek* article described how Saralyn Myers, a Dobbs Ferry, New York, mother of two children, worked to change the school menu. "We insist on high academic standards, why not have high standards for the kind of food we eat?" She started a committee and persuaded the school to use whole wheat bread and add a salad bar and veggie burgers to the menu. You can also raise the issue at a PTA meeting and propose that a committee be formed to look into the food being served in local schools. You might encounter some resistance if vending machines and fast food fund some school programs. Groups such as the National School Boards Association and the National Association of Secondary School Principals have opposed any policy change, apparently preferring to risk the future health of the students in order to maintain current funding. But with increasing awareness of the childhood obesity and diabetes epidemic, this position will be harder to justify.

Although Congressional legislation to limit sales of sodas haven't been successful on a national level, in New York the State Assembly passed a bill that would restrict the foods and drinks that could be sold in school vending machines. While the bill passed by a vote of 139 to 5, one legislator was worried that, "You have to be twenty-one to buy a Ho-Ho." You can let elected officials know that they needn't worry; you'd be willing to sacrifice your child's access to Ho-Hos in school. If the school won't give up the revenue from vending machines, have them include healthy snacks such as fruits, nuts, and yogurt at attractive prices while raising the cost of the nutritionally worthless foods. One study of vending machines conducted at twelve high schools and twelve work sites found that reducing the price of low-fat snacks and posting educational signs increased the proportion of low-fat snacks purchased without reducing the vending machine profits.

If you feel that you lack the expertise to challenge the school's policies, you can discuss your concern with your child's pediatrician. According to Dr. David Kessler, the former commissioner of the FDA, the medical profession has "missed the most important epidemic facing the vast majority of Americans," but recently the American Academy of Pediatrics issued a policy statement urging the restriction of soft drinks in schools. Your pediatrician may be familiar with the policy statement and is probably concerned about the increasing number of obese kids he or she is treating. With a little prodding he or she might be willing to get involved. You can also enlist the support of the local dental society since most dentists are concerned about the effects of sodas on children's teeth. For more ideas check out the School Foods Tool Kit from the Center for Science in the Public Interest website cspinet.org/schoolfood.

In addition to the school cafeteria menu, as a concerned parent, you will want to check on the school's physical education programs. How frequent are gym classes, and how much of the time is spent in physical activity versus changing clothes and lining up to take attendance? Are sports teams limited to the athletically talented students, or does everyone get a chance to play? Are sports excessively competitive so that average students become discouraged? Winning is nice, but showing kids that they can have a good time using their bodies is more important. Are sports programs focused primarily on the boys, or are girls' athletics equally important? While the funds to add gym classes might not be available, it may be possible to change routines to increase the amount of actual activity in gym class and ensure that all children benefit.

Consider organizing a walking school bus. Communities from Chicago to Christchurch, New Zealand, have programs where adults take turns walking a small group of children to school. Typically the children are dropped off at the "driver's" house or "picked up" en route and walk to school in a group with adult supervision. The children and the "driver" get some exercise while other parents avoid the frustration of dealing with the traffic jams around the school. For more information on starting this type of program go to walkingbus.com.

Ideally parents could help schools encourage the development of healthy body images in their students. In practice this is more difficult since the goals are less concrete than say, removing sodas from vending machines, but there are elementary school curricula for preventing eating problems. In junior high and high school, health and science classes can include discussions on physical development and pubertal changes, the effects of heredity on weight and body shape, and the hazards of fad dieting. It is not unrealistic to expect that schools have policies that discourage harassment and teasing, especially about body size and features.

The Intelligent Workplace

While your kids are in school, you're probably at a job that may be just as fattening for you as school is for your children. Joan, a forty-four-year-old social worker, spent much of her time out in the field but dreaded being in the office because of all the food and food-related activities that were present. She felt obligated to participate in the office coffee fund that provided daily coffee and donuts. She found it difficult to resist this daily ritual since everyone else was involved, so she tried to assuage her guilt by asking that they order a bran muffin for her instead of a fried donut. During the day she tried to avoid walking by several desks that had bowls of candy prominently displayed. Whenever one of her coworkers had a birthday, there would be a cake in the break room, and frequently on Fridays someone would order pizza and offer Joan a slice.

If your workplace is anything like Joan's you should take action—you shouldn't need superhuman willpower to dodge the external eating cues at work. Although it may be difficult if you are the first one to raise the issue at your workplace, it may help to know that many businesses, concerned about the long-term health costs of overweight employees, are instituting programs to help their employees lose weight. For example, some companies subsidize on-site Weight Watchers meetings and offer rewards for employees who buy a low-fat meal in the cafeteria. Others have a fitness center and weight-loss programs for their employees. Encouraging fitness in the workplace is a growing trend that also can include providing wellness coordinators who lead daily fitness classes and subsidizing gym memberships.

Some companies have instituted rewards for weight loss. One manufacturing company weighs employees each quarter and awards $25 if there hasn't been any gain and gives an extra $25 with a paid day off for maintaining weight loss for a year. Companies have good reasons for promoting fitness: obese workers have higher rates of absenteeism and their health insurance expenditures are 38 percent higher than their nonobese colleagues. Motorola reports that it saves $3.93 for every dollar it spends on employee fitness. In addition to being cost-effective for the employer, preliminary evidence suggests that losing weight in a group at work may be more effective than doing it alone.

What You Can Do

Even if the company you work for seems oblivious to the obesity epidemic, don't assume that there is nothing you can do to promote fitness. Since an increasing number of firms have on-site fitness programs, your request to start one shouldn't be perceived as unreasonable. If a structured program is not feasible, perhaps your employer can make smaller changes to promote fitness. For example, it shouldn't be expensive for the company cafeteria to serve healthier meals and vending machines to include fruit and nuts. In many office buildings stairways are dreary and uninviting. If they were repainted and carpeted and had upbeat music, employees might enjoy getting off the elevator and walking up the last two flights. Posting a notice next to the elevator suggesting that walking up stairs is good for the heart and waistline might remind employees who have good intentions but "don't have the time to exercise" to use the stairs. One study found that an illustrated sign ("Your heart needs exercise . . . here's your chance") placed near stairs and an escalator resulted in doubling of stair usage. Sprint, the telecommunications company, is using a different method to encourage their employees to use the stairs; they installed slow elevators.

If your employer isn't willing to consider rewarding weight loss, you can propose an informal activity contest among your coworkers. For example, you could divide your coworkers into two teams with each member contributing a small amount to the kitty. Each team member would reset their pedometer at the start of the day and an impartial judge would record the number of steps taken at the end of the day. The team with the highest weekly total would win the prize.

Joan couldn't persuade her supervisor to start a fitness program, but she was able to organize several of her coworkers to take daily walks during their lunch hour. After this routine was established, she had some support when asking her coworkers to keep their candy in, rather than on their desks, and she wasn't the only one to resign from the coffee break fund.

The Intelligent Community

Dr. James Hill is the director of the Center for Human Nutrition at the University of Colorado Health Sciences Center and an expert on the relationship between the environment and obesity. He said:

> It is fine to tell someone to eat less and exercise more, but we have created an environment that makes it difficult to do that. . . . Our biology, which worked fine a few generations ago, is not working today.

Our biology has not changed—our environment has. . . . As the environment has changed to one where food is readily available and as technology has reduced the need for physical activity, fewer people can resist the push of the environment toward obesity.

Dr. Hill was speaking at a conference focusing on the effects the physical environment (our cities, homes, and workplaces) has on our weight. This is a new area of study that could lead to major changes in the world around us. Some of the changes in political, economic, and urban planning policies would be controversial, but they are certainly worthy of consideration.

The Physical Environment

Do you live in the suburbs and drive to work? Although millions of Americans do, much of the rest of the industrialized world doesn't. In Europe it's common to walk to work or use public transportation but to walk on both ends of the journey. Our grandparents did the same, assuming they weren't living and working on a farm. Although this may seem trivial, one recent survey of 10,500 Atlanta residents found that for each additional thirty minutes spent commuting there was a 3 percent increase in the likelihood of being obese. People who live less than half a mile from shopping are more likely to walk and are 7 percent less likely to be obese. Suburban houses with lawns and three-car garages connected to shopping, school, and work by ever larger systems of roads and parking lots may be hazardous to your health. These findings, if supported in future research, have far-reaching implications for how we design our cities. If future urban planners consider the health consequences when designing new developments, it is likely that housing, shopping, and workplaces will be clustered in ways that support walking and discourage driving. For example, the Stapleton development in Denver is a mixed-use community designed to encourage walking. The Transit Village in Oakland's Fruitvale district represents an attempt to revitalize a run-down area by developing housing and shopping near the BART (subway) station so that residents can walk and use public transit rather than drive.

The relationship between driving and obesity was recognized in a recent *New York Times* editorial criticizing a proposed transportation bill. The editorial noted, ". . . at a time when the nation is obsessively worrying about obesity, the bill seems to do everything it can to make sure that Americans continue sitting in their cars for as much time as possible" and suggested that more of the $300 billion allocated for road construction be redirected to build pedestrian and bicycle paths.

The Media Environment

In Chapter 11, I discussed how parents could "inoculate" their children to minimize the effects of advertising on their eating habits. In recent years there have been attempts to legislate restrictions on food advertising directed toward children so that parental inoculation would be less necessary. For example, in 2004 Senator Tom Harkin from Iowa introduced legislation that would allow the Federal Trade Commission to restrict advertising directed toward children, and the National Advertising Review Council published a paper promoting responsible food advertising to children. Although the bill didn't pass and the advertising review paper was just advisory, they are indications of a growing awareness of the problem. A Roper Poll found that 85 percent of the adults queried thought that there shouldn't be any advertising on children's television so it appears that legislators are being unnecessarily timid in standing up to the food and advertising industries.

An alternative to banning food advertising directed at children would be to require equal time for ads promoting a healthy diet. This approach has been used with cigarette advertising where the Fairness Doctrine requiring equal time for antismoking messages led the tobacco companies to voluntarily abandon television advertising. For every Ronald McDonald ad there could be a superhero who gets his or her strength from fruits and vegetables. Perhaps it's time for an updated version of Popeye and his can of spinach or an American version of the Food Dudes.

The media environment also includes the glorification of the tall, thin body shape contributing to rampant body dissatisfaction, especially among girls and women. Encouraging healthy eating and activity habits does not require the idealization of thinness. There could be public service ads directed to parents warning about the hazards of childhood obesity, offering suggestions for preventing excess weight gain while acknowledging and valuing the diversity of healthy body shapes. It is important that any public health messages are careful not to add to the stigmatization that obese kids already experience.

The Legal and Political Environment

Legislation, regulation, public education, and taxation are tools that have been used to decrease health risks. Who would find frequent reminders to "buckle up" offensive or complain that laws mandating seat belt use are an excessive infringement on personal freedom? A variety of federal and state regulations have been enacted to decrease health risks. Aside from seat belts, public health campaigns routinely admonish us to get flu shots in the winter, there are labels on alcoholic beverages warning that alcohol impairs your ability to drive and may cause health problems, and tobacco companies are required to include a Surgeon General's Warning in all their print advertising.

Similar efforts could be used to promote body intelligence. The Nutrition Facts label currently required on packaged foods is a good start but could be improved. The serving size is typically described in grams, ounces, or cups. The addition of a more visual description, such as "about the size of your fist" (or tennis ball or deck of cards) would help consumers regulate portion size. A warning about the health risks, similar to "Excessive consumption of this food could contribute to childhood obesity, diabetes, and other illnesses," could be prominently displayed on high-calorie foods along with the current nutritional information.

There are some early indications that the concern about the obesity epidemic coupled with the continuing legal challenges to the tobacco industry may be having an impact on food manufacturers. In 2004, McDonald's announced that it would phase out supersized fries and drinks. (Although it is not clear as to how many franchises will follow this corporate edict.) Several snack food manufacturers have removed saturated fats and trans-fatty acids from their chips. Kraft Foods is planning to cut the fat and sugar content of Oreos and some of their other products but the planned changes are likely to be minimal. A Kraft spokesman said, "We're not going to do anything radical. . . . We don't want to lose the tastes that people have come to love" so it's too early to judge the sincerity of their efforts.

Legal regulations and the threat of lawsuits are not the only policy tools available. Taxes are routinely used to discourage drinking and smoking. One study found that a 10 percent increase in the price of cigarettes decreased adult smoking by 3 to 5 percent and had a greater impact on adolescent smoking. In 1994, Dr. Kelly Brownell in a *New York Times* Op-Ed piece proposed putting a surcharge on foods that were high in fat and low in nutritional value:

> *Fatty foods would be judged on their nutritive value per calorie or gram of fat; the least healthy would be given the highest tax rate. Consumption of high-fat foods would drop, and the revenue could be used for public exercise facilities—bike paths and running tracks—or nutrition education in the schools.*

Taxing high-fat foods would also help to reduce the cost differential with healthy foods. The Sunday newspaper is full of coupons for discounts on cookies and other snack foods, but have you ever seen a coupon for 25 cents off a bag of carrots? The next time you're in a supermarket walk down the aisle with fruits and vegetables and count the number of "two for the price of one" or "buy three, get one free" offers you find. Then walk down the snack food aisle and compare. While the prices of fruits and vegetables decline during the harvest season, you rarely find the type of promotions that make snack foods comparatively cheap.

Although increasing taxes is always unpopular and can be hazardous to the politicians who propose them, if the taxes were limited to junk foods designed to appeal to children, the concept might be more acceptable. It's unlikely that many adults would miss Fruit Loops or feel that their children were being deprived if they had to eat Cheerios instead. With the dramatic increase in the number of obese children and diabetes in children in the last decade, perhaps it's time to seriously consider Dr. Brownell's proposal.

A less direct method of controlling the obesity epidemic was proposed by Michael Pollan, a University of California Berkeley professor. He notes that when food is cheap, people will eat more of it. Since the early 1970s federal farm subsidy programs costing $19 billion a year have encouraged farmers to produce more grain. The simplest thing to do with the surplus is to process it into more compact forms such as corn sweeteners and corn-fed meat and then sell it cheaply as Big Gulps or 99-cent hamburgers. Pollan suggests that when commodities are cheap, food producers would reduce their profits if they passed on the savings by cutting the price of their products. Instead, it costs them very little to increase the portion size while maintaining the price and profits. The current overproduction of grain works out to be an extra 500 calories per day for every American. Pollan suggests that if the government stopped subsidizing the production of grain, the surplus would decrease. With less of a surplus there would be fewer calorie-dense food "bargains."

What You Can Do

Although legal and political change usually requires either large numbers of people or significant funding of lobbying efforts, there are instances of a single person, or small group, effecting change. For example, Carole Carson went from 182 to 120 pounds and described her progress in the local newspaper. She challenged the thirteen thousand residents of her town to an eight-week fitness program that was called the Nevada County Meltdown Challenge. Local businesses participated; fitness centers offered free two-month memberships; restaurants offered Meltdown menus; and spas offered free treatments as rewards for significant weight loss. Participants were organized in groups of five to provide mutual support. At the end of eight weeks, 1,061 people had lost about four tons of weight.

In an Oakland, California, neighborhood two college students are trying to improve the community's nutrition. According to one of the students, Tony Douangviseth, "The number 1 cause of death in Oakland is not homicide. It's heart disease . . . you live five minutes away from fast food but twenty minutes away from a grocery store. . . . We know we eat real bad. How can we help the community eat better?" He and fellow student, Ed James, are trying to provide a healthier alternative to fast food. They received funding from the County Public Health Department to hire four high school students to sell meals of chicken and greens sandwiches with fruit salad and fresh squeezed lemonade at a neighborhood farmers market, and they plan on expanding the program to six recreation centers.

Whether it's talking to your P.T.A. or school principal, organizing a walking school bus, lobbying for a fitness program at work, or writing letters to your legislators, creating a community that fosters body intelligence is going to require major reversals of unhealthy trends that have developed during the last fifty years. Nostalgia for the "good old days" won't accomplish much. Very few of us would be willing to give up our garage-door openers, TV remotes, or the convenience of getting a meal from the drive-up window at a restaurant when we've had to work late. Instead it will be necessary to find new ways to create an environment that makes it more likely that we will eat healthy foods in reasonable amounts and increase physical activity in our daily routine. The culture has changed to discourage smoking. Changes to increase body intelligence may be more complex, but the terrible consequences of doing nothing make it essential that we try.

CHAPTER 13

INCREASING YOUR BODY INTELLIGENCE

Body intelligence can be complicated. It's much simpler to think about weight control in terms of a diet—just banish carbs (or fats) from your diet and you'll lose weight and be happy, healthy, and content. In contrast to this unrealistic, overly simplistic view, the process of increasing body intelligence is more involved. You need to know your specific patterns of thinking and behavior for your eating, your body image, and your physical activity.

- When you can identify whether your eating is prompted by external stimuli, emotional arousal, physical hunger, or enjoyment you can make deliberate decisions and gain control.
- When you can realistically evaluate your body, taking into account your genetic makeup, your childhood and adolescent experiences, and the prevailing cultural conceptions of beauty, you will be able to establish realistic weight goals and avoid discouragement that interferes with permanent weight control.
- When you have identified the sources of your discomfort with exercise you will be able to find activities that are enjoyable, fit in with your daily routine, and make you feel good about using your body.

Although more complex, thinking in terms of body intelligence rather than dieting is liberating. Your weight is not a function of whether you were "good" or "bad" in following your diet, rather it is determined by the interaction of your genetic makeup, the external environment, and your body intelligence. With increasing body intelligence you recognize the genetic boundaries affecting your weight loss and body shape. Your goals will be realistic, enabling you to lose weight, improve your health, and feel better about your body even if it doesn't match the current ideal physique. With body intelligence you are aware of the environmental influences, both at the societal level and in your daily routine, so that you can minimize both external eating and emotional eating while avoiding hunger and allowing yourself the pleasure that eating can provide.

Planning and Persistence for Body Intelligence

Although there isn't a single body intelligence score similar to an IQ score, after completing the questionnaires and exercises in this book you should have a good idea of your strengths and the areas that still need work. If you are like most frustrated dieters, you have had repeated unsuccessful experiences trying to limit your eating, but have only made a few attempts to increase physical activity and haven't tried to improve your body image. Regardless of your past experiences, recognize that permanent weight loss is rarely straightforward. Change is a lengthy process that can have many temporary setbacks. Inevitably, there are upsets, reversals, discouragement, and backsliding but successful weight losers are characterized by persistence. How do you persist, rather than give up, when you are discouraged?

Consider the methods used by two people who have successfully maintained their weight losses. Dr. Richard Wurtman directs the Clinical Research Center at M.I.T. Although he's an expert on diet and nutrition and has been in great shape for years, he still describes himself as a "fat person in a thin person's body." He attributes his success at weight maintenance to daily aerobics and keeping a mental tally of the calories he consumes each day. Mary Litman is equally successful in maintaining her weight loss. When a coworker brought homemade cannoli into the office, she didn't want to feel deprived. She said to herself, "I'm going to eat it," which she did. But the deal she made with herself was that she would walk home from work and have salad for dinner. She enjoys chocolate-covered mints but instead of buying a large mint patty, she buys a box of Junior Mints and eats a few at a time when she wants a treat. Dr. Wurtman and Ms. Litman illustrate body intelligence. Rather than losing weight and then going off their diets, they have developed new habits and strategies for maintaining their healthier behaviors. Your maintenance behaviors may be different, but the persistence and planning required will be the same.

Recall from Chapters 6 and 10 that the action stage of change requires the most effort. When you are in the maintenance stage there is less experimentation with new eating and exercise behaviors. You have developed new habits that feel more natural; however, vigilance is still required to ensure that you don't return to the contemplation or preparation stage. One study of 714 people who had an average weight loss of sixty-five pounds that was maintained for more than five years suggests that the first few years are the most difficult. If you can keep the weight off for a few years, the loss is more likely to become permanent.

As you enter the maintenance stage you can expect slips or lapses; no one does it perfectly. A lapse is a temporary episode in which you abandon your new eating and exercise habits. You can recover from a brief lapse and resume your progress. In contrast, a relapse isn't temporary. You give up and return to the contemplation stage. Fortunately, many of your potential lapses are predictable so you can develop contingency plans to ensure that the lapse doesn't become a relapse. Some of the most common lapses are discussed in the following sections.

The Holiday Season Lapse

From Thanksgiving to Christmas to New Year's and through Super Bowl weekend, there are parties and celebrations revolving around food. Often there is the expectation that to participate fully, you need to overeat. Also there are more external food cues during the holidays. In addition to being offered goodies and second helpings at social events, food appears in the most unlikely places. I can recall going into a locksmith shop one December day to get a key made. On the counter, under a small Christmas tree, was a plate of brownies. Although I wasn't planning on eating a brownie that morning, I made a deal with myself. I would do an extra ten minutes on the treadmill and forgo dessert later in the day so that I could respond to the powerful cue.

When you combine holiday overeating with winter weather that makes outdoor exercise more difficult, it's easy to lapse into old patterns. To minimize weight gain over the holidays, plan on temporarily resuming self-monitoring. One study demonstrated that consistent self-monitoring during the holiday season was associated with weight maintenance while participants in a weight-loss program who were inconsistent in self-monitoring gained weight.

The Vacation Lapse

There are at least three dangers when you go on vacation. First, when you are away from home you'll have less control of your eating environment since many of your meals will be in restaurants. Second, many vacations, including cruises and all-inclusive resorts, emphasize eating a wide variety of fattening foods as part of the experience, and third, a vacation will disrupt the eating and activity routines you have established at home. To reduce these dangers, discuss with your traveling companion how you will minimize unnecessary eating before you leave. For example, you could decide to have the hearty breakfast that is included in your hotel stay but compensate by having a light lunch. Also, plan what you will do when you get home to prevent any lapse from becoming a complete relapse. For example, if you belong to a gym or participate in an exercise program, you could prepay your dues before going on vacation to ensure that you resume exercising when you get back.

The Life Change Lapse

If you move, get a new job, or just get sick, your normal routine will be disrupted. Any of these changes can divert your attention and energy away from your new eating and exercise patterns. For example, if you change jobs, your new commute may take you past a particularly tempting bakery. When you move to a new city, you might feel that other responsibilities are more urgent than finding a gym or a new walking partner. Time passes while you are focused on other priorities and your healthy eating and exercise habits are forgotten. Instead of allowing life changes to undermine your body intelligence, give some thought to the effects of these changes and then plan ahead. Before your move visit several gyms in your new neighborhood, sign up for a trial membership, and go within the first few weeks of arrival.

You can't assume that you will automatically resume your new eating and exercise habits after your life has been disrupted. Instead, recognize the possible lapse and make a plan to pick up where you left off once your life becomes more settled.

The Emotional Upset Lapse

Chapter 4 described the role of emotional eating in gaining weight. In addition to weight gain, eating in response to emotional arousal can trigger a lapse that, if not reversed, can become a relapse. One study of participants in a hospital weight-control program found that when successful losers gave up and regained their lost weight about half of the time an emotional upset was responsible. To avoid falling into this trap, review the methods presented in Chapter 4. Identify the type of emotion you are experiencing, check the underlying thinking to correct any irrational assumptions, and use techniques such as relaxation and exercise to help get you through the difficult times. If you are still having trouble, consider counseling to help deal with the emotional turmoil before the lapse turns into a relapse.

The Plateau Lapse

One of the most frustrating experiences for dieters occurs when they reach a plateau. If you've had this experience you know how discouraging it is to be restricting your eating, feeling deprived because you are hungry, and missing favorite foods—yet despite all this effort, the scale stubbornly refuses to budge. The typical response is to give up. If your dieting isn't producing results, why bother?

With body intelligence you won't let a plateau undo your progress. Assuming that you haven't started taking any medication that has weight gain as a side effect, examine your thinking about plateaus. It isn't necessary to become discouraged since there can be advantages to a plateau. Recall from Chapter 7 that obese people tend to overestimate the size of their body. After losing weight you may still see yourself as fatter than you are. A stable period of reduced weight will give you the opportunity to adjust your body image to more accurately reflect your actual size. Likewise, if family and friends are accustomed to treating you as a fat person, it may take some time for them to change their thinking and recognize that your weight doesn't limit you the way it had before. A plateau may help them get used to your thinner body.

What is most important is how you think about a plateau. Since you haven't been dieting and you have allowed yourself to enjoy eating, you shouldn't be feeling deprived. As you continue in the Maintenance Stage, your new eating behaviors will become more natural and require less effort. With a healthy, realistic body image, the need to reach an arbitrary ideal weight is lessened. If you spend some time at a stable, lower, but less than ideal weight, it won't feel as bad as it did before when you hit a plateau while dieting.

Your Relapse Prevention Plan

When you are going through a rough time and are feeling stressed or depressed, or even if it's just a realization that you're in the middle of your vacation and have gained a few pounds, it will be difficult to stop what you are doing and focus on regaining control over your eating and exercise. Without preplanning it's more likely that your lapse will become a relapse. Instead, recognize that almost everyone going through the stages of change will have some reversals, but with realistic expectations and a little planning the inevitable lapses need not undermine all your efforts. The time to do the planning is now, when you're not on vacation or in the middle of an especially stressful time. Start by trying to anticipate circumstances that would cause a lapse. Review the five common lapses described above and consider your past attempts to lose weight. What happened to make you discouraged and give up? Looking ahead, what could interrupt the changes you've been making? In your notebook jot down several scenarios that could trigger a lapse.

For most lapses, the most effective strategy is to resume self-monitoring of your eating and activity. With careful self-monitoring your attention will be directed to the specific situations that you've let slide. The difficulty is that during a lapse you probably won't feel like making the effort to monitor your eating and activity. It's important to plan now to have a backup mechanism in place that will help you get started with self-monitoring. For example, you could post a sign inside your medicine chest or near your scale indicating the cutoff weight that will make you resume self-monitoring, and have the forms in the cabinet ready so there is no delay if you reach the cutoff weight. If you need more structure, you could tell a supportive friend or spouse the weight that will trigger self-monitoring and ask him or her to remind you if you reach that weight. Considering your past experiences with lapses, what would be the best strategy to minimize the impact of a future lapse? Try to come up with a specific plan and write it in your notebook.

Body Intelligence for Life

With academic intelligence, your genetic inheritance sets the boundaries for your intellectual functioning. Within those boundaries, your parents, your school experiences, and the rest of your environment will determine how much of your intellectual potential is fulfilled. Body intelligence functions the same way. Your genes set the boundaries of your weight. Your environment, habits, and thought patterns determine the weight that you will maintain within those boundaries.

With academic intelligence, you're always learning even when you're not in school. Sometimes the learning is effortless, as when a baseball fan memorizes the batting averages of the players on his favorite team. Other times, such as when you're figuring out a new computer program, the learning requires more concentration, but it's unlikely that you would decide to study all day, every day so that you could become the next Bill Gates. Body intelligence works the same way. Sometimes good eating and exercise habits become natural, but at other times they require a more deliberate effort. This effort is different from "going on a diet," which requires rigid restriction of your eating all day, every day so that you can try to override your genetic weight boundaries.

If you've followed the guidelines presented in this book, you're well on your way to increasing your body intelligence. As you continue you will reach a healthy weight that will allow you to look good and feel better without the struggle of dieting. You will overcome the barriers that have caused so much frustration in the past and will be able to maintain this weight permanently. It will require persistence and planning, but your health and well-being are worth the effort.

REFERENCES

Chapter 1

Angier, N. (1994, December 1). Researchers link obesity in humans to flaw in a gene. *New York Times*, A-1, A-13.

Arone, L. J. (2002). Current pharmacological treatments for obesity. In C. G. Fairburn & K. D. Brownell (eds.), *Eating disorders and obesity: A comprehensive handbook (2nd ed.)* (pp. 551–556). New York: Guilford.

Barinaga, M. (1995). "Obese" protein slims mice. *Science*, 269, 475–476.

Bennett, W., & Gurin, J. (1982). *The dieter's dilemma: Eating less and weighing more*. New York: Basic Books.

Bouchard, C. (2002). Genetic influences on body weight. In C. G. Fairburn & K. D. Brownell (eds.), *Eating disorders and obesity: A comprehensive handbook (2nd ed.)* (pp. 16–21). New York: Guilford.

Bray, G. A. (1998). *Contemporary diagnosis and management of obesity*. Newtown, PA: Handbooks in Healthcare.

Brownell, K. D., & Horgen, K. B. (2004). *Food fight: The inside story of the food industry, America's obesity crisis, and what we can do about it*. Chicago: Contemporary Books.

Brownell, K. D., & Wadden, T. A. (1991). The heterogeneity of obesity: Fitting treatments to individuals. *Behavior Therapy*, 22, 153–157.

Field, A. E., Barnoya, J., & Colditz, G. A. (2002). Epidemiology and health and economic consequences of obesity. In T. A. Wadden & A. J. Stunkard (eds.), *Handbook of obesity treatment* (pp. 3–18). New York: Guilford.

Flegal, K. M., Carroll, M. D., Ogden, C. L., & Johnson, C. L. (2002). Prevalence and trends in obesity among U.S. adults, 1999–2000. *Journal of the American Medical Association*, 288, 1723–1727.

Freudenheim, M. (2003, August 29). Hospitals pressured by soaring demand for obesity surgery. *New York Times*, A-1.

Goleman, D. (1995). *Emotional intelligence: Why it can matter more than IQ*. New York: Bantam.

Gorman, B. S., & Allison, D. B. (1995). Measures of restrained eating. In D. B. Allison (ed.), *Handbook of assessment methods for eating behaviors and weight-related problems: Measures, theory, and research* (pp. 149–184). Thousand Oaks, CA: Sage.

Grady, D. (2002, May 23). Hormone linked to appetite, weight control. *New York Times*. Retrieved May 28, 2002, from nytimes.com.

Grady, D. (2002, August 8). Hormone that causes full feeling is found. *New York Times*. Retrieved August 8, 2002, from nytimes.com.

Grady, D. (2003, November 13). Nasal spray's use to curb hunger is found safe in small test. *New York Times*. Retrieved November 12, 2003, from nytimes.com.

Grady, D. (2004, May 4). Operation for obesity leaves some in misery. *New York Times*. Retrieved May 4, 2004, from nytimes.com.

Grollman, A. P. (2003, February 23). Regulation of dietary drugs is long overdue. *New York Times*. Retrieved February 23, 2003, from nytimes.com.

Hellmich, N. (2003, August 14). For Raechel, "it's horrible to be heavy." *USA Today*, A-2.

Herman, C. P., & Polivy, J. (1980). Restrained eating. In A. J. Stunkard (ed.), *Obesity* (pp. 208–225). Philadelphia: Saunders.

Heymsfield, S. B., Greenberg, A. S., Fujioka, K., Dixon, R. M., Kushner, R., Hunt, T., et al. (1999). Recombinant leptin for weight loss in obese and lean adults: A randomized, controlled-dose escalation trial. *Journal of the American Medical Association*, 282, 1568–1575.

Institute of Medicine. (1995). *Weighing the options: Criteria for evaluating weight-management programs.* (p. 53). Washington, DC: National Academy Press.

Kahn, H. S., & Valdex, R. (2003). Metabolic risks identified by the combination of enlarged waist and elevated triacylglycerol concentration. *American Journal of Clinical Nutrition,* 78, 928–934.

Katz, D. L. (2003, November 19). The scarlet burger. *Wall Street Journal,* A-20.

Perusse, L., Chagnon, Y. C., Weisnagel, S. J., Rankinen, T., Snyder, E., Sands, J., & Bouchard, C. (2001). The human obesity gene map: The 2000 update. *Obesity Research,* 9, 135–169.

Polivy, J., & Herman, C. P. (2002). Experimental studies of dieting. In C. G. Fairburn & K. D. Brownell (eds.), *Eating disorders and obesity: A comprehensive handbook (2nd ed.)* (pp. 84–87). New York: Guilford.

Price, R. A. (2002). Genetics and common obesities: Background, current status, strategies and future prospects. In T. A. Wadden & A. J. Stunkard, (eds.), *Handbook of obesity treatment* (pp. 73–94). New York: Guilford.

Schmid, R. E. (2003, September 9). Pets putting on pounds, study says. *San Francisco Chronicle,* A-2.

Serdula, M. K., Mokdad, A. H., Williamson, D. F., Galuska, D. A., Mendlein, J. M., & Heath, G. W. (1999). Prevalence of attempting weight loss and strategies for controlling weight. *Journal of the American Medical Association,* 282, 1353–1358.

Sturm, R. (2003). Increases in clinically severe obesity in the United States, 1986–2000. *Archives of Internal Medicine,* 163, 2146–2148.

The truth about dieting. (2002, June). *Consumer Reports,* 26–31.

Urbszat, D., Herman, C. P., & Polivy, J. (2002). Eat, drink, and be merry, for tomorrow we diet: Effects of anticipated deprivation on food intake in restrained and unrestrained eaters. *Journal of Abnormal Psychology,* 111, 396–401.

Wadden, G. A., & Foster, G. D. (1992). Behavioral assessment and treatment of markedly obese patients. In T. A. Wadden & T. B. VanItallie (eds.), *Treatment of the seriously obese patient* (pp. 290–330). New York: Guilford.

Chapter 2

Attie, I., & Brooks-Gunn, J. (1989). The development of eating problems in adolescent girls: A longitudinal study. *Developmental Psychology*, 25, 70–79.

Barboza, D. (2003, August 3). If you pitch it, they will eat. *New York Times*. Retrieved August 3, 2003, from nytimes.com.

Berkowitz, R. I., & Stunkard, A. J. (2002). Development of childhood obesity. In T. A. Wadden & A. J. Stunkard (eds.), *Handbook of obesity treatment* (pp. 515–531). New York: Guilford.

Birch, L. L. (2002). Acquisition of food preferences and eating patterns in children. In C. G. Fairburn & K. D. Brownell (eds.), *Eating disorders and obesity: A comprehensive handbook (2nd ed.)* (pp. 75–79). New York: Guilford.

Birch, L. L., & Fisher, J. O. (1998). Development of eating behavior among children and adolescents. *Pediatrics*, 101 (Suppl.), 539–549.

Birch, L. L., & Fisher, J. O. (2000). Mothers' child-feeding practices influence daughters' eating and weight. *American Journal of Clinical Nutrition*, 71, 1054–1061.

Bowman, S. A., Gortmaker, S. L., Ebbeling, C. B., Pereira, M. A., & Ludwig, D. S. (2004). Effects of fast-food consumption on energy intake and diet quality among children in a national household survey. *Pediatrics*, 113, 112–118.

Brownell, K. D., & Horgen, K. B. (2004). *Food fight: The inside story of the food industry, America's obesity crisis, and what we can do about it*. Chicago: Contemporary Books.

Bruch, H. (1973). *Eating disorders: Obesity, anorexia nervosa, and the person within*. New York: Basic Books.

Byely, L., Archibald, A. B., Graber, J., & Brooks-Gunn, J. (2000). A prospective study of familial and social influences on girls' body image and dieting. *International Journal of Eating Disorders*, 26, 156–164.

Fisher, J. O., & Birch, L. L. (2001). Early experience with food and eating: Implications for the development of eating disorders. In J. K. Thompson & L. Smolak (eds.), *Body image, eating disorders, and obesity in youth: Assessment, prevention, and treatment* (pp. 23–39). Washington, DC: American Psychological Association.

Fomon, S. J., Filer, L. J., Thomas, L. N., Anderson, T. A., & Nelson, S. (1975). Influence of formula concentration on caloric intake and growth of normal infants. *Acta Pediatrca Scandinavica*, 64, 172–181.

Graber, J. A., Archibald, A. B., & Brooks-Gunn, J. (1999). The role of parents in the emergence, maintenance, and prevention of eating problems and disorders. In N. Piran, M. P. Levine, & C. Steiner-Adair (eds.), *Preventing eating disorders: A handbook of interventions and special challenges* (pp. 44–62). Philadelphia: Brunner/Mazel.

Johnson, S. L., & Birch, L. L. (1994). Parents' and children's adiposity and eating style. *Pediatrics*, 94, 653–661.

Lawrence, C., & Thelen, M. (1995). Body image, dieting, and self-concept: Their relation in African-American and Caucasian children. *Journal of Clinical Child Psychology*, 24, 41-48.

Mellin, L., Irwin, C., & Scully, S. (1992). Prevalence of disordered eating in girls: A survey of middle-class children. *Journal of the American Dietetic Association*, 92, 851–853.

Moore, L. L., Lombardi, D. A., White, M. J., Campbell, J. L., Oliveria, S. A., & Ellison, R. C. (1991). Influence of parents' physical activity levels on activity levels of young children. *The Journal of Pediatrics*, 118, 215–219.

Murnen, S., & Smolak, L. (2000). The experience of sexual harassment among grade-school students: Early socialization of female subordination? *Sex Roles*, 43, 1–17.

Ravussin, E. (2002). Energy expenditure and body weight. In C. G. Fairburn & K. D. Brownell (eds.), *Eating disorders and obesity: A comprehensive handbook (2nd ed.)* (pp. 55–61). New York: Guilford.

Richardson, B. L., & Rehr, E. (2001). *101 ways to help your daughter love her body*. New York: Quill.

Roberts, S. B., Savage, J., Coward, W. A., Chew, B., & Lucas, A. (1988). Energy expenditure and intake in infants born to lean and overweight mothers. *New England Journal of Medicine*, 318, 461–466.

Robinson, T. N. (1999). Reducing children's television to prevent obesity: A randomized controlled trial. *Journal of the American Medical Association*, 282, 1561–1567.

Ryan, J. (2002, May 28). Planet Twinkie weighs on us. *San Francisco Chronicle*, A-17.

Severson, K., & May, M. (2002, May 12). Growing up too fat. *San Francisco Chronicle*, A-1, A-14–A-15.

Smolak, L., & Levine, M. P. (2001). Body image in children. In J. K. Thompson & L. Smolak (eds.), *Body image, eating disorders and obesity in youth: Assessment, prevention, and treatment* (pp. 41–66). Washington, DC: American Psychological Association.

Smolak, L., Levine, M. P., & Schermer, F. (1999). Parental input and weight concerns among elementary school children. *International Journal of Eating Disorders, 25*, 263–272.

Stice, E. (2002). Sociocultural influences on body image and eating disturbance. In C. G. Fairburn & K. D. Brownell (eds.), *Eating disorders and obesity: A comprehensive handbook (2nd ed.)* (pp. 103–107). New York: Guilford.

Stice, E., Cameron, R. P., Killen, J. D., Hayward, C., & Taylor, C. B. (1999). Naturalistic weight-reduction efforts prospectively predict growth in relative weight and onset of obesity among female adolescents. *Journal of Consulting and Clinical Psychology, 67*, 967–974.

Taylor, W. C., Baranowski, T., & Sallis, J. F. (1994). Family determinants of childhood physical activity: A social-cognitive model. In R. K. Dishman (ed.), *Advances in exercise adherence* (pp. 319–342). Champaign, IL: Human Kinetics.

U.S. Department of Health and Human Services. (1987). National children and youth fitness study II. *Journal of Physical Education, Recreation, and Dance, 58*, 85–96.

Chapter 3

Cannon, W. B. (1929). *Bodily changes in pain, hunger, fear and rage (2nd ed.)*. New York: Appleton.

Drewnowski, A. (2002). Taste, taste preferences, and body weight. In C. G. Fairburn & K. D. Brownell (eds.), *Eating disorders and obesity: A comprehensive handbook (2nd ed.)* (pp. 50–54). New York: Guilford.

Eisenstein, J., & Greenberg, A. (2003). Ghrelin update: 2003. *Nutrition Review*, 61, 101–104.

Goode, E. (1998, November 10). Study links food desire to memory. *New York Times*, F-7.

Kischenbaum, D. S. (1996, November). Preventing weight gain during the holidays: The critical role of self-monitoring. Paper presented at the annual meeting of the Association for Advancement of Behavior Therapy, New York.

Logue, A. W. (1986). *The psychology of eating and drinking*. New York: Freeman.

Mellin, L. (1998). *The diet-free solution*. New York: Regan Books.

Pinel, J. P., Assanand, S., & Lehman, D. R. (2000). Hunger, eating, and ill health. *American Psychologist*, 55, 1105–1116.

Pliner, P., & Iuppa, G. (1978). Effects of increasing awareness on food consumption in obese and normal weight subjects. *Addictive Behaviors*, 3, 19–24.

Rodin, J. (1980). The externality theory today. In A. J. Stunkard (ed.), *Obesity* (pp. 226–239). Philadelphia: Saunders.

Rolls, B., & Barnett, R. A. (2000). *The volumetrics weight-control plan: Feel full on fewer calories!* New York: HarperCollins.

Ross, L. (1974). Effects of manipulating the salience of food upon consumption by obese and normal eaters. In S. Schachter & J. Rodin (eds.), *Obese humans and rats*. Washington: Erlbaum/Halsted.

Roth, G. (1984). *Breaking free from compulsive eating*. New York: Signet.

Schachter, S. (1968). Obesity and eating. *Science*, 161, 751–756.

Schachter, S., & Gross, L. P. (1968). Manipulated time and eating behavior. *Journal of Personality and Social Psychology*, 10, 98–106.

van Strien, T., Frijters, J. E. R., Bergers, G. P. A., & Defares, P. B. (1986). The Dutch Eating Behavior Questionnaire (DEBQ) for assessment of restrained, emotional, and external eating behavior. *International Journal of Eating Disorders*, 5, 295–315.

Wardle, J. (1987). Eating style: A validation study of the Dutch Eating Behaviour Questionnaire in normal subjects and women with eating disorders. *Journal of Psychosomatic Research*, 31, 161–169.

Chapter 4

Agras, W. S., & Telch, C. F. (1998). The effects of caloric deprivation and negative affect on binge eating in obese binge-eating disordered women. *Behavior Therapy, 29,* 491–503.

Alberti, R. E., & Emmons, M. L. (1978). *Your perfect right: A guide to assertive behavior.* San Luis Obispo, CA: Impact.

Beck, A. T. (1976). *Cognitive therapy and the emotional disorders.* New York: New American Library.

Burns, D. D. (1990). *The feeling good handbook.* New York: Plume.

Carlson, J. G., & Hatfield, E. (1992). *Psychology of emotion.* Fort Worth, TX: Harcourt Brace.

Dallman, M. F., Pecoraro, N., Akana, S. F., la Fleur, S. E., Gomez, F., Houshyar, H., et al. (2003, September 30). Chronic stress and obesity: A new view of "comfort food." *PNAS, 100,* 11696–11701.

Ellis, A., & Harper, R. A. (1975). *A new guide to rational living.* N. Hollywood: Wilshire Books.

Ganley, R. M. (1989). Emotion and eating in obesity: A review of the literature. *International Journal of Eating Disorders, 8,* 34–361.

Grilo, C. M. (2002). Binge eating disorder. In C. G. Fairburn & K. D. Brownell (eds.), *Eating disorders and obesity: A comprehensive handbook (2nd ed.)* (pp. 178–182). New York: Guilford.

Lazarus, R. S. (1991). *Emotion & adaptation.* New York: Oxford.

Martinsen, E. W., & Stephens, T. (1994). Exercise and mental health in clinical and free-living populations. In R. K. Dishman (ed.), *Advances in exercise adherence* (pp. 55–72). Champaign, IL: Human Kinetics.

McGowan, K. (2003, September/October). The science of scrumptious. *Psychology Today,* 54–56, 58, 60.

Polivy, J., & Herman, C. P. (2002) *Experimental studies of dieting.* In C. G. Fairburn & K. D. Brownell (eds.), *Eating disorders and obesity: A comprehensive handbook (2nd ed.)* (pp. 84–87). New York: Guilford.

Sanftner, J. L., & Crowther, J. H. (1998). Variability in self-esteem, moods, shame, and guilt in women who binge. *International Journal of Eating Disorders, 23,* 391–397.

Schafer, W. (1987). *Stress management for wellness.* New York: Holt.

Springen, K. (2002, November 4). Taking a bite out of Hershey's. *Newsweek*, 12.

van Strien, T., Frijters, J. E. R., Bergers, G. P. A., & Defares, P. B. (1986). The Dutch Eating Behavior Questionnaire (DEBQ) for assessment of restrained, emotional, and external eating behavior. *International Journal of Eating Disorders*, 5, 295–315.

Tavris, C. (1989). *Anger: The misunderstood emotion*. New York: Touchstone.

Wardle, J. (1987). Eating style: A validation study of the Dutch Eating Behaviour Questionnaire in normal subjects and women with eating disorders. *Journal of Psychosomatic Research*, 31, 161–169.

Wilson, G. T. (2002). *Eating disorders and addictive disorders*. In C. G. Fairburn & K. D. Brownell (eds.), *Eating disorders and obesity: A comprehensive handbook (2nd ed.)* (pp. 199–203). New York: Guilford.

Wilson, G. T. (1994). Food: Can it become addictive? *Weight Control Digest*, 4, 313, 316–318.

Chapter 5

Abramson, E. (1999). *To have and to hold: How to take off the weight when marriage puts on the pounds*. New York: Kensington.

Baker, R. C., & Kirschenbaum, D. S. (1993). Self-monitoring may be necessary for successful weight control. *Behavior Therapy*, 24, 377–394.

Baumeister, R. F. (2003). Ego depletion and self-regulation failure: A resource model of self control. *Alcoholism: Clinical & Experimental Research*, 27, 281–284.

Bennett, W., & Gurin, J. (1982). *The dieter's dilemma: Eating less and weighing more*. New York: Basic Books.

Blackburn, G. L. (2002). Weight loss and risk factors. In C. G. Fairburn & K. D. Brownell (eds.), *Eating disorders and obesity: A comprehensive handbook (2nd ed.)* (pp. 484–489). New York: Guilford.

Boutelle, K. N., & Kirschenbaum, D. S. (1998). Further support for consistent self-monitoring as a vital component of successful weight control. *Obesity Research*, 6, 219–224.

Brasher, P. (2000, February 25). Diet heavyweights clash on best way to slim down. *San Francisco Chronicle*, A-9.

Brownell, K. D., & Wadden, T. A. (1992). Etiology and treatment of obesity: Understanding a serious, prevalent, and refractory disorder. *Journal of Consulting and Clinical Psychology, 60*, 505–517.

Cooper, Z., Fairburn, C. G., & Hawker, D. M. (2003). *Cognitive-behavioral treatment of obesity: A clinician's guide*. New York: Guilford.

D'Adamo, P. (1997). *Eat right 4 your type*. New York: Putnam.

Dansinger, M. (2003, November). One-year effectiveness of Atkins, Ornish, Weight Watchers and Zone diets in decreasing body weight and heart disease risk. Paper presented at the meeting of the American Heart Association, Orlando, FL.

Doell, S. R., & Hawkins, R. C. (1982). Pleasures and pounds: An exploratory study. *Addictive Behaviors, 7*, 65–69.

Foster, G. D., Wadden, T. A., Vogt, R. A., & Brewer, G. (1997). What is a reasonable weight loss? Patients' expectations and evaluations of obesity treatment outcomes. *Journal of Consulting and Clinical Psychology, 65*, 79–85.

Greene, P., Willett, W., Devecis, J., & Skaf, A. (2003). Pilot 12-week feeding weight-loss comparison: Low-fat vs. low-carbohydrate (ketogenic) diets. *Obesity Research, 11*, A-23.

Health Magazine. (2000). *The diet advisor: The complete guide to choosing the right diet for you*. Alexandria, VA: Time-Life.

Heber, D. (2002). Meal replacements in the treatment of obesity. In C. G. Fairburn & K. D. Brownell (eds.), *Eating disorders and obesity: A comprehensive handbook (2nd ed.)* (pp. 529–533). New York: Guilford.

Hill, A. J. (2002). Prevalence and demographics of dieting. In C. G. Fairburn & K. D. Brownell (eds.), *Eating disorders and obesity: A comprehensive handbook (2nd ed.)* (pp. 80–83). New York: Guilford.

Hill, A. J., Weaver, C. F., & Blundell, J. E. (1991). Food craving, dietary restraint and mood. *Appetite, 17*, 187–197.

Kirschenbaum, D. S. (1996, November). Preventing weight gain during the holidays: The critical role of self-monitoring. Paper presented at the annual meeting of the Association for Advancement of Behavior Therapy, New York.

Kleinfield, N. R. (2004, February 11). Weight-loss guru Atkins weighed 258 at death. *San Francisco Chronicle*, A-3.

Kolata, G. (2000, October 18). Days off are not allowed, weight experts argue. *New York Times*. Retrieved December 24, 2000, from nytimes.com.

Kolata, G. (2004, February 22). Vegetarians vs. Atkins: Diet wars are almost religious. *New York Times*. Retrieved February 22, 2004, from nytimes.com.

Mazel, J. (1982). *The Beverly Hills diet*. New York: Berkley.

McCord, H. (2001). *The peanut butter diet*. New York: St. Martin's.

McGuire, M. T., Wing, R. R., & Hill, J. O. (1999). The prevalence of weight loss maintenance among American adults. *International Journal of Obesity*, 23, 1314–1319.

Melanson, K., & Dwyer, J. (2002). Popular diets for treatment of overweight and obesity. In T. A. Wadden & A. J. Stunkard (eds.), *Handbook of obesity treatment* (pp. 249–282). New York: Guilford.

Polivy, J., & Herman, C. P. (2002). If at first you don't succeed: False hopes of self-change. *American Psychologist*, 677–689.

Puhn, A. (1996). *The 5-day miracle diet*. New York: Ballentine Books.

Rating the diets. (1993, June). *Consumer Reports*, pp. 353–357.

Raynor, H. A., & Epstein, L. H. (2001). Dietary variety, energy regulation, and obesity. *Psychological Bulletin*, 127, 325–341.

Ross, E. (2004, May 29). Weight watchers does well in study. *San Francisco Chronicle*, A-6.

Squires, S. (2001, January 10). Only high-carb, modest-fat diets work for long. *San Francisco Chronicle*, A-2.

Stacey, M. (1994). *Consumed: Why Americans love, hate, and fear food*. New York: Touchstone.

Stern, L., Iqbal, N., Seshadri, P., Chicano, K. L., Daily, D. A., McGrory, J., et al. (2004). The effects of low-carbohydrate versus conventional weight loss diets in severely obese adults: One-year follow-up of a randomized trial. *Annals of Internal Medicine*, 140, 778–785.

Stunkard, A. J., & McLaren-Hume, M. (1959). The results of treatment of obesity. *Archives of Internal Medicine*, 103, 79–85.

Wadden, T. A., & Phelan, S. (2002). Behavioral assessment of the obese patient. In T. A. Wadden & A. J. Stundard (eds.), *Handbook of obesity treatment* (pp. 186–226). New York: Guilford.

Wells, M. (2004, April 26). Life after Atkins. *Forbes*, 174, 119.

Wilson, G. T. (1996). Behavioral and psychological predictors of treatment outcome in obesity. In D. B. Allison & F. X. Pi-Sunyer (eds.), *Obesity treatment* (pp. 183–190). New York: Plenum.

Yancy, W. S., Olsen, M. K., Guyton, J. R., Bakst, R. P., & Westman, E. C. (2004). A low-carbohydrate, ketogenic diet versus a low-fat diet to treat obesity and hyperlipidemia: A randomized, controlled trial. *Annals of Internal Medicine*, 140, 769–777.

Zernike, K. (2004, December 26). Fatkins. *New York Times*. Retrieved December 26, 2004, from nytimes.com.

Zernike, K., & Burros, M. (2004, February 19). Low-carb boom isn't just for dieters anymore. *New York Times*. Retrieved February 19, 2004, from nytimes.com.

Chapter 6

Ballard, C. (2003, August 31). That stomach is going to make you money someday. *New York Times*. Retrieved September 6, 2003, from nytimes.com.

Cho, S., Dietrich, M., Brown, C. J. P., Clark, C. A., & Block, G. (2003). The effect of breakfast type on total daily energy intake and body-mass index: Results from the Third National Health and Nutrition Examination Survey (NHANES III). *Journal of the American College of Nutrition*, 22, 296–302.

Gibson, E. L., & Desmond, E. (1999). Chocolate craving and hunger state: Implications for the acquisition and expression of appetite and food choice. *Appetite*, 32, 219–240.

Jebb, S. A. (2002). Energy intake and body weight. In C. G. Fairburn & K. D. Brownell (eds.), *Eating disorders and obesity: A comprehensive handbook (2nd ed.)* (pp. 37–42), New York: Guilford.

Katz, D. L. (2002). *The way to eat: A six-step path to lifelong weight control.* Naperville, IL: Sourcebooks.

Mellin, L. (1998). *The diet-free solution: 6 winning ways to permanent weight loss.* New York: Regan Books.

Nielsen, S. J., & Popkin, B. M. (2003, January 22). Patterns and trends in food portion sizes, 1977–1998. *Journal of the American Medical Association*, 289, 450–453.

Pereira, M. A., Kartashov, A. I., Van Horn, L., Slattery, M., Jacobs, D. R., & Ludwig, D. S. (2003, March). Eating breakfast may reduce the risk of obesity, diabetes, heart disease. Paper presented at the American Heart Association's Annual Conference on Cardiovascular Disease Epidemiology and Prevention, Miami, FL.

Polivy, J., & Herman, C. P. (1976). The effects of alcohol on eating behavior: Disinhibition or sedation? *Addictive Behaviors*, 1, 121–125.

Polivy, J., & Herman, C. P. (1976). Effects of alcohol on eating behavior: Influences of mood and perceived intoxication. *Journal of Abnormal Psychology*, 85, 601–606.

Pollan, J. (2003, January 12). Fat land: Supersizing America. *New York Times*. Retrieved January 12, 2003, from nytimes.com.

Prochaska, J. O., DiClemente, C. C., & Norcross, J. C. (1992). In search of how people change. *American Psychologist*, 47, 1102–1104.

Raynor, H. A., & Epstein, L. H. (2001). Dietary variety, energy regulation, and obesity. *Psychological Bulletin*, 127, 325–341.

Rolls, B. (2003, October). Salad and satiety: Do portion size and energy density of a first course affect lunch intake? Paper presented at the annual meeting of the North American Society for the Study of Obesity, Fort Lauderdale, FL.

Rolls, B., & Barnett, R. A. (2003). *The volumetrics weight-control plan*. New York: HarperTorch.

Smiciklas-Wright, H., Mitchell, D. C., Mickle, S. J., Goldman, J. O., & Cook, A. (2003). Foods commonly eaten in the United States, 1989–1991 and 1994–1998: Are portion sizes changing? *Journal of the American Dietetic Association*, 103, 41–47.

Smith, C. F., Williamson, D. A., Womble, L. G., Johnson, J., & Burke, L. E. (2000). Psychometric development of a multidimensional measure of weight-related attitudes and behaviors. *Eating and Weight Disorders*, 5, 73–86.

Spiegel, T. A., Wadden, T. A., & Foster, G. D. (1991). Objective measurement of eating rate during behavioral treatment of obesity. *Behavior Therapy*, 22, 61–67.

Wansink, B. (2004). Environmental factors that increase the food intake and consumption volume of unknowing consumers. *Annual Review of Nutrition*, 24, 455–479.

Wansink, B., & Seabum, P. (2001). At the movies: How external cues and perceived taste impact consumption volume. *Food Quality and Preference*, 12, 69–74.

Wing, R. R., & Jeffery, R. W. (1999). Benefits of recruiting participants with friends and increasing social support for weight loss and maintenance. *Journal of Consulting and Clinical Psychology*, 67, 132–138.

Young, L. R., & Nestle, M. (2002). The contribution of expanding portion sizes to the U.S. obesity epidemic. *American Journal of Public Health*, 92, 246–249.

Chapter 7

Associated Press. (2004, August 3). Halle Berry decries nation's obsession with beauty, youthfulness. *San Francisco Chronicle*, E-4.

Brownell, K. D. (1991). Dieting and the search for the perfect body: Where physiology and culture collide. *Behavior Therapy*, 22, 1–12.

Cash, T. F., Counts, B., & Huffine, C. E. (1990). Current and vestigial effects of overweight among women: Fear of fat, attitudinal body image, and eating behaviors. *Journal of Psychopathology*, 12, 157–167.

Collins, J. K. (1987). Methodology for the objective measurement of body image. *International Journal of Eating Disorders*, 6, 393–399.

Collins, J. K., Beumont, P. J. V., Touyz, S. W., Krass, J., Thompson, P., & Philips, T. (1987). Variability in body shape perception in anorexic, bulimic, obese, and control subjects. *International Journal of Eating Disorders*, 6, 393–399.

Duenwald, M. (2003, June 22). One size definitely does not fit all. *New York Times*. Retrieved June 22, 2003, from nytimes.com.

Fisher, S. (1986). *Development and structure of the body image*. Hillsdale, NJ: Lawrence Erlbaum.

Freedman, R. (1986). *Beauty bound*. Lexington, MA: Lexington.

Garner, D. M. (1997). The 1997 body image survey results. *Psychology Today*, 30(1), 30–44, 75–84.

Glassner, B. (1988). *Bodies: Why we look the way we do and how we feel about it*. New York: Putnam.

Hangen, J. D., & Cash, T. F. (1991, November). Body-image attitudes and sexual functioning in a college population. Paper presented at the annual meeting of the Association for Advancement of Behavior Therapy, New York.

Katzmarzyk, P., & Davis, C. (2001). Thinness and body shape of *Playboy* centerfolds from 1978 to 1998. *International Journal of Obesity*, 25, 590–592.

King, T. K., & Clark, M. M. (2002, November). Improving clinical outcomes in obesity treatment. Paper presented at the annual meeting of the Association for Advancement of Behavior Therapy, Reno, NV.

McCarthy, M. (1990). The thin ideal, depression and eating disorders in women. *Behaviour Research and Therapy*, 28, 205–215.

Miller, T. B., Coffman, J. G., & Linke, R. A. (1980). Survey on body image, weight, and diet of college students. *Journal of the American Dietetic Association*, 77, 561–566.

Naik, G. (2004, December 29). New obesity book in Arab countries has old ancestry. *Wall Street Journal*, A1-A2.

Puhl, R., & Brownell, K. D. (2002). Stigma, discrimination, and obesity. In C. G. Fairburn & K. D. Brownell (eds.), *Eating disorders and obesity: A comprehensive handbook (2nd ed.)* (pp. 108–112). New York: Guilford.

Rodin, J., Silberstein, L. R., & Striegel-Moore, R. H. (1985). Women and weight: A normative discontent. In T. B. Sondereggar (ed.), *Nebraska symposium on motivation: Psychology and gender*. Lincoln, NE: University of Nebraska Press.

Rosen, J. C., Orosan, P., & Reiter, J. (1995). Cognitive behavior therapy for negative body image in obese women. *Behavior Therapy*, 26, 25–42.

Sarwer, D. B., & Thompson, J. K. (2002). Obesity and body image disturbance. In T. A. Wadden & A. J. Stunkard (eds.), *Handbook of obesity treatment* (pp. 447–464). New York: Guilford.

Sarwer, D. B., Wadden, T. A., & Foster, G. (1998). Assessment of body image dissatisfaction in obese women: Specificity, severity and clinical significance. *Journal of Consulting and Clinical Psychology*, 66, 651–654.

Schindehette, S. (1999, October 16). Going to extremes. *People*, 110–114, 116, 119–120.

Siever, M. D. (1994). Sexual orientation and gender as factors in socioculturally acquired vulnerability to body dissatisfaction and eating disorders. *Journal of Consulting and Clinical Psychology*, 62, 252–260.

Wilfley, D. E., Schreiber, G. B., Pike, K. M., Striegel-Moore, R. H., Wright, D. J., & Rodin, J. (1996). Eating disturbance and body image: A comparison of a community sample of adult black and white women. *International Journal of Eating Disorders*, 20, 377–387.

Chapter 8

Allon, N. (1982). The stigma of overweight in everyday life. In B. B. Wolman (ed.), *Psychological aspects of obesity: A handbook* (pp. 130–174). New York: Van Nostrand Reinhold.

American Psychiatric Association. (2000). *Diagnostic and statistical manual of mental disorders (4th ed., text revision)*. Washington: American Psychiatric Association.

Cooper, Z., Fairburn, C. G., & Hawker, D. M. (2003). *Cognitive-behavioral treatment of obesity: A clinician's guide*. New York: Guilford.

Gordon, R. A. (2000). *Eating disorders: Anatomy of a social epidemic (2nd ed.)*. Oxford: Blackwell.

Leon, G. R., & Roth, L. (1977). Obesity: Psychological causes, correlations, and speculations. *Psychological Bulletin*, 84, 117–139.

Wadden, T. A., & Stunkard, A. J. (1987). Psychopathology and obesity. *Annals of the New York Academy of Sciences*, 499, 55–65.

Chapter 9

Allen, M. (2002, August 23). Bush says running clears his mind. *San Francisco Chronicle*, A-3.

American Heart Association. (1997). *Fitting in fitness*. New York: Times Books.

Andersen, R. (1994). Conveniences: The physical activity component. *Weight Control Digest*, 4, 369–370.

Barnes, P. M., & Schoenborn, C. A. (2003, May 14). Physical activity among adults: United States, 2000. Retrieved November 3, 2004, from cdc.gov/nchs/data/ad/ad333.pdf.

Bassett, D. R., Schneider, P. L., & Huntington, G. (2004). Physical activity in an Old Order Amish community. *Medicine & Science in Sports & Exercise*, 36, 79–85.

Blair, S. N., & Leermakers, E. A. (2002). Exercise and weight management. In T. A. Wadden & A. J. Stunkard (eds.), *Handbook of obesity treatment* (pp. 283–300). New York: Guilford.

Blair, S. N., Wells, C. L., Weathers, R. D., & Paffenbarger, R. S. (1994). Chronic disease: The physical activity dose-response controversy. In R. K. Dishman (ed.), *Advances in exercise adherence* (pp. 31–54). Champaign, IL: Human Kinetics.

Blundell, J. E. (2002). A psychobiological system approach to appetite and weight control. In C. G. Fairburn & K. D. Brownell (eds.), *Eating disorders and obesity: A comprehensive handbook (2nd ed.)* (pp. 43–49). New York: Guilford.

Brody, J. E. (1995, February 8). Personal health: How to experience the benefits of regular exercise without working up a sweat. *New York Times*, B-5.

Doyne, E. J., Ossip-Klein, D. J., Bowman, E. D., Osborn, K. M., McDougall-Wilson, I. B., & Neimeyer, R. A. (1987). Running versus weight lifting in the treatment of depression. *Journal of Consulting and Clinical Psychology*, 55, 748–754.

Greene, B., & Winfrey, O. (1996). *Make the connection: Ten steps to a better body and a better life*. New York: Hyperion.

Haney, D. Q. (2004, March 30). Exercise seems to help fight breast cancer. *San Francisco Chronicle*, A-4.

Kalb, C. (2003, January 20). Health for life: Get up and get moving. *Newsweek*, 59–60, 62–64.

Kayman, S., Bruvold, W., & Stern, J. S. (1990). Maintenance and relapse after weight loss in women: Behavioral aspects. *American Journal of Clinical Nutrition*, 52, 800–807.

Levine, J. A., Lanningham-Foster, L. M., McCrady, S. K., Krizan, A. C., Olson, L. R., Kane, P. H., Jensen, M. D., & Clark, M. M. (2005, January 28). Interindividual variation in posture allocation: Possible role in human obesity. *Science*, 37, 584–586.

Manson, J. E., Skerrett, P. J., & Willet, W. C. (2002). Epidemiology of health risks associated with obesity. In C. G. Fairburn & K. D. Brownell (eds.), *Eating disorders and obesity: A comprehensive handbook (2nd ed.)* (pp. 422–428). New York: Guilford.

Martinsen, E. W., & Stephens, T. (1994). Exercise and mental health in clinical and free-living populations. In R. K. Dishman (ed.), *Advances in exercise adherence* (pp. 55–72). Champaign, IL: Human Kinetics.

McAuley, E., Poag, K., Gleason, A., & Wraith, S. (1990). Attrition from exercise programs: Attributional and affective perspectives. *Journal of Social Behavior and Personality*, 5, 591–602.

McGuire, M. T., Wing, R. R., Klem, M. L., Seagle, H. M., & Hill, J. O. (1998). Long-term maintenance of weight loss: Do people who lose weight through various weight loss methods use different behaviors to maintain their weight? *International Journal of Obesity*, 22, 572–577.

Plante, T. G. (1992, September). The psychological benefits of exercise: How and why does exercise make us feel so good? *Weight Control Digest*, 2, 194–195.

Ross, R., Janssen, I., Dawson, J., Kungl, A., Kuk, J. L., Wong, S. L., et al. (2004). Exercise-induced reduction in obesity and insulin resistance in women: A randomized controlled trial. *Obesity Research*, 12, 789–798.

Saris, W. H. (2002). Metabolic effects of exercise in overweight individuals. In C. G. Fairburn & K. D. Brownell (eds.), *Eating disorders and obesity: A comprehensive handbook (2nd ed.)* (pp. 495–499). New York: Guilford.

Shapiro, S., Weinblatt, E., Frank, C. W., & Sager, R. V. (1965). The H.I.P. study of incidence and prognosis of coronary heart disease. *Journal of Chronic Diseases*, 18, 527–558.

Thayer, R. E. (2001). *Calm energy.* New York: Oxford.

The truth about dieting. (2002, June). *Consumer Reports*, 26–31.

Wilfley, D. E., & Brownell, K. D. (1994). Physical activity and diet in weight loss. In R. K. Dishman (ed.), *Advances in exercise adherence* (pp.361–393). Champaign, IL: Human Kinetics.

Chapter 10

Buchowski, M. S., & Sun, M. (1996). Energy expenditure, television viewing and obesity. *International Journal of Obesity*, 20, 236–244.

Cooper, Z., Fairburn, C. G., & Hawker, D. M. (2003). *Cognitive-behavioral treatment of obesity: A clinician's guide.* New York: Guilford.

Dishman, R. K. (1982). Compliance/adherence in health-related exercise. *Health Psychology*, 1, 237–267.

Epstein, L. H., Wing, R. R., Koeske, R., & Valoski, A. (1985). A comparison of lifestyle exercise, aerobic exercise, and calisthenics on weight loss in obese children. *Behavior Therapy*, 16, 345–356.

Hu, F. B., Li, T. Y., Colditz, G. A., Willett, W. C., & Manson, J. E. (2003, April 9). Television watching and other sedentary behaviors in relation to risk of obesity and type 2 diabetes mellitus in women. *Journal of the American Medical Association*, 289, 1785–1791.

Kendzierski, D. (1990). Exercise self-schemata: Cognitive and behavioral correlates. *Health Psychology*, 9, 69–82.

Klem, M. L. (1996). Lessons from successful losers. *Weight Control Digest*, 6, 553, 561–562.

Neergaard, L. (2003, April 13). U.S. rethinking the rewards of luxury. *San Francisco Chronicle*, C-2.

Perri, M. G., Martin, A. D., Leermakers, E. A., Sears, S. F., & Notelovitz, M. (1997). Effects of group- versus home-based exercise in the treatment of obesity. *Journal of Consulting and Clinical Psychology*, 65, 278–285.

Prochaska, J. O., & Marcus, B. H. (1994). The transtheoretical model: Applications to exercise. In R. K. Dishman (ed.), *Advances in exercise adherence* (pp. 161–180). Champaign, IL: Human Kinetics.

Chapter 11

American Psychiatric Association. (2000). *Diagnostic and statistical manual of mental disorders (4th ed, text revision)*. Washington, DC: American Psychiatric Association.

Arria, S., & Welch, L. (2003, September 7). Balancing act. *New York Times*. Retrieved September 7, 2003, from nytimes.com.

Asimov, N. (2003, November 12). 1 million kids fail fitness test. *San Francisco Chronicle*, A-15, A-22.

Birch, L. L. (2002). Acquisition of food preferences and eating patterns in children. In C. G. Fairburn & K. D. Brownell (eds.), *Eating disorders and obesity: A comprehensive handbook (2nd ed.)* (pp. 75–79). New York: Guilford.

Dietz, W. H. (2002). Medical consequence of obesity in children and adolescents. In C. G. Fairburn & K. D. Brownell (eds.), *Eating disorders and obesity: A comprehensive handbook (2nd ed.)* (pp. 473–476). New York: Guilford.

Fisher, J. O., & Birch, L. L. (2001). Early experience with food and eating: Implications for the development of eating disorders. In J. K. Thompson & L. Smolak (eds.), *Body image, eating disorders, and obesity in youth: Assessment, prevention, and treatment* (pp. 23–39). Washington, DC: American Psychological Association.

Freedman, D. S., Kahn, L. K., Dietz, W. H., Srinivasan, S. R., & Berenson, G. S. (2001). Relationship of childhood obesity to coronary heart disease risk factors in adulthood: The Bogalusa Heart Study. *Pediatrics*, 103, 1175–1182.

Goldfield, G. S., Raynor, H. A., & Epstein, L. H. (2002). Treatment of pediatric obesity. In T. A. Wadden & A. J. Stunkard (eds.), *Handbook of obesity treatment* (pp. 532–555). New York: Guilford.

Goode, E. (2003, June 22). How to talk to teenage girls about weight? Very carefully. *New York Times*. Retrieved June 22, 2003, from nytimes.com.

Haney, D. Q. (2003, April 18). Inactivity, overeating mean more kids have adult diabetes. *San Francisco Chronicle*, D-3.

Hirsch, J. M. (2003, December 7). Healthy meals seldom show up at many schools. *San Francisco Chronicle*, A-11.

Killen, J. D., Taylor, C. B., Hayward, C., Haydel, K. F., Wilson, D. M., Hammer, L., et al. (1996). Weight concerns influence the development of eating disorders: A 4-year prospective study. *Journal of Consulting and Clinical Psychology*, 64, 936–940.

Maynard, L. M., Galuska, D. A., Blanck, H. M., & Serdula, M. K. (2003). Maternal perceptions of weight status of children. *Pediatrics*, 111, 1226–1231.

Moore, L. L., Lombardi, D. A., White, M. J., Campbell, J. L., Oliveria, S. A., & Ellison, R. C. (1991). Influence of parents' physical activity levels on activity levels of young children. *The Journal of Pediatrics*, 118, 215–219.

Muntner, P., Jiang, H., Cutler, J. A., Wildman, R. P., & Whelton, P. K. (2004, May 5). Trends in blood pressure among children and adolescents. *Journal of the American Medical Association*, 291, 2107–2113.

Nagourney, E. (2002, July 30). Regimens: When P.E. class includes exercise. *New York Times*. Retrieved July 30, 2002, from nytimes.com.

Neumark-Sztainer, D., Story, M., & Fabisch, L. (1988). Perceived stigmatization among overweight African American and Caucasian adolescent girls. *Journal of Adolescent Health*, 23, 264–270.

O'Connor, A., & Grady, D. (2003, December 16). FDA moves to let drug treat obese teenagers. *New York Times*. Retrieved December 16, 2003, from nytimes.com.

Piscatella, J. C. (1997). *Fat-proof your child*. New York: Workman Publishing.

Rorty, M., Yager, J., Rossotto, E., & Buckwalter, G. (2000). Parental intrusiveness in adolescence recalled by women with a history of bulimia nervosa and comparison women. *International Journal of Eating Disorders*, 28, 202–208.

Schwartz, M. B., Chen, E. Y., & Brownell, K. B. (2003). Trick, treat, or toy: Children are just as likely to choose toys as candy on Halloween. *Journal of Nutrition Education and Behavior*, 35, 207–209.

Severson, K. (2002, December 29). Epidemic of child obesity puzzles experts. *San Francisco Chronicle*, A-3.

Shunk, J. A., & Birch, L. L. (2004). Girls at risk for overweight at age 5 are at risk for dietary restraint, disinhibited overeating, weight concerns, and greater weight gain from 5 to 9 years. *Journal of the American Dietetic Association*, 104, 1120–1126.

Staffieri, J. R. (1967). A study of social stereotype of body image in children. *Journal of Personality and Social Psychology*, 7, 101–104.

Stice, E., Cameron, R. P., Killen, J. D., Hayward, C., & Taylor, C. B. (1999). Naturalistic weight-reduction efforts prospectively predict growth in relative weight and onset of obesity among female adolescents. *Journal of Consulting and Clinical Psychology*, 67, 967–974.

Stice, E., Mazotti, L., Weiberl, D., & Agras, W. S. (2000). Dissonance prevention program decreases thin-ideal internalization, body dissatisfaction, dieting, negative affect, and bulimic symptoms: A preliminary experiment. *International Journal of Eating Disorders*, 27, 206–217.

Stradmeijer, M., Bosch, J., Koops, W., & Seidell, J. (2000). Family functioning and psychosocial adjustment in overweight youngsters. *International Journal of Eating Disorders*, 27, 110–114.

Troiano, R. P., Flegal, K. M., Kuczmarski, R. J., Campbell, S. M., & Johnson, C. L. (1995). Overweight prevalence and trends for children and adolescents. *Archives of Pediatrics and Adolescent Medicine*, 149, 1085–1091.

Zimmerman, J., & Reavill, G. (1998). *Raising our athletic daughters: How sports can build self-esteem and save girls' lives*. New York: Doubleday.

Chapter 12

Abate, T. (2003, February 22). Surgeon general targets obesity. *San Francisco Chronicle*, A-5.

Barboza, D. (2003, July 10). Food makers trim fat as lawsuits and regulations loom. *New York Times*. Retrieved July 10, 2003, from nytimes.com.

Barboza, D. (2003, August 3). If you pitch it, they will eat. *New York Times*. Retrieved August 3, 2003, from nytimes.com.

Barclay, L. (2004, May 19). Obesity and the built environment: A newsmaker interview with James O. Hill, Ph.D. *Medscape.com*. Retrieved May 27, 2004, from medscape.com/viewarticle/478315.

Brownell, K. D. (1994, December 15). Get slim with higher taxes. *New York Times*, A-23.

Brownell, K. D. (2002). The environment and obesity. In C. G. Fairburn & K. D. Brownell (eds.), *Eating disorders and obesity: A comprehensive handbook (2nd ed.)* (pp. 433–438). New York: Guilford.

Brownell, K. D., & Horgen, K. B. (2004). *Food fight: The inside story of the food industry, America's obesity crisis, and what we can do about it*. Chicago: Contemporary Books.

Brownell, K. D., Stunkard, A. J., & Albaum, J. M. (1980). Evaluation and modification of exercise patterns in the natural environment. *American Journal of Psychiatry*, 137, 1540–1545.

Colliver, V. (2004, May 23). One business. *San Francisco Chronicle*, A-16.

DeFao, J. (2004, August 1). 2 youths work to cure city of fast-food habit. *San Francisco Chronicle*, B-2.

Durbin, D. A. (2004, August 11). Seat belt use cited in decline in highway deaths. *San Francisco Chronicle*, A-7.

Editorial. (2004, March 24). The path to a healthier America. *New York Times*. Retrieved March 24, 2004, from nytimes.com.

Ellin, A. (2004, August 10). Shed some pounds (and get a bonus). *New York Times*. Retrieved August 10, 2004, from nytimes.com.

Frank, L. D., Andresen, M. A., & Schmid, T. L. (2004). Obesity relationships with community design, physical activity, and time spent in cars. *American Journal of Preventive Medicine*, 27, 87–96.

French, S. A., Jeffery, R. W., Story, M., Breitlow, K. K., Baxter, J. S., Hannan, P., & Snyder, M. P. (2001). Pricing and promotion effects on low fat vending snack purchases: The CHIPS study. *American Journal of Public Health*, 91, 112–117.

Holland, J. (2004, March 7). "Cheeseburger bill" expected to pass. *San Francisco Chronicle*, A-7.

Ives, N. (2004, July 21). Obesity and National Geographic. *New York Times*. Retrieved July 21, 2004, from nytimes.com.

Johnson, L. A. (2003, September 2). More businesses tackling obesity. *San Francisco Chronicle*, B-1, B-4.

Knight, H. (2004, May 23). One nutritionist. *San Francisco Chronicle*, A-17.

Krisberg, K. (2004, June 17). Unhealthy foods bulk of school vending machine choices. *Medscape.com*. Retrieved June 23, 2004, from medscape.com/viewarticle/479970.

Lucas, G. (2004, May 23). One quest. *San Francisco Chronicle*, A-17.

Markel, H. (2004, March 8). Soft drinks, schools, and obesity. Retrieved March 17, 2004, from medscape.com/viewarticle/470344.

National Cancer Institute. (1993). *The impact of cigarette excise taxes on smoking among children and adults: Summary report of a National Cancer Institute expert panel*. Bethesda, MD: National Cancer Institute, Division of Cancer Prevention and Control, Cancer Control Science Program.

Pollan, M. (2003, October 12). The (agri)cultural contradictions of obesity. *New York Times*. Retrieved October 12, 2003, from nytimes.com.

Rothstein, R. (2002, August 21). School's chosen cure for money ills: A sugar pill. *New York Times*. Retrieved August 21, 2002, from nytimes.com.

Santora, M. (2004, June 2). Taking candy from pupils? School vending bill says yes. *New York Times*. Retrieved June 2, 2004, from nytimes.com.

Schlosser, E. (2002). *Fast food nation: The dark side of the all-American meal*. New York: Harper Perennial.

Smolak, L. (1999). Elementary school curricula for the primary prevention of eating problems. In N. Piran, M. P. Levine, & C. Steiner-Adair (eds.), *Preventing eating disorders: A handbook of interventions and special challenges* (pp. 85–104). New York: Brunner/Mazel.

Tahmincioglu, E. (2004, May 23). Paths to better health (on the boss's nickel). *New York Times*. Retrieved May 23, 2004, from nytimes.com.

Tapper, K., Horne, P. J., & Lowe, C. F. (2003). The food dudes to the rescue! *The Psychologist*, 16, 18–21.

Tyre, P. (2002, August 5). Fighting "big fat." *Newsweek*, 38–40.

Zernike, K. (2004, October 12). Companies force employee fitness. *San Francisco Chronicle*, A-20.

Chapter 13

Grilo, C. M., Schiffman, S., & Wing, R. R. (1989). Relapse crises and coping among dieters. *Journal of Consulting and Clinical Psychology*, 57, 488–495.

Kirschenbaum, D. S. (1996, November). Preventing weight gain during the holidays: The critical role of self-monitoring. Paper presented at the annual meeting of the Association for Advancement of Behavior Therapy, New York.

Kolata, G. (2000, October 18). Days off are not allowed, weight experts argue. *New York Times*. Retrieved December 24, 2000, from nytimes.com.

McGuire, M. T., Wing, R. R., Klem, M. L., Lang, W., & Hill, J. O. (1999). What predicts weight regain in a group of successful weight losers. *Journal of Consulting and Clinical Psychology*, 67, 177–185.

INDEX